WOMEN, AGENCY AND THE LAW, 1300–1700

The Body, Gender and Culture

Series Editor: Lynn Botelho

Titles in this Series

1 Courtly Indian Women in Late Imperial India
Angma Dey Jhala

2 Paracelsus's Theory of Embodiment: Conception and Gestation in Early Modern Europe
Amy Eisen Cislo

3 The Prostitute's Body: Rewriting Prostitution in Victorian Britain
Nina Attwood

4 Old Age and Disease in Early Modern Medicine
Daniel Schäfer

5 The Life of Madame Necker: Sin, Redemption and the Parisian Salon
Sonja Boon

6 Stays and Body Image in London: The Staymaking Trade, 1680–1810
Lynn Sorge-English

7 Prostitution and Eighteenth-Century Culture: Sex, Commerce and Morality
Ann Lewis and Markman Ellis (eds)

8 The Aboriginal Male in the Enlightenment World
Shino Konishi

9 Anatomy and the Organization of Knowledge, 1500–1850
Matthew Landers and Brian Muñoz (eds)

10 Blake, Gender and Culture
Helen P. Bruder and Tristanne J. Connolly (eds)

11 Age and Identity in Eighteenth-Century England
Helen Yallop

12 The Politics of Reproduction in Ottoman Society, 1838–1900
Gülhan Balsoy

13 The Study of Anatomy in Britain, 1700–1900
Fiona Hutton

14 Interpreting Sexual Violence, 1660–1800
Anne Greenfield (ed.)

Forthcoming Titles

Sex, Identity and Hermaphrodites in Iberia, 1500–1800
Richard Cleminson and Francisco Vázquez García

The English Execution Narrative, 1200–1700
Katherine Royer

British Masculinity and the YMCA, 1844–1914
Geoff Spurr

WOMEN, AGENCY AND THE LAW, 1300–1700

EDITED BY

Bronach Kane and Fiona Williamson

Routledge
Taylor & Francis Group

LONDON AND NEW YORK

First published 2013 by Pickering & Chatto (Publishers) Limited

Published 2016 by Routledge
2 Park Square, Milton Park, Abingdon, Oxfordshire OX14 4RN
711 Third Avenue, New York, NY 10017, USA

First issued in paperback 2015

Routledge is an imprint of the Taylor & Francis Group, an informa business

BRITISH LIBRARY CATALOGUING IN PUBLICATION DATA

Women, agency and the law, 1300–1700. – (The body, gender and culture)
1. Women – Legal status, laws, etc. – England – History – to 1500. 2. Women
– Legal status, laws, etc. – England – History – 16th century. 3. Women – Legal
status, laws, etc. – England – History – 17th century. 4. Women – Legal status,
laws, etc. – Wales – History – to 1500. 5. Women – Legal status, laws, etc. –
Wales – History – 16th century. 6. Women – Legal status, laws, etc. – Wales
– History – 17th century.
I. Series II. Kane, Bronach Christina editor of compilation. III. Williamson,
Fiona editor of compilation.
342.4'20878'09-dc23

ISBN-13: 978-1-138-66217-9 (pbk)
ISBN-13: 978-1-8489-3384-2 (hbk)

Typeset by Pickering & Chatto (Publishers) Limited

CONTENTS

List of Contributors   ix
List of Abbreviations   xiii
Preface   xv

Introduction – *Bronach Kane with Fiona Williamson*   1
Part I: Shaping Women's Testimony
   1 Your Oratrice: Women's Petitions to the Late Medieval Court of
     Chancery – *Cordelia Beattie*   17
   2 Echoes, Whispers, Ventriloquisms: On Recovering Women's Voices
     from the Court of York in the Later Middle Ages – *Jeremy Goldberg* 31
   3 Women, Memory and Agency in the Medieval English Church Courts
     – *Bronach Kane*   43
Part II: Encountering the Law
   4 'Utterly and Untruly He Hath Deceived Me': Women's Inheritance in
     Late Medieval England – *Rosemary Horrox*   63
   5 'She Hym Fresshely Folowed and Pursued': Women and Star Chamber
     in Early Tudor Wales – *Deborah Youngs*   73
   6 Women and the Hue and Cry in Late Fourteenth-Century Great
     Yarmouth – *Janka Rodziewicz*   87

Part III: Women's Voices and Women's Spaces
   7 Gender and the Control of Sacred Space in Early Modern England
     – *Amanda Flather*   99
   8 The Travails of Agnes Beaumont – *Bernard Capp*   113
   9 Parish Politics, Urban Spaces and Women's Voices in Seventeenth-
     Century Norwich – *Fiona Williamson*   125
   10 'With a Sword Drawne in Her Hande': Defending the Boundaries of
     Household Space in Seventeenth-Century Wales – *Nicola Whyte* 141
Appendix   157

Notes   159
Index   203

LIST OF CONTRIBUTORS

Cordelia Beattie is Senior Lecturer in Medieval History at the University of Edinburgh. She is the author of *Medieval Single Women: The Politics of Social Classification in Late Medieval England* (Oxford: Oxford University Press, 2007) and a number of essays on medieval women and gender. She is also co-editor, with Anna Maslakovic and Sarah Rees Jones, of *The Medieval Household in Christian Europe, c. 850–c. 1550: Managing Power, Wealth and the Body* (Turnhout: Brepols, 2003); with Kirsten A. Fenton, of *Intersections of Gender, Religion, and Ethnicity in the Middle Ages* (London: Palgrave Macmillan, 2011) and, with Matthew Frank Stevens, of *Married Women and the Law in Premodern Northwest Europe* (Woodbridge: The Boydell Press, 2013).

Bernard Capp, FBA, is Emeritus Professor of History at the University of Warwick, where he has taught since 1968. His research centres on early modern social and cultural history. His books include *When Gossips Meet: Women, Family and Neighbourhood in Early Modern England* (Oxford: Oxford University Press, 2003) and *England's Culture Wars: Puritan Reformation and its Enemies in the Interregnum,1649–1660* (Oxford: Oxford University Press, 2012), with articles forthcoming on 'The Religious Market-Place: Public Disputations in England in the 1640s and 1650s' in *English Historical Review* (2014) and '"Jesus Wept" but did the Englishman?', exploring masculinity and the display of emotion in the early modern period.

Amanda Flather is Lecturer in History at the University of Essex. Her first book, *Gender and Space in Early Modern England* (Woodbridge: The Boydell Press, 2007), explored the influence of gender on the use and organization of space amongst early modern English men and women below the level of the elite. She was awarded the John Nichols Prize in English Local History by the University of Leicester in 1998, and has published on the organization of sacred space, the sexual division of labour and the spatial experience of servants in early modern England. Her current project, which is in preparation, is a monographic study of gender, material culture and the Church in early modern England.

Jeremy Goldberg is a social and cultural historian of the English later Middle Ages who actively writes and researches in the areas of gender, family, childhood, work, sexuality and so forth. Current interests include exploring the relationship between people and buildings. His publications include *Women, Work, and Life Cycle in a Medieval Economy* (Oxford: Clarendon Press, 1992); *Medieval England: A Social History c. 1250–1550* (London: Arnold, 2005); *Communal Discord, Child Abduction and Rape in the Later Middle Ages* (New York: Palgrave Macmillan, 2008) and an edition of translated sources, *Women in England c. 1275–1525* (Manchester: Manchester University Press, 1995). He currently teaches in the Department of History at the University of York and is a member of the Centre for Medieval Studies which has helped inspire his commitment to interdisciplinary approaches to the past.

Rosemary Horrox is a Fellow and Director of Studies in History, at Fitzwilliam College, Cambridge. She has written or edited numerous works on aspects of medieval history, including *A Social History of England, 1200–1500* (Cambridge: Cambridge University Press, 2006) with W. M. Ormrod; *Pragmatic Utopias: Ideals and Communities, 1200–1630* (Cambridge and New York: Cambridge University Press, 2001) with S. Rees Jones and *Fifteenth-Century Attitudes: Perceptions of Society in Late Medieval England* (Cambridge, Cambridge University Press, 1994). Her research interests encompass medieval British identities and perspectives, women and the concept of 'queenship'.

Bronach Kane is Lecturer in Medieval History at Cardiff University. She has held fellowships from the Leverhulme Trust, the Institute of Historical Research (IHR) and the Economic History Society. She has published on gender, sexuality and lay–Church relations in medieval England, and is currently completing a monograph on memory and gender in the English church courts.

Janka Rodziewicz completed her thesis investigating order and society in Great Yarmouth 1366–1381 at the University of East Anglia (UEA) in 2009. She has since worked as an Associate Tutor at the UEA and as a Research Assistant on a British Academy funded project at the University of Oxford. Most recently, Janka successfully completed a Knowledge Transfer Partnership project jointly hosted by the UEA and the Norwich Heritage Economic and Regeneration Trust (HEART) which sought to make information about Norwich's built heritage more accessible to the public. She now works as an Internship and Mentoring Officer at the UEA.

Nicola Whyte is Senior Lecturer in History at the University of Exeter. She specializes in the landscape and social history of the early modern period and recently held an Early Career Fellowship from The Leverhulme Trust, investigating landscape, memory and identity in early modern Wales. Her first book, *Inhabiting the Landscape: Place, Custom and Memory 1500–1800* was published with Oxbow Books in 2009. Her research is concerned with developing cross-disciplinary engagements between the fields of landscape studies and early modern social history. She is currently working on a number of projects including researching attitudes towards the material evidence of the past in the landscape and contemporary perceptions and experiences of landscape and environmental change.

Fiona Williamson is currently Senior Lecturer in History at the National University of Malaysia. Her research interests include seventeenth-century social history, gender and popular politics. She is in the process of finishing a monograph on the theme of communities and identities in seventeenth-century Norwich, a text that reflects the influence of the spatial turn of social history on her writing. She has recently moved to Malaysia to pursue research into Asian social, environmental and climatic history. This will be her second edited collection of essays.

Deborah Youngs is Senior Lecturer in Medieval History at Swansea University. Her interests lie in the social and cultural history of Britain from the late fourteenth to the early sixteenth century. She has written on a range of topics, including the English aristocracy, literary culture and the life cycle. Her latest project explores the social and political history of women in Wales, *c.* 1350–1550.

LIST OF ABBREVIATIONS

BI	Borthwick Institute for Archives
BL	British Library
CCA	Canterbury Cathedral Archives
ERO	Essex Record Office
HMSO	Her/His Majesty's Stationary Office
MED	*Middle English Dictionary*
NCC	Norwich Consistory Court
NRO	Norfolk Record Office
ODNB	*Oxford Dictionary of National Biography*
TNA	The National Archives, Kew

PREFACE

Bronach Kane and Fiona Williamson

In October 2009, scholars working in the field of gender studies in Britain met at the University of East Anglia (UEA), Norwich, to discuss the problems of reclaiming women's words from the historic record. The one-day event, a conference organized jointly by Fiona Williamson and Janka Rodziewicz, was titled 'Women's Voices: The Power of Words in Medieval and Early Modern Europe'. It was the product of ongoing discussions between scholars interested in recovering women's voices from textual sources, such as letters and, particularly, legal documents in line with the contemporary work of scholars such as Alexandra Shepard, Jeremy Goldberg, Garthine Walker, Tim Stretton and Cordelia Beattie, amongst others. Their work has highlighted the importance of legal documents, such as secular and ecclesiastic court proceedings, in understanding women's agency and ability to negotiate their own roles and contest those of others at law. In particular, this work has sought to move beyond the restrictions of prescriptive literature and dominant narratives of female identities to reconstruct women's real lived experiences through the in-depth analysis of their own words. The conference brought together leading names in the field, along with new scholars and postgraduate students, who engaged in discussion about the future of the field and the ways in which it might usefully build.

It is from these discussions that the idea for this collection was formed. This volume is not a conference proceeding per se, but a collection of essays inspired by the dialogue that took place during the event. As such, the scholars gathered here all share a common interest in recovering the female voice and revealing how women counterbalanced their knowledge of the legal system with the restraints of prevailing stereotypes about women's role, in many cases actively engaging in a process of manipulating these limitations to their best advantage. In so doing, the women in the cases highlighted in this volume demonstrate women's agency to negotiate and achieve their goals, or to take part in the male dominated world of the law, in often very difficult circumstances. These women were not always successful but their cases reveal much about women's agency in practice.

The editors wish to thank those people who, although not contributing to this volume, helped to make the 'Women's Voices' conference a success and whose research collectively inspired this collection, particularly John Arnold, Anne Laurence, Wendy Perkins and Alexandra Shepard. The editors are also indebted to the anonymous reviewers of the collection, whose perceptive comments helped shape the final structure of the volume. We also wish to thank the Centre for East Anglian Studies (CEAS), the Norfolk Record Office (NRO), the Royal Historical Society (RHS) and the UEA Graduate Students Association, for providing the funds to make the conference possible. Finally, we would also like to thank all the contributors for their efforts in making this volume a reality.

INTRODUCTION[1]

Bronach Kane with Fiona Williamson

The field of women and the law in later medieval England and Wales has witnessed a number of significant historiographical advances in the past two decades, many of which build on arguments advanced by social historians of women and gender in the 1980s and 1990s. The essays in this volume are chiefly concerned with recent developments and consider the relationship between women and the law, seeking to identify continuities and changes in their legal encounters. Ultimately, this collection assesses the capacity of women to negotiate the legal systems of pre-modern England. As such, this study of women's agency aims to investigate avenues of female influence in legal cultures, focusing on the ability to interject in trial accounts, litigation or through legal and illegal acts. The contributors employ innovative methods in social and cultural history to draw new meanings from legal records that have traditional historiographical pasts. From gender history to feminist theory, and from the history of memory to landscape archaeology and the spatial turn, the collection generates novel ways of discussing women's agency and action in pre-modern settings.

The focus of this collection is influenced by a wider set of developments in historiography on later medieval and early modern social relations. Work by Judith Bennett, Marjorie McIntosh and Stephen Rigby has emphasized the nexus of status, authority, gender and the law that shaped later medieval experiences among non-elites.[2] Focused on social relations in early modern England, Keith Wrightson's concept of the 'politics of the parish' proposed a number of interrelated areas through which historians might explore 'social history with the politics put back in'.[3] The experience of authority has similarly emerged as a crucial context in which medieval and early modern individuals exercised agency. The work of James C. Scott and Antonio Gramsci, for example, has underpinned a number of studies on peasant and 'subaltern' experiences of state governance in late medieval and early modern England.[4] This focus on culture as a field of power influences the concept of agency applied in this volume as it explores women operating within the hegemonic paradigm of patriarchal authority. The legal testimony attributed to women in later medieval and early modern judicial records, as well as women's experiences of the law, should be explored anew from this perspective.

Court officials recorded, interpreted and mediated female speech in ways that reflected contemporary thought on gender and prescribed forms of behaviour. Central to this project is the belief that legal records do not faithfully represent women's 'voices', but rather offer unparalleled insights into female encounters with the law. From these mediated sources emerge the choices, decisions and actions of women as litigants, witnesses and suspects. Nevertheless, even after a couple of decades of development, the conceptual tools of gender history are not perfectly attuned to social histories of non-elites or fully engaged with women's voices in legal contexts. In a special issue of *Gender & History* in 2008, also published as an edited collection, Alexandra Shepard and Garthine Walker note the neglect of contexts in which women were able to act as agents and thus effect change in their own right.[5] A related methodological problem surrounds the place of post-structuralism and cultural theory in gender history, with criticisms that these developments shift the analytic focus towards language at the expense of social practice. Shepard and Walker noted this move, commenting that many studies of masculinity have 'similarly prioritised representation above the material and subjective realities of men's lives'. It is this focus on experience over language that 'provides the key to understanding historical agency' and is the premise upon which this collection builds.[6]

A persistent concern in historiography on women's voices and agency is female 'resistance to social norms and oppressive power relations, namely male dominance'.[7] A number of theorists advocate the rejection of agency as a category of analysis, criticizing its lack of analytical precision as well as the supposed tendency towards abstraction.[8] While acknowledging these criticisms, this volume aims to demonstrate the underlying value of this concept in the context of women's use of the law. The concept of agency, however, encapsulates the theoretical relation between individuals, language and social practice, operating as the 'site of mediation between discourses and experience'.[9]

Female agency has also been highlighted since the 1990s in a series of studies that have debated the extent of women's empowerment.[10] Historians of later medieval and early modern women have explored the constraints and fields of influence that shaped women's choices and legal activities. Bennett, in particular, considers medieval women and their experiences of authority, through manorial fines, limited labour opportunities and socio-cultural marginalization. Bennett also underlines women's ability to alleviate elements of these restrictions, noting that historians must attend to 'women's agency within and against these constraints'.[11] Jeremy Goldberg, for example, emphasized the economic opportunities that young women may have gained while employed as 'life-cycle' servants in urban households.[12] Barbara Hanawalt similarly explored women's agency in the context of family and the law in peasant communities, and more recently in medieval London.[13] For the sixteenth and seventeenth centuries, Laura Gowing, Susan Kingsley Kent and Garthine Walker, among others, have argued for widening the understanding of women's roles and, thus, addressing a broader range of roles and spaces for developing and exercising female agency.[14]

The analysis of gender and agency in tandem provides a powerful tool for exploring not only women's actions, but also the relationship between gender, the law and social practice. As Padma Anagol notes of colonial India, women's agency does not exist as an independent and autonomous force.[15] A number of overlapping structures shaped the degree of choice that women exercised, from their position under the law and their ability to access resources, to societal expectations of female behaviour at each level of society. Thus, for the late medieval and early modern periods, female agency operated within dominant religious and intellectual frameworks, as well as the broad range of women's own actions. Studies of gender, then, should also account for hierarchies of status, economic power, or social and cultural capital, as well as competition between women themselves. As an analytic tool, the concept of agency also helps to explain how women upheld modes of oppression or colluded with oppressive hierarchies that constrained other women. The collection aims to avoid attributing women's agency solely to the experience of gender, noting how a number of other factors influenced participation in legal cultures. The ability to negotiate legal jurisdictions was influenced by sets of structures and processes – social, economic and religious – as well as the expectations of the law.

A persistent concern in women's history, to a greater extent than in historical studies of gender, is the relationship between continuity and change, with the latter often emphasized at the expense of the former. Bennett underlines the imperative to distinguish 'between *changes* in women's *experiences* on the one hand and *transformations* in women's *status* on the other'.[16] More work is needed on the historiography of gender relations in the century and a half after the arrival of plague. Previous studies have focused on the degree of improvement that women experienced from the late 1340s onwards in the wake of the first pestilence, with economic gains in urban areas balanced by repressive socio-cultural perceptions of women.[17] The decades before the plague merit similar attention, with further study needed of long-term patterns of litigation and economic engagement among women in urban and rural areas.[18] Likewise, gender historians of the 1980s and early 1990s were preoccupied with the idea that the position of women deteriorated during the early modern period, as many conventions governing women, and female behaviour, were consolidated in law.[19] Concerns over the problematic boundaries imposed by periodization are similarly highlighted by Shepard and Walker, whose 2009 collection questions the applicability of conventional chronologies for the study of gender.[20] There is a particular need for more detailed understandings of women's legal agency that account for long-term continuity and change in women's property rights, the application of coverture and their use of courts. In addition, the influence of different jurisdictions, court processes and structures on women's agency varied across this period, with distinctive legal voices and narratives emerging at different points.

Although the present collection concentrates largely, though not exclusively, on women's experiences of litigation, the contributors address methodological concerns raised in recent historiographies of gender, crime and the law. A series of important works in the 1990s, including a collection of essays by Jenny Kermode and Garthine Walker, focused on the way in which women participated in both criminal activity and litigation, analysing patterns in different jurisdictions.[21] Since then, fundamental concerns in the study of women and the law have shifted from female participation in litigation to roles and power relations in wider legal cultures, following in part the innovative agenda set by Kermode and Walker.

Historians of women, agency and the law draw on methodological approaches from the broader field of social and cultural history, applying these to readings of women's activities in legal records. A number of important works concentrate on the construction of identities in court material, identifying the discursive influence of power relations on narratives attributed to parties, witnesses and suspects. Noting the different ontologies of early modern culture, for example, Lyndal Roper produced a psychoanalytic reading of witch accusations in Reformation Germany, interpreting these as 'mental productions' that reflected aspects of actors' subjectivities.[22] In his study of power relations in heresy trials, John Arnold explores the subjectivities of peasants in thirteenth- and fourteenth-century Languedoc, arguing that interrogations produced the 'confessing subject'.[23] From this perspective, the inquisitor's hegemonic position enabled the control of linguistic contexts, which in turn generated the identities of suspects in court transcripts.

The intersections of identity, power relations and the law provide the focus for several important studies of women in late medieval and early modern court records. Analysing patterns of crime in early modern Cheshire, Walker argues that perceptions of gender shaped prosecutions of social disorder, with physical violence associated with male suspects, while verbal insult and infanticide were interpreted as particularly female crimes.[24] Narratives deployed in legal defences relied on gender-specific discourses, as suspects adopted 'subject positions' that broadened the extent of their legal agency.

Aspects of the law which sought to police female bodies, particularly in cases of suspected pregnancy and infanticide, have also been considered by scholars. In her pioneering study of the politics of touch in seventeenth-century England, Laura Gowing analyses legal records relating to women and sexuality from a range of jurisdictions, including the church courts, quarter sessions, the assizes and the Bridewell.[25] Drawing on contemporary prescriptive and religious literature, Gowing addresses the regulation of female bodies, interpreted as unfinished and porous, and requiring specific control and management. Much of this policing was accomplished between women themselves, as forms of knowledge regarded as particularly feminine were transformed into methods of control. The politics of touch emblematized the hierarchies of power and authority that constrained female experiences of sexuality, pregnancy and desire.

Domestic violence was similarly regulated in legal actions, particularly the ecclesiastical courts where separation could be sought on the grounds of marital cruelty. Expanding the implications of domestic abuse to include male reputation, Sara Butler, Jeremy Goldberg and Derek Neal use church court records to show that violence against wives could tarnish husbands' reputations in late medieval England.[26] Similarly, Francis Dolan considers the practical implications of early modern spousal abuse, arguing that marriage operated according to an 'economy of scarcity', whereby worth was vested in only one spouse at the expense of the other, usually the wife.[27] Recent works have begun to explore how emotions were regulated and shaped in the course of legal actions. Gowing and Malcolm Gaskill both acknowledge the narrative construction of emotions in legal and trial records, which were described according to the type of suit and legal argument.[28]

Analytical categories drawn from post-structuralist theories have influenced a number of key works on legal records, women and identity, particularly those which apply methods of discursive analysis.[29] This approach influences several contributors to this volume in their explorations of the dissonance between language in legal records and social practice. The majority of these studies consider women's voices and agency through close readings of individual cases, drawing on micro-historical approaches in order to detect female action where it might otherwise be obscured. Others, such as Bernard Capp and Amanda Flather, focus on less traditional spheres of women's legal activity such as autobiographical religious writing and female iconoclasm in ecclesiastical court records. In their choice of source, these chapters address women's legal voices in a similar fashion to essays in an important collection on medieval women and the law edited by Noël James Menuge.[30] A key question is the level of self-consciousness present in women's exercise of agency. The methodological legacy of the linguistic turn, and the tensions that it emphasized, implicitly shapes this volume's focus on the intersections of agency, voices, discourse and lived experience.

Women, Coverture and Agency

The wealth of recent works on women and the law, including those within this volume, signifies the importance of broadening the contexts for women's use of the law in relation to marriage. A growing literature relating to coverture and property rights explores how women negotiated the patriarchal structures of the household, particularly inheritance practices and networks of debt and credit, the settlement of which often occurred through litigation.[31] In many instances, later medieval and early modern women engaged with legal cultures in disputes that interacted with the market and control over resources or property. Attempts to alienate women from the market economy were accompanied by misogynistic cultural images of the 'woman on top', or married women who could 'displace men as heads of household and ... could transfer property from one man to another'[32]. Between the thirteenth and seventeenth centuries, Martha Howell argues, 'marital property and inheritance law was also enlisted in the effort to limit women's control of property'.[33]

Several contributors in this volume explore how women asserted rights over property through the law and brought suit in cases where redress was otherwise limited. A series of factors combined in order to restrict female legal activity in these contexts, not least the presumption of coverture whereby the legal identity of a married woman became incorporated into the person of her husband.[34] Noting several misinterpretations of the concept, Frederick Pollock and Frederic Maitland emphasized the husband's legal guardianship over the wife's property, as opposed to the 'unity of person' that earlier accounts associated with coverture.[35] The wife's loss of legal personhood upon marriage was accompanied by practical limits on female economic and legal engagement, whereby wives were prohibited from suing in the common law courts. The theoretical implications of coverture also included the protection of married women from certain kinds of prosecution, particularly those concerning financial transactions.[36]

The extent to which coverture influenced female agency in legal practice is questioned, however, in recent studies.[37] While male control over property and economic resources restricted married women's actions in the market economy, a more expansive and flexible attitude towards marital goods pertained beyond the formal law. Amy Erickson and Joanne Bailey both note that married women maintained attachments with personal goods and property.[38] Erickson observes that it 'is unlikely that wives stopped thinking of certain property as theirs simply for the duration of the marriage'.[39] The ability to extend credit and accrue debts was circumscribed under the legal condition of coverture, as part of a broader schema that endowed the husband with sole responsibility for fiscal matters. Shepard, however, notes that married women arranged credit and conducted financial transactions 'both with men and with other women, often as a result of independent business concerns'.[40] Müller emphasizes regional experiences of customary law among peasant women, noting differences in the tenor of lordship and local custom that influenced the importance of coverture.[41] Chris Briggs suggests that after 1550 the role of women in relation to credit and debt may have altered, 'aided perhaps by the rise of the equity courts, which created greater scope for exceptions to the *coverture* doctrine'.[42]

The inconsistent application of coverture in the period this volume covers indicates that women's legal agency was marked by variation and depended on marital status, jurisdiction and region. Although the common law applied the designation *femme covert* to women after marriage, other jurisdictions interpreted the position of women differently. Thus, women could bring suits in other jurisdictions, namely in the courts of equity, under customary law and in the ecclesiastical courts.[43] The degree of agency that women exercised in litigation therefore depended on the jurisdiction in which their action was initiated. Female litigants brought only a small number of actions in the common law courts of the late fifteenth and early sixteenth centuries, figuring in 5 per cent of the business that reached the King's Bench and the Court of Common Pleas.[44] Although women brought fewer cases than men in the common law courts, many of these related to economic matters as did suits initiated by male litigants.[45] The ecclesiastical courts similarly facilitated a greater number of female litigants than in other courts in both the later medieval and early modern periods.[46] The pursuit of grievances relating to marriage and defamation in the church court afforded late medieval and early modern women a considerable degree of agency.

Shaping Women's Testimony

Since the publication of Natalie Zemon Davis's ground-breaking study on pardons for homicide in seventeenth-century France, historians using legal records have increasingly sought to understand the narrative construction of legal documents.[47] The apparent immediacy conveyed by legal documents, particularly petitions and witness depositions, obscures the process of legal mediation that structured court records.[48] Arnold cautions that there 'is little more seductive in social history than the promise of access to the "voices" of those normally absent from the historical record'.[49] A number of chapters in this collection address the relationship between testimony, narrative and subjectivity, but each interprets legal records as documents constructed according to cultural discourses, narratives and tropes.

Legal records of trials hold specific methodological problems, several of which concern their linguistic and textual nature as official documents.[50] Linguistic categories and terms prevalent in social practice are seldom reproduced in the vernacular in court records before the mid-fifteenth century. Yet narrative elements are not mere filters upon the words and intentions of women actors. Criminal prosecutions, heresy trials and litigation in the common law and church courts occurred in the context of complex power relations that shaped, forced and emphasized speech in various ideological ways. As Gaskill notes for witchcraft accusations, depositions in these trials may be seen 'to overlay reality with fantasy as a conscious or subconscious means of influencing courts'.[51] Women accused of witchcraft, such as Margaret More of Cambridgeshire, may have adopted the subject position assigned to them during court proceedings, thus gaining a sense of empowerment through assuming this identity.[52] Arnold similarly remarks that 'language is not a veil over subjectivity: it is the arena in which subjectivity is provoked, contained, and performed'.[53]

Recent studies on the narrative construction of legal documents depend on discourse analysis in order to interpret various influences on their final form. Legal narratives were generated through the conjunction of different discourses, with particular narratives depending not only on the sex of the petitioner, party or deponent, but also on their occupation and social status.[54] Both Arnold and Walker interpret legal records using Mikhail Bakhtin's concepts of 'heteroglossia' and 'multivocality', focusing on the way in which medieval and early modern people presented themselves within particular subject positions.[55] In his study of medieval heresy trials, Arnold describes Bakhtin's concept of 'heteroglossia', as the analysis of 'multiple discourses that are at work within a culture, but which are not synonymous with the personal voices of individuals'.[56] He examines heresy trials for 'excesses of speech' where suspects responded at length to inquisitors' questions, perhaps demonstrating a greater degree of agency in their speech.

In this collection, Cordelia Beattie engages with such arguments and theories. Interpreting individuals seeking redress from Chancery as 'petitioning subjects', her chapter explores shifts in narrative in order to detect the female petitioner's involvement in drafting the bill. By reading closely narrative and symbolic descriptions of a violent assault, Beattie argues that that the concept of subject positions enables subtle readings of petitioners' narratives.

Narratives were ordered not only according to cultural tropes, but also in the context of processes specific to each court. Beattie notes that the discursive composition of bills submitted to the court of Chancery depended in part on the stages of their production. In addition, Beattie argues that historians need not make definitive interpretive choices between the textual and the social in legal records, identifying areas where the collaborative nature of writing petitions becomes evident. As an equity court, Chancery produced a complex dynamic between legal advisors, women using the law, and common cultural expectations, particularly since Chancery was regarded as especially receptive to female petitioners.[57] Tim Stretton comments that judges in equity courts 'recognised the injustices that could flow from the common law fiction that a married woman had virtually no legal identity separate from her husband', introducing processes that circumvented these limitations.[58]

In a similar vein, both Jeremy Goldberg and Bronach Kane emphasize the comparative agency afforded to women in the medieval ecclesiastical courts, a jurisdiction that permitted women both to testify and initiate suits, despite informal and occasional restrictions. In his chapter, Goldberg suggests that the composition of witness statements altered during this period, such that fifteenth-century depositions were revised rather less than fourteenth-century statements, perhaps producing documents that resembled more closely the direct speech of witnesses. Although in one fifteenth-century suit the translation of reported speech into Latin, along with the main body of the statement, may indicate the rhetorical crafting of clerical personnel.

The historiographical concern with narrative analysis in legal records has been accompanied by a number of studies on memory practice, forming part of a broader turn towards memory studies in cultural history.[59] Several works explore the memories of male jurors in late medieval proof of age statements from inquisitions *post mortem*, documents that often represent 'stock memories' and only record male perspectives.[60] Both Goldberg and Kane analyse aspects of remembrance in church court litigation, with the former focusing on memory strategies of female witnesses as elements of interiority elicited by church authorities concerned with extracting 'truth'. In her chapter, Kane argues that women's testimony drew on wider perceptions of female memory in clerical-authored writings as much as the memorial responsibilities afforded to them. Female testimony relied on gendered expertise gained in a variety of contexts, imbuing their evidence with authority that drew on women's roles in the household, parish and community. Situating women's remembrance in the context of broader cultural assumptions, Kane indicates the ways in which female testimony alludes to a broader base of customary memory in communal contexts.

Walker and Kermode note that traditional methods for interpreting legal activity often fail to register tactics employed by women beyond formal litigation.[61] In a similar vein, Kane emphasizes women's legal expertise on the margins of suits, while the 'extra-curial' efforts of women involved in cases coming before the common law courts have been noted for the later fifteenth and early sixteenth centuries. As wives and kin, women gathered evidence, administered bonds and sureties, and often controlled the financial resources that facilitated legal actions.[62] Since men sued in greater numbers than women in the majority of jurisdictions, analysis of related legal activities is therefore necessary in order to plot women's engagement with the law more extensively.

As a number of contributors argue, the narrative construction of trial and litigation records often occurred in the process of developing legal arguments, and varied depending on the apparatus consulted. In considering legal records for the eighteenth century, Bailey proposes comparisons of deposition material with related contemporary documentation including family papers, journals and letters.[63] While extensive supplementary records become more patchy for later medieval England and Wales, understandings of women's agency in legal settings may be explored through analysis of related legal documents, such as solicitors' papers for the eighteenth century, and proctors' books and drafts for the later medieval and early modern centuries.

Encountering the Law

Several chapters in this volume address the experiences of women using the law, despite a number of significant formal restrictions. As the inconsistent application of coverture suggests, the experiences of women varied according to jurisdiction and in relation to litigation in particular. Regional variations similarly shaped the application and use of legal recourse. In medieval Wales, for example, local customary law operated alongside marcher law where this suited the fiscal interests of the Crown and the marcher lords. Practices under the law of Hywel Dda thus occasionally coexisted with the law of the marches, including several that concerned women's sexual activities and marital status, such as the virginity fine of *amobr*.[64] In this volume, Deborah Youngs draws on cases initiated in Star Chamber by Welsh complainants in the early Tudor period, arguing that although far fewer women used this court than the consistory courts or Chancery, their suits suggest how women negotiated the law when other methods of redress had failed. The inability of inhabitants of the Welsh marches to bring suit in the central common law courts of the King's Bench and Common Pleas meant that complaints were judged in prerogative courts instead, such as Star Chamber. Difficulties in securing justice in the southern lordships of Wales stemmed in part from the corruption of local administrative officers. The related cases in Youngs's study concern complaints of the murder of a husband, and accusations of rape, both of which afforded female litigants forceful positions in a jurisdiction where few women prosecuted. Exploring the women's appropriation of specific gendered identities, the chapter focuses on discursive strategies that alternated between agency and passivity in order to construct convincing narratives.

The legal activities identified by Rosemary Horrox and Youngs in particular demonstrate how widows obtained justice despite restrictions on women's ability to wage law. Marriage caused a theoretical contraction in women's ability to access the law, but opportunities returned upon widowhood.[65] The economic vulnerability of widows in the thirteenth century was borne out in the high numbers of bereaved women suing to enforce their rights over dower.[66] By the fourteenth century, however, the royal courts saw increasing numbers of widows suing with the additional expertise of attorneys.[67] In her chapter, Horrox analyses the difficulties of Jane Stapleton, a gentry widow, in recovering lands of which she was deprived by her son. The inheritance of estates among the late medieval gentry often depended on types of land tenure, as well as the intentions outlined in the relevant testament. These might specify its diversion to another branch of the family or delineate particular forms of tenure that precluded its passage. Where recourse to common law was unavailable, women might pursue grievances in the court of Chancery. In a comparable vein to women's 'extra-curial' engagement with the law, many gentry families resolved disputes through informal means. Yet, as Horrox notes, Stapleton's decision not to pursue the case through common law or Chancery may have prompted the detailed account of the deception, and her subsequent response in her testament. Horrox's study demonstrates how life cycle and marital status influenced the degree of agency available to women.

Beyond the avenue of formal litigation, women were able to use the law in less structured ways. At the level of the parish and community, for example, women's speech operated both as a forceful weapon of reproach and as a site of anxiety for local authorities. In this collection, Janka Rodziewicz analyses the use of the hue and cry in late fourteenth-century Great Yarmouth as a means of exploring women's agency in local communities that otherwise limited female regulatory roles. The control of crime and misbehaviour in the fourteenth century depended in part on the obligations of mutual surety embedded in the system of frankpledge and tithings, processes from which women were excluded.[68] The capacity for female inhabitants to raise the hue and cry in their communities provided women with the opportunity to engage in communal policing. Sandy Bardsley maintains that the decline of the hue and cry as an 'empowering institution' in the late fourteenth century coincided with increased prosecutions of female speech in the church courts.[69] It has been suggested that harsher penalties were instituted in dealing with a variety of crimes from the second half of the sixteenth century onwards, in response to female speech in particular.[70] Yet, in a reassessment of early modern scolding, Martin Ingram argued that rates of prosecution against women perceived as troublesome were low compared to other offences, crimes and misdemeanours with which men and women were charged in Tudor and Stuart England.[71] In this volume, Rodziewicz notes that women's voices did not witness a significant decline in the value accorded them, as both men and women experienced difficulties in pressing justified claims of hue-raising at the leet court in Yarmouth.

Litigation over insult, Gowing suggests, 'provided a way of shifting personal, semi-public disputes into a much broader, official sphere to which women rarely had access'.[72] A number of contributors address the relationship between women's speech, authority and reputation in this period. The limitations imposed on women's actions under the law influenced perceptions in related spheres of authority. In local society, attitudes towards reputation, its construction and maintenance, differed between the sexes, with women more vulnerable to attacks on their sexual honour. Kane suggests that forms of customary memory under-pinned insults of theft and disorder that women levelled at male neighbours, drawing on the same source of authority that allowed female use of the hue and cry. Similarly, Fiona Williamson examines the role of insult in seventeenth-century defamation suits, in which slander was used to critique and undermine social status and sexual reputations in neighbourhood conflicts. In his study of scolds, Ingram noted that women were able to engage in policing local relations, acting as 'brokers of gossip, makers and breakers of reputation, [and] sharers in the process whereby both men and women could be reported to the ecclesiasti-cal and secular courts for sexual misbehaviour and other offences'.[73] Accounts of women's moral worth previously emphasized sexuality as a marker of respecta-bility, without analysing comparable arenas where ideological concerns could be negotiated. The use of sexual insult as a 'mundane response' in disputes involving women ensured that the origins and context of such conflicts were neglected.[74] Female honour evidently depended not only on sexual reputation, but also on virtuous domestic management.[75]

Women's Voices and Women's Spaces

The chapters that comprise the final section emphasize the ways in which women participated in the regulation of communal relations, focusing on the household, parish and local community as spheres of functional and symbolic meaning. The studies approach these areas as sources of authority, exploring the extent to which women's legal action depended on their engagement with infor-mal elements of social relations. Many of these themes touch on areas included in Wrightson's influential concept of the 'politics of the parish' which argued for a political analysis of patriarchy, the neighbourhood, custom, the Reformations and state formation, and subordination and meaning.[76] While a growing body of literature addresses the extent of agency in parochial contexts throughout the period covered in this volume, the position of women in these spheres remains understudied.[77]

Bernard Capp considers religious identity as a key component of female agency, using piety as the context in which to explore women's narrative voices. Religion was one of the few areas where women gained autonomy outside of a domestic setting, with potential for informal influence in parochial organization. In seventeenth-century England, however, the bounds of religious conformity were rapidly shifting once again, such that dissenting groups faced consider-able hostility from the episcopate and Church authorities.[78] In his study, Capp analyses the providential narrative through which Agnes Beaumont, a pious nonconformist, interpreted her own life in an autobiographical work outlining her tribulations.[79] While the engagement of women in religious reform movements has been noted, few studies explore the relation between female piety and subjective religious experiences.[80] In his chapter, Capp analyses how devotion underpinned Beaumont's personal and religious autonomy, shaping the work's textual format which resembled other dissenting scriptural autobiographies. Recording her experiences later in life, perhaps writing it herself, Beaumont's account retained oral inflections evident in conversational phrasing. Despite familial opposition, particularly from her father, Beaumont favoured the spiritual rewards of radical religion over relations with her kin, choices that embroiled her in several legal suits, including the accusation of poisoning her father. The encounters detailed in her account offer first-hand explanations of her own use and experiences of the law, framed in scriptural narrative terms.

The final chapters engage with related aspects of the household, religion and local politics, engaging with the 'spatial turn' of recent historiography to explore the material settings of agency. Driven by attempts to account for the influence of the material and symbolic in everyday life, this analytic focus aims to recover past dynamics of political power from beyond the written archive. Influential, here, have been explorations of 'how human bodies occupy and move through the built and natural landscapes'.[81] The methodological developments of the 'spatial turn' in social history hold particular significance for the study of agency and legal voices among late medieval and early modern women. For gender historians, a novel focus on the spatial contexts of gender relations further challenges the framework of 'separate spheres' that aligned female experiences with the private, domestic sphere in opposition to male engagement with the public arena of governance outside the home.[82] In a reassessment of the notion of 'separate spheres' for women, Amanda Vickery emphasized its persistence since classical society, albeit in different guises, and with varying reasons and consequences.[83] Nevertheless, historians influenced by the 'spatial turn' have demonstrated just how fluid and dynamic concepts of gendered spaces were in practice.[84]

The law interacted with the physical environment in various ways during this period, shaping and being shaped by spatial practices and representations.[85] In this volume, Flather, Williamson and Nicola Whyte explore women's engagement with the law through the function and meaning of gendered spaces, interpreting material culture and places as active agents in the articulation of identities. The primary spheres of analysis are the household, parish, neighbourhood and the surrounding landscape, yet ideological perceptions of each of these areas overlapped as did experiences of the law through their lenses.

The parish offered laypeople, especially women, opportunities to participate in economic and political organization through channels that were reconfigured at various stages of the sixteenth-century religious reformations. Flather thus explores the understudied motivations of female iconoclasts, noting how such actions represented the ritual and symbolism that accompanied these gestures. Female involvement in parish life often paralleled patterns of women's activity in the household.[86] In later medieval England, contact with the material culture of parochial religion through 'church-keeping' allowed women to transform constraints on their agency into authority, gaining 'proximity to the sacred' and incorporating piety into everyday routine.[87] The religious upheavals of the sixteenth and seventeenth centuries profoundly influenced changes in the material appearance of church interiors. The actions of female iconoclasts allowed laywomen to engage in the reconstruction of spatial meaning in local sacred spaces. In this context, Flather interprets the destruction of church interiors by women as their active engagement in reconfiguring pious places. In her chapter, women emerge as conscious and dynamic actors in religious change, imbued with the agency to direct and manage religious practice in their own communities.

The parish and the neighbourhood were symbolic units of worship and organization which operated to include and exclude individuals in later medieval and early modern communities. The social ties that underpinned female networks of belonging are considered in Williamson's chapter, which focuses on discourses of inclusion and exclusion in defamation cases. Through the micro-study of a set of suits presented at the Norwich Diocesan Court, the essay explores the 'politics of the parish' in seventeenth-century Norwich. Steve Hindle emphasizes the processes of incorporation and belonging in local settings but notes that by 1550 the oligarchic parish was assuredly male.[88] In this volume, however, Williamson argues that women emerged as key actors in determining the range of behaviours and social relationships that operated within urban spaces. The uses of the law by women of non-elite social status is a theme common to many of the chapters in this volume. Williamson also considers the spaces of the parish as key points in the formation of female agency, drawing on Gowing's work that has highlighted the importance of doorways and thresholds in defamation suits during the early modern period.[89]

As the chapters by Whyte and Williamson indicate, the household and its inhabitants often figure in legal narratives in this period, drawing on a number of practical and symbolic associations relating to gender and the law. Operating not only as a residential and economic unit, the household was also a site where affective and conjugal bonds were established, negotiated and occasionally rejected. In late medieval English urban areas, masters as heads of households exercised authority over male dependents in ways that led to conflicts relating to manhood.[90] Extolled in sermons and other prescriptive texts, the model of the husband and father as governor of his 'state' was rarely embodied in domestic settings without adaptation or negotiation.[91] As a marker of respectability, property-holding was infused with the attributes of successful male adulthood; male parties and witnesses often referenced land-holding and household status as signs of economic and moral worth.[92] Yet notions of female honour also depended on the reputation of the household, with early modern women's authority 'invested in their daily labours and household position'.[93] The boundaries of the marital home were associated with honour, both masculine and feminine, and, as Beattie notes in this volume, these meanings might be emphasized in legal narratives. Similarly, Whyte emphasizes that the household was a space through which Welsh families articulated senses of identity and agency. In early modern Wales, the household was both physical sanctuary and the symbolic site of gendered identities.

Using methodologies informed by landscape studies, Whyte analyses instances of boundary-breaking in relation to property and household spaces, exploring how these influenced women's roles as defenders of household space. Her study argues for the extension of the material and symbolic limits of the household, which should be interpreted in the wider setting of the landscape. In this way, Whyte's chapter draws on recent work, by early modernists in particular, on non-elite engagement with the law through popular understandings of the landscape. Andy Wood, for example, emphasizes the ways in which popular perceptions of custom underpinned plebeian senses of the environment.[94] A number of important works have begun to consider custom and the landscape from the perspective of female parties and witnesses, providing a counterbalance to studies that focus on common law. Stretton, for example, considers the place of custom in women's appeals to the Court of Requests during the reign of Elizabeth.[95] Though custom offered flexibility and relative parity to women, it was also 'capable of absorbing, as it was of withstanding, the prejudice against women that is so often associated with the common law'.[96] Elsewhere, Whyte reveals how women participated in the development and defence of customary rights in local communities. A number of roles and identities were therefore adopted by women, who operated as 'informal brokers' of memory in cases concerning tithes and enclosure.[97] In this volume, Whyte explores the implications of everyday violence in order to situate modes of resistance and assertion in the broader context of landscape, dwelling and power in early modern Wales.

Conclusion

The studies collected in this volume concentrate on women's experiences of the law for a number of reasons already outlined.[98] The imperative to analyse female participation in legal cultures, for instance, demonstrates the contributors' willingness to eschew the homogeneity of collective 'women's experiences'.[99] The essays in this volume represent a wide range of themes and periods but all engage with methodologies and ideas that inform the study of women and the law. The unifying factor is a concern with the extent of women's agency in the contexts of testifying in the courts, encountering the law and shaping communal relations.

Addressing an extended chronology from the late thirteenth to the seventeenth centuries, they aim to explore the range of legal experiences available to women over the longue durée. Regardless of their social status or personal circumstances, women, through the medium of the law, were active in negotiating and creating their own identities alongside commonly recognized stereotypes and norms of gender expectations.

1 YOUR ORATRICE: WOMEN'S PETITIONS TO THE LATE MEDIEVAL COURT OF CHANCERY

Cordelia Beattie

Beseecheth meekly your poor oratrice Denise Gros of London, widow.

[Chancery bill, 1443–56]

Right meekly beseecheth your gracious lordship your poor oratice and bedewoman Elizabeth the wife of one Joce Lamanva.

[Chancery bill, c. 1471]

Meekly beseecheth your good lordship your daily oratrice and poor maiden Johanne Fowler.

[Chancery bill, 1475–80 or 1483–5][1]

The late medieval court of Chancery has often been held to be a court that was particularly accessible to women.[2] Married women, for example, such as Elizabeth the wife of Joce Lamanva (quoted above), could bring cases to Chancery in their own right, rather than having to be represented by their husbands, as the restrictions of common law did not apply.[3] Petitioners would ask the Chancellor to provide redress for problems that could not be resolved fairly in another legal jurisdiction. If accepted into the court, the Chancellor (usually a bishop or archbishop in this period) would judge cases according to 'conscience', some contemporary notion of what was fair, rather than strict rules of evidence, making Chancery an early 'equity' court.[4] Cases were begun by a complaint, which could be made orally, although our main source for how this court operated are the written bills that were submitted to it by lawyers, on behalf of petitioners.[5] As the court did not make decisions based on legal precedents it did not have to store its records. While some of the bills that initiated a case have survived, it is rare that they are endorsed with process notes or stored with related records such as writs or depositions relating to the same case. Although this means we usually do not know how any individual case progressed, the evidence that we do have is written from the perspective of the petitioner rather than the court and, from 1443, usually in Middle English.[6] For Barbara Hanawalt, 'Because they are

written in English instead of Latin, they give the reader a sense of the way people narrated their own pathetic tales'.[7] Chancery bills, then, should be an ideal
source for those interested in the female litigant and her 'voice' under the law.

As with all legal material, though, we need to think carefully about the relationship between the written document and the persons and events it describes.
The frequent identification of the petitioner in the opening line of a Chancery bill
as 'your oratour' or 'oratrice' suggests a speaking subject but the bill's formulaic
language, and the third person format, also nods towards the involvement of a
lawyer or scribe. The stance taken in this essay is that one need not choose utterly
between the 'textual' and the 'social'. First, we will briefly consider how other historians have tackled the question of what legal records can reveal of past societies,
particularly women's voices and agency. Second, we will discuss the composition of Chancery bills and the process of petitioning the late medieval court of
Chancery in order to elucidate my own approach. Third, this approach will be
demonstrated by way of a particular case study, the Chancery bill of Humphrey
and Johanne Bawde, *c.* 1480 (see the appendix, p. 157, for a transcript).[8]

Legal Records and the Historian

Historians are aware of both the problems as well as possibilities of the sources
that they use, but some approaches stress one more than the other. For Joanne
Bailey, social and cultural historians have tended to approach legal records in one
of two ways: they act either as '"story-tellers", constructing stories of individuals,
relationships, and communities from legal testimony', or as '"translators" ... seeking to decode the symbol and form' of the language used in court records.[9] In
this typology, the 'story-tellers' –aware that the juridical context both shapes the
legal record and distorts our view of life outside the court – hold that the court
records nevertheless permit us to recover the experiences of people in the past
and even to access 'mental worlds' and 'voices' that would otherwise be lost.[10]
Or they emphasize reading trial narratives for the information that they contain. This was Marjorie McIntosh's approach to equity court bills in her study on
working women: 'The accounts were constructed to present the claims of that
party in a positive legal light ... The secondary information provided by the narrative ... was less apt to be deliberately re-worked.'[11]

By contrast, the 'translators' focus on the distortions. For some it is a matter
of identifying these 'filters' – such as the lawyer's or scribe's formulaic language
– so that they can be removed, allowing us access to an individual's voice and
agency.[12] Some scholars even alter their source material when quoting in order
to emphasize the female voice: 'repetitive and formulaic legal phrases have sometimes been removed without ellipses, and narratives returned to the first person
singular'.[13] For others, the filters are so effective that all we can reconstruct is the

'narrative of a trial', rather than the events that preceded it.[14] Christopher Cannon argues that the distortions in the records themselves signify by suggesting the *life lived at law*:

> The constricting lines of force that work to obscure women's voices in court – the rules of law and its procedural forms, attorneys and their linguistic influences, scribes and their distorting Latin formulae – are crucial forces determining the part of life lived *at law*: in the court, in the process of pleading, on the way to asserting the rights to plead and appeal that women had. [original emphasis][15]

Perhaps a little confusingly considering the nomenclature of her typology, Bailey's 'translators' – such as Laura Gowing and Tim Stretton – often focus on *storytelling* in the legal records. The seminal work in this respect is Natalie Zemon Davis's *Fiction in the Archives*, which analyses the stories told by those seeking a royal pardon for murder in sixteenth-century France. For Davis, the supplicant's voice was 'the primary one in a collective endeavor', that involved a royal notary and his clerks and possibly a lawyer or attorney, but the stories were 'determined by the constraints of the law and approaches to narratives learned in past listening to and telling of stories or derived from other cultural constructions'.[16] Stretton – in his study of the Elizabethan Court of Requests, which shared similar procedures with the court of Chancery – argues that it would be wise to focus attention on 'the story-telling, rather than the story-teller' as this allows one to set aside 'the eternal problem of separating the contributions (and values) of litigants and lawyers'.[17] But there are other approaches which, as Garthine Walker puts it,

> aim to be sensitive to the ways in which the content of legal tales was culturally mediated and structured by law ... yet ... also strive to hear individual women's voices in these texts, in keeping with conventional women's history that seeks to recover women's agency from a past of structural inequalities.[18]

Gowing's analysis of women's depositions from the church courts of early modern London is one such example, while Walker's approach to legal narratives in early modern England is another.[19] Walker stresses the multivocality of her legal texts. By this she does not just mean the woman's dialogue with the legal system, with specific laws, and with the persons judging her story, but she is also referring to the different discourses that the woman might invoke within a legal narrative:

> In speaking in or through intersecting or competing discourses, they constituted and positioned themselves as subjects within various and multiple subjectivities ... Their stories therefore provide us with access to a range of female subject positions, subjectivities as they were both performed and recorded in the particular context of legal procedures.[20]

The approach adopted in this essay aligns me with the 'translators', with its emphasis on analysing the structure and language of Chancery bills. Further, it strives to uncover the input of female petitioners. Although it will also discuss stories, tropes and subject positions, its methodology is tailored to the specific legal arena and records under discussion: the court of Chancery and its bills.

Chancery Bills and the Petitioning Subject

Although some scholars have thought about Chancery bills from the perspective of the petitioners, much of the previous scholarship on this source has been on their language and composition, that is, the role of scribes and lawyers.[21] The Six Clerks of Chancery were involved in drawing up the bills and could act as attorneys for petitioners.[22] Timothy Haskett has argued that lawyers outside of Chancery also composed some bills, although in such cases – if the bills were not written in Chancery hand – the bills would have been recopied by a Chancery clerk once submitted.[23] Formal petitions follow a universal set of epistolary principles in terms of their structure: *salutatio* (formal greeting to the addressee), *exordium* (introduction of the petitioner(s)), *narratio* (narration of the circumstances leading to the petition), *petitio* (presentation of request) and *conclusio* (final part).[24] Chancery bills are also presented as the kinds of cases that the Chancellor could deal with; for example, petitioners frequently claimed that they were too poor or too powerless to get justice at common law because such a claim allowed the Chancellor to intervene. In terms of both the generic elements of a petition and a bill's specific claims, we find many examples of formulaic language. For example, most bills begin with a version of 'your poor orator' or 'oratrice' and the actions of opponents are often explained as stemming from 'malice', leading to the petitioner's 'utter undoing' unless the Chancellor intervened.[25] Thus there was a distinct canon of form for a Chancery bill, which was applied to a petitioner's complaint by a Chancery clerk or another lawyer.

Chancery bills, though, obviously contain individualizing features that relate to specific petitioners and their problems. Haskett, in a study of Chancery cases for which more than one bill pertaining to the same matter survives, has argued that such examples 'demonstrate the nuances of presentation that were thought to ensure the greatest chance of success for a case in chancery'.[26] These nuances include presenting two different petitioners concerned with a single problem in different ways, the modification of bills after they were initially drawn but before submission and the modification and resubmission of failed bills. It was not acceptable for petitioners to alter the substance of their bills after they had been submitted; some bills included a memorandum of surety stating that the petitioner must prove the matter as specified in that particular bill to be true.[27]

Haskett is keen to emphasize how hard lawyers and scribes worked in order to give petitioners the best chance of success. However, his findings also enable us to envisage what role an individual petitioner might play in this process. For example, for a case to be successful it was imperative that a petitioner could substantiate her claims in court when required, although this stage – if it came – was much further on.[28] After a petition was handed in to Chancery, and if its case was appropriately set out, the requested writ would be issued, for example, to summon or secure the person of whom the bill complains or, directed to officials and holders of courts, asking them why the petitioner had been arrested and sometimes to produce the same petitioner from prison.[29] The next stage was for the defendant to answer the charges made. The petitioner then had the option of submitting a replication responding to the answer, which might in turn produce a rejoinder from the defendant, and so on, until the allegations of the bill had been whittled down to a set of agreed points at issue. These were then used for the next stage, the gathering of evidence. Witnesses could be examined and depositions produced. By the mid-fifteenth century, it seems that all these elements were presented to the Chancellor in written form, as some of these documents have been preserved. The Chancellor could then make a decision on the evidence that was before him, order a search for further evidence, examine further any of the parties involved, or delegate some of these tasks.[30] It is likely that not all cases lasted the distance, with some being dismissed, and others lapsing due to lack of funds or because the defendants had settled out of court, although this is hard to quantify when we only have the initial bill.[31] While written documents were the main means by which petitioners (and their opponents) could communicate their versions of events, then, they also needed to ensure that they could defend in person whatever was alleged therein.

The petitioner's presentation of the case to the lawyer or scribe could also be the origin of some of the bill's distinctive features, whether these relate to the story told, the subject positions adopted or to some of the language that is used. As discussed, one approach towards legal records has been to focus on *stories*, the common plots, literary tropes and vivid details that make the legal narratives plausible and familiar to a contemporary audience. The intention of a Chancery bill was not to tell a compelling story, though, but to get a case moved to Chancery, usually from another jurisdiction. Thus bills tend to outline what should have happened in another court and what had happened instead, but do not always elaborate on the events that led up to the earlier legal process, although we might discern a common narrative frame.[32] Nevertheless, whether a Chancery bill tells a coherent story or not, the events related work to position the petitioner in one or more ways. For example, Chancery bills from servants who were being sued in another court by former employers position the petitioners as 'good servants', 'honest workers' and 'virtuous maidens' who had been exploited in some way. 'Poor maiden Johanne Fowler', whose bill was quoted at the outset, counters her mistress' accusation of theft with the statement that, 'she was but a poor maiden having ... no help but only of almighty God through her virtuous living and maidenly disposition'.[33] Johanne Lytle, whose master pursued serial actions of trespass against her when she tried to leave his service at the end of an agreed term, is described in her bill as 'being a poor maiden and nothing hath to live by but only by her true service'.[34]

While one could debate if the subject position constructed in a bill, as with the narrative, was the creation of the petitioner, a lawyer or someone else, if the petitioner wanted her complaint to be redressed she needed to ensure that she could occupy the subject position(s) adopted in the bill – such as the 'poor maiden', or the 'chaste wife' – for any potential court appearance. What we get in a Chancery bill, then, is primarily a *textual* subject, which we might think of as a *petitioning subject*. The petitioning subject is produced by the process of petitioning Chancery, rather than being a fictive persona or an *a priori* self 'revealed' through writing.[35] Thus understanding that process enables us to make a link between the text and the lived life.

Although it can be problematic to separate out the petitioner's contribution from that of the lawyer, there are occasions when the bill's writer slips and the collaborative nature of the petition is exposed. It is in these slips that we might discern something of the petitioner's voice. For example, the bill of Denise Gros begins, as we have seen, in conventional manner ('Beseecheth meekly your poor oratrice Denise Gros of London, widow') but just over halfway through it switches from the usual third person representation of the petitioner and allows Denise to address the Chancellor directly:

> Whereby your oratrice is destroyed and undone by untrue maintenance the law may not be observed as law and conscience requireth less than ye gracious lord be my good lord now standing in my great mischief ... Beseeching you gracious lord of your merciful grace and of tender pity to have compassion on my long suit and of my great poverty and set me on a way how I shall speak in my right for I dare not go home for doubt of my life.[36]

This bill is a particularly unusual example where the crafted nature of the Chancery bill has broken down and we appear to have a female petitioner's direct complaint to the Chancellor. The bill to be examined in more detail here, that of Humphrey Bawde and his wife Johanne, also includes hints that the Chancery clerk or other lawyer who drew it up was not in complete control of its narrative. Of course the lawyer composed the bill by incorporating elements of the story his clients must have told him. But in this example we will see that the lawyer's role as listener is revealed in the bill itself and the voice he was listening to seems to have been Johanne's.

The Chancery Bill of Humphrey Bawde and his Wife Johanne

In a Chancery bill, as in other formal petitions, we can expect an address to the Chancellor, an identification of the petitioner(s), a narration of the problem, a request for redress and a conclusion.[37] In this example, the petitioners are named as Humphrey Bawde and his wife Johanne and the bill is addressed to the Archbishop of York. The address to the Chancellor is usually the key to dating a bill (bills are undated and Chancellors are not named but just titled in bills), and dates this bill to 1465–7, 1470–1 or 1480–3.[38] However, London's consistory court was also considering an allegation in 1480 that Humphrey Bawde and his wife had defamed one 'Matilda Olyve' by calling her *meretricem* (whore) and *pronubam* (bawd; go-between), which allows us to date the bill more narrowly to *c.* 1480.[39] The third element, the narration of the problem, takes up the vast majority of the bill. It tells a detailed and dramatic story, which sets it apart from many other Chancery bills.

According to the bill, one Maud Olyff (Maud is a variant of Matilda) was aware that Humphrey Bawde lived in service with one Thomas Hart, baker, in Smithfield, leaving his wife, Johanne, residing alone in the parish of St Giles without Cripplegate. Maud told Johanne that there was a man (unnamed) who was in love with her and wanted an introduction, which Johanne refused because she did not want any damage to her reputation. Maud – said to be of 'false living and uncleanly disposition' – then set out to help the man have his 'foul lust and will of the said Johanne' by bringing him to the Bawdes' house. Maud made the man lie down upon a bench, and then seems to have left him alone in the house. Johanne at this time was working in another little house, perhaps a shed, and returned home to find, to her surprise, the man lying on the bench. The man jumped up, took Johanne in his arms, and said 'he would have a doo with her or else he would die for it'. Johanne struggled hard with him and managed to escape with her chastity intact. She grabbed a staff, gave him a dozen blows with it, and drove him out of the house. The next scenario we are presented with is Johanne's subsequent encounter with Maud, at which she gave her 'a knappe [sharp blow] upon the cheek' and warned her never to bring any such men into Johanne's house again. The bill then gets to the crux of the matter: Maud Olyff had taken a plaint of trespass against the Bawdes in the sheriffs' court, alleging that Johanne had beaten her with a staff, and asking for damages of twenty pounds. The common law process in the sheriffs' court would not allow the aforementioned provocation as a justification of Johanne's actions.

The bill then moves on to the request for redress: the Chancellor is asked to intervene by sending a writ of *certiorari* to the sheriffs of London, requiring them to produce a 'certification' of the reason for Johanne's arrest, so that the case could be heard in Chancery 'according to conscience'. There are no concluding words to this bill. The endorsement on the bill reveals that the Bawdes' request was accepted but we do not know how the case progressed after that.[40]

As one might expect, the evidence for the Bawdes' – particularly Johanne's – input is in the narration of the problem, the largest part of the bill. First, as we shall see, there are shifts in whose perspective it was written from: Humphrey's, the married couple's, Johanne's. Second, in similar fashion, there are shifts in who is assigned ownership of the house in which some of the alleged events took place. These latter shifts can be linked with different stages in the story and different subject positions for Johanne Bawde. Third, the bill seems to include some examples of reported speech, albeit transposed – like the rest of the bill – into the third person. The linguistic shifts, or slips, suggest that the bill and its story are not one seamless construction, and they point up interaction between the bill's composer and the petitioners, particularly Johanne, as does the inclusion of reported speech.

First, to whom did the petition belong? The petitioners are identified at the start of the bill as being Humphrey Bawde and Johanne his wife. Then, near the start and end of the narration of the problem, it is Humphrey who is said to be the 'beseecher' while Johanne is described as 'his wife' (see appendix in this volume, ll. 4, 23–4), as she is on l. 24. Yet, in the final line of the narration, it is Johanne who is referred to as 'your oratrice' (l. 26). Moreover, although Humphrey is formulaically referred to as the petitioner, he is actually absent from all the events that the bill relates. Indeed, his only role in the story is to be away working in Smithfield as a baker's servant. It is this absence that allowed the other man to come into his house in Cripplegate, where Johanne was living alone, and attempt to have sex with her. The story is told, then, from Johanne's perspective, with lots of references to 'Johanne', 'she' and 'her' throughout.

The second indication that the narrative belongs more to Johanne than to Humphrey, and that the lawyer did not have complete control over it, is more subtle: there are switches in how Humphrey and Johanne's house is referred to in the bill. First it is 'the house of your said beseecher' (l. 11), which is probably the phrasing of the lawyer, as it follows from how Johanne is described, as the 'wife of your said beseecher' (l. 4). However, then it is 'her ... house' (ll. 14–15), 'her husband's house' (l. 19) and 'the house of the same Johanne' (ll. 21–2). These inconsistencies suggest that we are seeing here traces of the story that Johanne reported to the lawyer.[41] If we look at where these three references to the house appear in the overall narrative, how the house is described seems to be tied in with the events narrated and how Johanne is presented. These can be summarized in the following way: the house as the location of Johanne's honest labour, the house as chaste marital home and the house as Johanne's domain. We will consider if there are any other parallels, legal and otherwise, for the different elements of this dramatic story but, while it is possible that the adaptation of common stories and tropes could have suggested themselves to a lawyer as much as to Johanne, the inconsistencies in presentation point to Johanne's narrative role.[42]

The context for the reference to 'her ... house' is the period immediately preceding the alleged sexual attack on Johanne. She was working in 'another little house' and, when she 'had done her business she came into her other house', not knowing that a man had been smuggled in and was lying on one of her benches, presumably hidden from sight. This evocation of the moments leading up to the attack presents Johanne as a working woman, going about her everyday business, and the house – her house – is part of this picture of normality, of domesticity, about to disturbed. The subject position is that of the 'good housewife'. This was perhaps a deliberate strategy, as other scholars working on legal narratives about violence, sexual and otherwise, have identified similar tropes. Davis found that when women appealed for a pardon for murder in sixteenth-century France they tended to excuse their supposedly out-of-character actions by invoking the setting of everyday life, whereas men tended to use ritual and festive contexts in their accounts. In many of their stories of homicide, for example, wifeliness and/ or sexual honour were at stake. These letters of remission tended to emphasize housewifely activities at the start of their narratives as a way of showing that these women had not encouraged any sexual advances.[43] Similarly, Miranda Chaytor – in an analysis of rape narratives in depositions to the Northern Circuit assizes in late seventeenth-century England – argues that females stressed how, at the time of the attack, they were engaged in some useful activity such as taking hay to the calves in the barn or fetching ale from the alehouse. For Chaytor, this was because 'for a woman reporting a rape, honour ... was, had to be, metaphorically transposed from the sexual body to the body that worked'.[44] Walker's study of narratives of sexual violence heard by a range of seventeenth-century English law courts found frequent recourse to the motif of open, closed and locked doors and chambers. Walker contends that 'the household was where non-sexual feminine honour resided', and so violation of this space also served as a metaphor for the violation of the household's women.[45]

The second reference to the Bawdes' house in the Chancery bill is to 'her husband's house' (l. 19). The context here is the alleged sexual attack on Johanne. The household might be where non-sexual feminine honour resides but it is also usually the marital home. Thus the man's sexual advances, and Maud's role in them, are made worse by the fact that Johanne was a married woman and that they happened in her husband's house. The phrasing seems particularly deliberate given that we know Humphrey Bawde actually lived with his master in Smithfield. Similarly, when the house was first described as 'the house of your said beseecher' (l. 11), meaning Humphrey, the context was Maud bringing the unnamed man into the property with the intention of helping the latter 'have his foul lust and will of the said Johanne'. Therefore, there seems to be a correlation between the labelling of the house as Humphrey's and the reported attempts on Johanne's marital chastity.

The description of the attack also emphasizes Johanne's position as a 'chaste wife' in other ways. She 'struggled sore [hard] with him and by the help and grace of our lady that blessed virgin broke from him a clean woman not defiled' (ll. 17–18). Not only is Johanne referred to as 'a clean woman' and 'not defiled' but an association is made with the Virgin Mary, the ultimate touchstone in female chastity. The reference to the Virgin Mary is unusual in a Chancery bill. The only other example I have seen is in a bill belonging to a female servant, who claimed she was being falsely accused of theft by a hosteller with her master's backing, which relates that she had asked her master 'at the reverence of Our Lady, comfort of all women, to be from thenceforth her good master'.[46] In the Bawdes' bill, though, the Virgin is said to have helped Johanne escape from her attacker's clutches. Given that Johanne was being prosecuted in London's sheriffs' court for her attack on Maud, it was perhaps a sensible – if atypical – tactic to claim that Johanne escaped from the man because of the help and grace of the Virgin Mary, rather than because she hit him a dozen times with a staff. While invoking the help of the Virgin was not a common legal trope, it does occur in other narratives, most notably the miracle stories associated with the Virgin Mary, which were used in sermons in the late medieval period.[47] Indeed, A. Wallensköld argued that the chaste-wife tale – in which a wife, whose husband is away, spurns a man's advances but is then falsely accused of adultery and persecuted, which entails more unwelcome sexual advances – took one of five different forms in the West, of which the Marian-miracle subgroup is one (the other four being *Gesta romanorum*, *Florence of Rome*, *Crescentia* and *Hildegard*).[48] In the Marian-miracle subgroup, the wife (usually an Empress) prays to the Virgin on two occasions and on both is saved from an attempted rape.[49] In *Florence of Rome*, a related subgroup, Florence's prayers to the Virgin Mary save her from gang rape in that they produce a miraculous storm and even when she prays to God to stop another attempted rape it is Mary who is credited with saving her.[50] There were therefore a number of literary, if not legal, parallels for the claim that the Virgin Mary helped a woman avoid an attempted rape.

In the Chancery bill's third reference to the house, when Johanne confronts Maud, it is described once more as Johanne's house. Maud is given 'a knappe upon the cheek' and told 'never bring into the house of the same Johanne any man of such condition as the foresaid man was' (ll. 20–2). In this woman versus woman confrontation, the offence is quite clearly represented as being against Johanne rather than her husband, who is still absent from the events of the narrative. In this scene Johanne is not presented as a victim but rather as a woman who is asserting her rights. In order for her defence to work, then, this image needed to follow on from the previous presentation of her as the good housewife, hard at work, not looking for any trouble, and as a chaste wife, attacked in her husband's own home and saved by the Virgin Mary. The bill is perhaps wise not to dwell on Johanne's attack on Maud but it is worth noting that Davis also found that all-female conflicts 'stay matter-of-fact, commonplace' in her legal narratives, unlike in male–female or male–male ones and unlike the representations of women fighting in contemporary images and literary texts. She wonders if this was in part due to lack of *serious* models for female fighting.[51] Karen Jones put forward a complementary argument in her study of gender and crime in Kent's local courts, 1460–1560: 'Didactic literature, which is so full of injunctions to women to avoid disorderly speech, has nothing to say about female violence' with the result that women's brawls were more likely to appear in court as scolding or defamation rather than assault.[52]

The third element of the bill that suggests the input of Johanne, alongside that of a lawyer, is the inclusion of reported speech in the narration of the problem. In the church court records discussed in this book by Jeremy Goldberg and Bronach Kane, reported speech is usually signalled by the scribe switching from Latin into Middle English to convey the words in the vernacular.[53] Inevitably, reported speech will be less evident in a Middle English petition but there are three occasions in this bill that can be read that way, all introduced by the words 'saying that', which are not typically found in Chancery bills. They refer, in order, to what Maud allegedly said to Johanne, to Johanne's response and to what the unnamed man had said to Johanne.[54] The key issue is not whether any of the individuals had actually said these words but rather whether they represent what Johanne had reported to her lawyer. Although, like the rest of the bill, they have been transposed into the third person and the past tense, the variety of language used in the three statements suggests that they were meant to represent the spoken words of others. The speech attributed to the male attacker is the most striking and dramatic of the three. As noted above, it is reported that – when he grabbed hold of Johanne – he said 'he would have *a doo* with her or else he would die for it'. An example from a defamation case, heard in London's consistory court around the same time as the bill was presented, indicates the use of 'a doo' in contemporary speech, presumably to refer to sexual intercourse: Alice Barbour, for instance, defamed Elizabeth Braudnam saying in English 'thou had *adoo* with my husband in my garden'.[55] We would expect a clerk or lawyer to use clearer and more formal language where an attempted rape was concerned, thus suggesting that the unnamed man's assertion is an example of reported speech.[56] The other two examples represent the conversation that took place between Maud and Johanne. Maud allegedly said, 'there was a man the which ought to her *hertly luf* and gladly would be with her acquainted' (ll. 6–7) and Johanne replied 'she were loath to have any such acquaintance by the which she in any way might be hurt of her good name' (ll. 8–9). Johanne's response is quite a formal one. This reported speech is perhaps part of the presentation of Johanne as an upstanding and chaste wife. Maud's words, though, while not giving away the full extent of what was to come, are more lively, with her reference to 'hertly luf' and the adverb 'gladly'. 'Hertly luf' can be translated as heartfelt love; a fifteenth-century Middle English verse begins 'My hertly love is in your governance'.[57] However, there is perhaps a hint of euphemism for the unnamed man's physical feelings for Johanne as 'hertly' could also mean 'violent'; Maud is described here as having 'laboured subtly' (l. 6) to set up the extramarital encounter.[58]

The contention that this Chancery bill includes reported speech is reinforced by an examination of a commissary court act book, also from late fifteenth-century London (the same one in which the Bawdes' alleged defamation of Maud Olyff appears).[59] The act book records a large number of defamation cases, for the most part in Latin, in which the alleged defamatory words are given in Middle English, with some introduced by the words 'saying that', as in the Chancery bill. For example, one entry reads:

> *Johanna Mate diff. Elisabeth Adale vocando eam* hore and harlot' and **seying that** she schulde logge gentylmen of the kynges howse in her bed.[60]

> (Johanna Mate defamed Elisabeth Adale calling her whore and harlot and saying that she should lodge gentlemen of the king's house in her bed.)

In this act book reported speech has also been transposed into the third person. Such transpositions, in the Chancery bill as well as the act book, remind us that we are dealing with a written record of reported speech rather than direct speech. Nevertheless, the original source of the reported conversations must have been the litigants.

Conclusion

The Chancery bill of Humphrey and Johanne Bawde tells a compelling story because of its verisimilitude: its vivid, apparently authentic detail. However, we must be careful not to read it as a transparent account of events that had taken place in Johanne's life. If we pay attention to the common form of Chancery bills, their structure and language, we can sometimes find fissures in their careful crafting. In this example, shifts in whose perspective the bill was written from and, in particular, shifts in who was assigned ownership of the house at the centre of the narrative reveal Johanne's key role not only in the events that the bill narrates but also in the construction of the bill. Despite the formulaic references to Humphrey as 'your said beseecher', the story is largely told from Johanne's perspective and it positions her as a respectable woman, a good housewife and chaste wife. We also hear echoes of her conversations with Maud and the unnamed man, even if these have been changed in the retelling, first when Johanne recounted them to her lawyer and then when he transposed them into the third person for the Chancery bill.

Although reported speech is unusual in Chancery bills, the approach of analysing the subject positions offered in such bills is one that can be applied more generally. These positions (sometimes linked with common stories and/ or tropes), whether they were the conscious or unconscious creation of the petitioner or the lawyer or some combination, are revealing of cultural norms such as what it might mean to be a good wife or servant and thus of deep-rooted ideologies of gender. They are also positions that petitioners would have had to be prepared to adopt for their appearances in court. While the chaste-wife tale can be found in different cultures, periods and genres, Johanne Bawde took on the subject position of 'chaste wife' in a way that both befitted the wife of a baker's servant in late fifteenth-century London and a woman who was appealing to the Archbishop of York as Chancellor for help in avoiding a conviction and damages for trespass in the city's sheriffs' court.[61] Johanne's story and voice, such as they exist for us, are produced by her experience of petitioning Chancery with her husband via a Chancery clerk and perhaps another lawyer. The petitioning subject that we find in a Chancery bill is a textual one but it gives us, in most cases, our only insight into the women who brought their complaints to Chancery. By understanding the process of petitioning Chancery we need not choose utterly between the 'textual' and the 'social' or 'lived'. A methodology that pays attention to this is revealing not only of gender ideologies but also of women's experiences of and interactions with the law.

2 ECHOES, WHISPERS, VENTRILOQUISMS: ON RECOVERING WOMEN'S VOICES FROM THE COURT OF YORK IN THE LATER MIDDLE AGES

Jeremy Goldberg

The records of Inquisition and of instance (or private) litigation within the church courts are singularly attractive to scholars. Both are associated with the production of depositions, the written records of the responses given by deponents to questions put to them. Such depositions offer the tantalizing – but perhaps elusive – possibility of recovering the actual words, thoughts, beliefs and experience of a variety of people, female and male, old and young, poor and wealthy.[1] John Arnold, however, has used Inquisition records to argue that deponents' responses were shaped by the questions posed and that the questions posed in turn reflected the Inquisitors' own agenda and understanding of the nature of heresy and of heretics. We are permitted to see, therefore, those who were subjected to the process of Inquisition only as they are represented within an inquisitorial discourse, which, in Arnold's words, 'cannot recapture the "true" voices of the past'.[2] Arnold's statement is of course a truism. How can we ever recapture 'true' voices and how would we recognize one if we did? In the absence of archival recordings we can never access past speech directly. We are dependent at best on voices as ventriloquized by the clerks who recorded the depositions more or less conscientiously and often in a language – Latin – other than the vernacular of the deponent. Arnold goes on, however: 'to leave the possibilities of speech in silence seems to me a recapitulation of failure and defeat in the face of power.'

In the context of this present volume, another attraction of church court depositions, as also Inquisition records, is that it is not just men's voices that are recorded or at least ventriloquized. Inquisitors were interested in detecting heretics whether male or female. The church courts and the canon law differed from the English royal courts and the common law tradition. Common law very significantly curtailed women's agency to bring actions. In essence only in pleas of rape or the death of a husband where he died in the woman's arms – and of course they always did, since otherwise a widow cruelly robbed of her spouse risked having no opportunity for justice – were permitted to bring an action before royal justices.[3] There was much less limitation on actions being brought against women, though a married woman might be acquitted if her crime were committed with her husband and hence on his orders.[4] Customary courts and borough courts were more permissive, at least to women without husbands, notably widows, but married women usually might bring actions only with their husbands. The canon law courts created no such obstacles and allowed female litigants the same access to the law as men regardless of marital status. They seem also to have been equally willing to admit women as deponents and, regardless of the perception of the laity using the courts, to have given their testimony essentially equal weight with that of men.[5]

This present chapter will explore evidence from the Court of York, which Bronach Kane also discusses in her own chapter in this collection. During the course of the later Middle Ages, and indeed for several centuries thereafter, the Church provided a network of courts at both archidiaconal and diocesan level. Much lower-level jurisdiction saw the courts act in a policing capacity enforcing canon law *ex officio*, mostly in respect of presentments for fornication or adultery. Whereas the extant records of this *ex officio* jurisdiction are invariably formulaic and rather bald, the records generated by private (instance) litigation can be fairly voluminous. One case from York concerning burial rights disputed between the church of Sutton on Hull and the mother church of Wawne fills a whole volume.[6] This present chapter will several times refer to another substantial case, that of *Marrays* v. *Rouclif*. Here John Marrays asked the court to restore his wife, Alice de Rouclif, to him after she was abducted by men acting for Brian de Rouclif, who appears to have asserted rights of wardship as feudal suzerain over the young heiress.[7] The case was defended in the name of Alice by the counter-argument that Alice was too young to have lawfully consented to marriage and so could not be married to Marrays. The case is remarkable for the very large number of deponents appearing on either side, a high proportion of which were female.[8]

The most common instance actions brought by the laity, like the Rouclif case, concerned marriage, though defamation and probate disputes are also found and the laity were usually defendants in tithe litigation. By their nature, women are conspicuous in matrimonial disputes, usually as litigants and most commonly trying to enforce contracts of marriage. We also find suits to annul marriage and, much more rarely, to provide for legal separation on grounds of cruelty.[9] Though thousands of such cases passed through the network of church courts during the course of the later Middle Ages, it is only from the diocesan courts of Canterbury in the thirteenth and earlier fifteenth centuries, of London in the late fifteenth century, and of York from 1301 that records of actual litigation including depositions survive in any quantity. Whereas at Canterbury and London in the fifteenth century it is books of depositions alone that survive, for

York much related material – libels, articles, judgements, etc. – add significantly to the value of the records for the historian.

The Court of York records bear some relation to Inquisitorial records. Both are the product of the Church acting in a judicial capacity. The language of record, moreover, is the Latin of the Church rather than the vernaculars of the actual deponents. There are some very significant differences, however. The private litigation that results in the collection of depositions within the Court of York is not the product of fear. Those who give testimony do not endanger their own lives or the lives of their kin, friends and neighbours. They do not have to balance anxieties and uncertainties about what evidence the Inquisitors have already gathered against them. Rather, they are there to support litigants pursuing essentially private disputes that fall within, or can be made to fall within, the realm of canon law. In brief, witnesses in the Court of York, as in similar instance litigation in other ecclesiastical courts throughout Latin Christendom, appeared because they had in principle agreed to, not because they were made to. Some servants, employees or other dependents or subordinates may have been pressured by their masters or superiors, but this represents a very different order of compulsion or fear and radically changes the dynamics of power outlined in Arnold's analysis of Inquisition records.[10]

These profound differences, I will argue, make the recorded depositions from the Court of York a rather less opaque window onto the witnesses whose testimony they purport to reproduce than is true of Inquisitorial depositions. Nevertheless, church court depositions do present many challenges. We need to consider the process by which the depositions were produced; the evidence of the extant depositions, which vary considerably in quality, from neat and carefully written texts to rather scrappy and much crossed out scribbles; as well as the evidence of the actual contents. My discussion will stress the fictive nature of the process. Witnesses did not testify as if chatting to a close friend. They were well aware of the work their testimony was designed to perform and may often have been – to borrow transatlantic jargon – suitably 'prepped'. Similarly clerks were not stenographers charged with producing a verbatim transcript, but rather a legal deposition that might be used by the Official – the presiding officer of the court – in reaching his judgement.[11]

There were almost no restrictions on the testimony of women (or men) beyond that they were of free status and of canonical age.[12] Depositions associated with women survive in considerable number from the Court of York, though those associated with men are significantly more common. Indeed, for certain kinds of litigation such as disputes about tithes or parochial rights where cases were made or broken on communal memory of local custom, female deponents are hardly found. Even for matrimonial litigation, male deponents outnumbered women in the extant fourteenth- and fifteenth-century records by three to one (713 male deponents to 230 female). This imbalance grew over the period and is more marked in rural cases – the ratio here is nearly four to one – than urban.[13] Women's testimony, then, was permitted, but social and cultural prejudices, strongest in the more ideologically conservative countryside, worked to their disadvantage. Older, male witnesses seem generally to have been preferred, though women were used as expert witnesses in respect of recalling childbirth and impotence. As already observed, such prejudice against the testimony of women appears not to have been shared by the courts.[14]

Ages of deponents are regularly recorded from the later fourteenth century, though rarely before. We can also surmise something of the social standing of witnesses from the details invariably supplied at the beginning of each deposition or from clues provided within the body of the deposition or elsewhere within the extant documentation. The description of 'Joan Symkyn Woman of Rawcliffe, having almost nothing in goods save her clothing for body and bed, and a small brass pot, tenant of Sir Brian de Rouclif' is unusually informative, but we can still often distinguish between peasant women, bourgeois women, ladies, and more generally the wealthy and the poor. What is apparent is that persons of comparatively high social rank are rarely found as witnesses. Most witnesses were probably artisans and their wives, landed peasants and (to a rather lesser degree) their wives, and, in an urban context, male and female adolescent and young adult servants. Teenage witnesses tend not to be especially common other than in respect of urban servants. Despite this, the extant depositions do record a broad social and age range of women witnesses.

Rather than being cross-examined, witnesses responded to questions that had been drawn up in advance though sometimes the court officer charged with questioning witnesses was instructed to ask additional questions. All questions were put and answered in the vernacular, but, before about the middle of the sixteenth century, recorded only in Latin.[15] Sometimes, however, reported speech such as the words used in a matrimonial contract or alleged defamatory words may be recorded additionally in the vernacular.[16] This process of converting verbal responses into written depositions prompts a number of questions. How far did the clerk attempt a verbatim transcript that was then reworked as a Latin text? Fourteenth-century York church court depositions tend to be neatly written in abbreviated Latin. By the fifteenth century the actual documents become conspicuously messier. Text is crossed through, insertions are added, and the quality of the hand deteriorates. At the same time, as just noted, reported speech is sometimes recorded in English. This is suggestive of contemporaneous note-taking that may not have been true earlier. The apparent neatness and uniformity of fourteenth-century depositions may, of course, simply represent a neat copy produced for the court and not the original transcript. More likely, depositions were reworked from some kind of contemporaneous transcript or notes; there are some indications that this was indeed the case.

The tone of the Latin depositions is formal. Witnesses appearing within the consistory court might adopt a more formal register than they would use in everyday speech, but this does not seem sufficient explanation. In the Rouclif case from 1366 that revolved around whether one Alice de Rouclif was of sufficient age to have lawfully married, a deposition by Anabilla Wascelyne reads:

> concerning the first and second articles she says that they contain the truth [*continent veritatem*] and this she knows by confession of the parties in dispute [*inter quos agitur*] and by the account of others and common report [*communem famam*] circulating about them.[17]

The phrases where I have given the original Latin text in parenthesis can all be recognized as belonging to a legal rather than a vernacular discourse. The implication is that the clerk, whilst conveying the original sense, has substituted these familiar phrases for whatever less concise or orderly words were actually proffered.

Other than phraseology that constitutes a form of legal discourse, the wording of depositions made few gestures to literary elegance or cleverness and tends to suggest that the Latinity of the court's clerks was not of a particularly high standard. A relatively limited range of vocabulary is deployed. In this way the translation from the vernacular feels more like a fairly literal translation, as if the thought processes were in English rather than Latin. Much the same could be said of the way dates were recorded. In the same case, for example, Maud de Herthill related that she gave birth 'on the morrow of St Bartholomew twelve years ago'. Several witnesses placed Alice de Rouclif's birth on 'the Saturday before the first Sunday in Passiontide'.[18] The use of major saints' days to locate events in time probably tends to follow social practice and reflects a society in which work days were punctuated by the more important feasts of the Church.[19] But we should be a little cautious of presuming that the depositions always convey dates as given by witnesses. The use of feast days was very much the calendar norm of the Church and hence of the ecclesiastical courts. It is likely that dates would have been recast to conform to this ecclesiastical norm where they did not originally and certainly that they achieved much greater uniformity at the hands of recording clerks than would always have been true of the actual spoken words of the witnesses.

Thus far I have implied that clerks merely standardized text by adopting certain common phrases, standardizing dates and the like, but otherwise did little to undermine our confidence that the resultant depositions broadly represent what the witness said. In fact, their intervention can sometimes be shown to be more intrusive. In imposing some standardization of the text and converting hesitant circumlocutions into regular Latin phrases, the clerk may also have cut out words and phrases. Clerks were not trained stenographers. They do not reproduce the 'ums' and 'ahs' and repetitions that characterize ordinary speech. Rather, they may have seen their job primarily to produce text that accurately conveyed the salient points. Indeed, it is hard not to suspect that the frequent iteration of '*dicit*' and '*ut dicit*' – 'he says,' 'so she says', etc. – which supposedly conveys the orality of the deposition process and which effectively characterizes depositions as a distinctive genre of writing, actually serves to deflect attention from the fact that these are not the actual words of the deponent. As I have stated elsewhere, 'the more the depositions reiterate their origin in speech, the more they ... draw attention to their fictive nature as texts'.[20]

This argument may be elaborated. The answers that witnesses give to the questions asked of them – the 'articles' as they are regularly described in the depositions – are remarkably, even suspiciously, focused. Rarely does the witness stray from the subject. To no small degree this is probably a product of the careful 'prepping' of witnesses, but it may also follow from tacit editing by the clerk. Returning to the Rouclif case, Agnes Quysteler knew Alice de Rouclif's birthdate from 'her neighbours' and Eufemia de Rouclif 'from the relation of women'.[21] The importance of their testimony is thus marginal because second-hand, but the women themselves are hardly likely to have realized this. These witnesses may have attempted to offer lists of names and anecdotal detail about who said what, where and when, but any such detail was discarded.

The degree to which the words of witnesses have been shaped or reworked by the clerk is but one consideration in what we may regard as an essentially fictive process. Indeed, the clerk is not the most important, merely the most recent player in this process. The deposition as a fictive text is in fact shaped by a number of different agents. Witnesses testified in response to set questions composed in advance by proctors – legal counsel – who were employed by the litigants. These questions derived ultimately from the plaintiff's original 'plaint', conveyed in the 'libel', or the counter case made by the defendant, written down as the 'exception'. Both documents were composed by men trained in the canon law on the basis of information supplied by the parties for whom they worked.[22] It follows that the questions were designed not to find out what the witness might or might not know, but specifically provide answers that substantiate one version of events or the other. The value of the witnesses' responses thus lay solely in how far they supported and gave credence to the points raised by the questions. In effect, it was the answer required that dictated the initial question just as the question itself prompted and helped determine the desired testimony.

The example of William Pottell, another witness in the Rouclif case, and his rather flawed and confused deposition offers telling illustration of the point and reflects the degree to which legal counsel might 'prep' witnesses.[23] Pottell was the lowly factotum of John Marrays, the man who claimed Alice de Rouclif as his wife. A series of questions was put to him with a view to establishing that Alice was of sufficient age to marry and that she really wanted John for her husband, i.e. that their alleged marriage satisfied the canonical yardsticks that indicated consent. The fourth question posed asked if Alice had achieved puberty. Pottell replied that he had brought her various gifts from John Marrays, his master, and that he had asked her why her husband was away all the time. Pottell's enigmatic response only makes sense once we come to question number six which specifically asked about the giving and receiving of gifts. What is apparent is that Pottell had been 'prepped' for the questions that were put to him, but mistook his cues – the opening of the fourth and sixth questions is superficially similar – and had proffered his prepared answer to the sixth question when asked the fourth question, only to have to recover himself rapidly when confronted with the actual sixth question. One can sympathize with Pottell's anxiety to please – his job may well have been on the line – and his nervousness in an unfamiliar situation. But we should also note that the clerk seems to have made little effort to rectify Pottell's error. We know he fluffed his answer because the clerk has conscientiously recorded it. That gives us a little more confidence in the degree to which the deposition does indeed reflect the witness's testimony.

Although Pottell had his responses prepared and there is a clear sense more generally that the form of the question did much to shape most responses, deponents did not always simply repeat back words and phrases from the questions put to them. As with William Pottell's deposition, personal experience and individual testimony can move beyond the limited outlines suggested by the question. When, for example, Maud Katersouth, who was Maud de Bradelay's witness in another marriage case from 1355, was asked both if John de Walkyngton had contracted Maud de Bradelay by words of future consent followed by intercourse and if this were known in the locality, i.e. North Street, York, she introduced many details that were not contained in these two initial questions.[24] Her account, which was prompted by the questions and no doubt anticipated by Maud's legal counsel, explained how she had been in Maud's home together with her teenage son. She was there when John got into bed and called for Maud de Bradelay to 'come to bed' and heard Maud decline. John responded by telling Maud 'you are mine and I am yours ... I refuse to seek permission from you to do my will with you', but Maud responded that she would only get into bed if he exchanged words of matrimony with her. They then contracted and Maud concluded with 'now you can do your will with me'. When Maud was asked the time at which the couple contracted she replied that it was 'about the ringing of the curfew bells on Pavement'.

Maud Katersouth gives us – and gave to the court – a vivid vignette of a supposed encounter between a man and a woman that brings together remembered words and eyewitness account of actions. By itself it would seem convincing testimony were we to overlook the question of why Maud and her teenage son were present in the first place to witness the exchange and indeed to remain in the house to witness the couple get up out of bed the next morning. Her deposition is in fact not so distinctive. The deposition of Maud's son, Robert, is similar in a way that cannot be explained simply by the commonality of their experience. The point is not that the likeness of wording and phraseology undermines the credibility or historicity of the events described – they may or may not have happened and they may or may not have been so witnessed – but that the witnesses have been 'prepped'. The vividness of the narrative is thus in part an artifice, just as the similarity of the two depositions is a deliberate strategy to satisfy the canon-legal understanding that consistency of testimony was the benchmark of credibility.[25]

Medieval canon lawyers did not rely solely on witnesses parroting one another. There was room for individual experience where this could provide suitably compelling testimony. Beatrix de Morland in the Rouclif case, for example, offered tragic reason for remembering the date of Alice's birth: her husband had been killed the same year.[26] When Lady Margery de Rouclif was asked how she was able to remember the birthdate of Alice's deceased older brother, she replied

> because on the one hand William Fairfax, who married this witness' daughter, had that year a son born of his wife who was called John before he was baptised because his imminent death was feared, and on the other hand she remembers by the dates of writings and indentures by which she demised certain of her lands at farm, and otherwise by the births of other children at Rawcliffe who were born a short time before and after the birth of John of women neighbours of the village of Rawcliffe where this witness was then living.[27]

Lady Margery's evidence is impressive. It deploys a mnemonic strategy commonly enough found in Proof of Ages testimony on the part of male jurors that explains how even after the passage of fourteen years she was able to locate so precisely in time John de Rouclif's birth.[28] It also enhances her credibility. Not only is she a mature, aristocratic widow – and hence immediately a more substantial witness than William Pottell – but through her deposition she is able to project herself variously as a good estate manager who took an informed interest in her property, as a caring mother and grandmother, and as an exemplary landlord and gentlewoman who took an interest in and kept herself informed about the lives of her peasant women neighbours.

The deposition of Alice de Beleby, who was Alice de Rouclif's godmother, is similarly impressive in its construction. She remembered how Alice's birth had taken place:

> at least twelve years ago before the Saturday before the first Sunday in Passiontide last, according to what she dares say on oath before God. Alice was baptised that Saturday and was born that day or the Friday before, and she knows no other reason to offer for her knowing other than that she has thought it out thus in her heart, and according to what this witness has calculated from her memory, so she remembers that the year in which Alice was born fell in the third or fourth year at most after the great pestilence,

and that this witness has a son of the Carmelite order who was made a brother in the order in the year before Alice's birth, and fourteen years or more have gone by from the year he was made a friar. She says further that at the time her son was made a friar, William la Zouche of happy memory was archbishop of York and she believes, as she says, that Alice was born in the time of Archbishop William.[29]

What is striking about Alice's deposition is not so much the carefully garnered detail, but its general and very distinctive tenor. Whereas Lady Margery's deposition could almost have been borrowed from a Proof of Age inquest, Alice de Beleby's seems to owe rather more to devotional writing. Where other women recall the giving birth to a son or daughter, or remember the births of other women's children, Alice tells of her son's spiritual birth as a member of the Carmelite order. Whereas other depositions hardly ever reference what we know as the Black Death – invariably described as the great pestilence – as if this event were so traumatic, people tended to shy away from mentioning it, Alice has no such inhibition. The pestilence was, of course, understood as divine punishment for sin and those who survived had a duty to repent. Her dating of her son becoming a Carmelite friar is with reference to the office of the then archbishop, a method of dating I have discovered in no other later medieval matrimonial cause from York.

The whole tone of Alice de Beleby's testimony is one of pious devotion. Her recollection of the particular moment is not based on life-changing events – childbirth, the death of a spouse or close relative – but on what she has thought out 'in her heart' and 'calculated from her memory', the same introspective processes demanded of the penitent sinner against confession. This is not simply a pious discourse designed to impress an ecclesiastical court, but rather a brilliant strategy to present as inherently trustworthy the crucial, but fragile testimony that Alice de Rouclif was of canonical age. Is this merely a reflection of the skill of the legal counsel and is Alice de Beleby's testimony essentially a fabrication? That must be a possibility, but it is one I feel unlikely. Rather it is that de Beleby's testimony takes her actual knowledge and experience and shapes it into a form that is most effective for the party for whom she is appearing. It is thus not spontaneous testimony given in response to the questions posed, but pre-rehearsed drama. It is, however, drama for which she, as Alice's godmother, is ideally cast since it finds her playing herself.

Our final example continues the theme of drama, but reiterates our argument that we should be ever watchful of the fictive nature of testimony and reported speech. In an early fifteenth-century matrimonial case Agnes Grantham, a recent York widow, claimed she had been ambushed as she walked through woodland on her way to Acomb Grange from York, violently abducted, and forced into marriage entirely against her will.[30] As she was bundled away, Agnes allegedly cried out:

Oh, men! What do you mean to do with me? Alas that I left the city of York today! Alas that I rose from my bed today, or that my father begot me, or that my mother brought me into the world.

By rendering the Latin of the record into modern English we are, of course, in danger of understanding this primarily as an historical record of what was supposedly said at the time. In fact, the sentiment seems more akin to Greek drama than an accurate record of what she might actually have called out. The reported speech should rather be understood in the context of its original audience – not those who may or may not have heard whatever Agnes may or may not have exclaimed, but the ecclesiastical court. As such we need then to return to the original Latin, the language of the court, which reads, '*O homines, quid mecum proponitis facere? Heu quod hodie de civitate Ebor' exivi. Heu quod hodie de meo lecto surrexi, aut quod pater me genuit, seu mater in mundum me produxit.*'[31]

The fictive nature of the proffered words becomes even starker once we see this as the original text as opposed to trying to recover a lost vernacular original behind the Latin. The Latin is carefully crafted for maximum impact. We may note the alliteration of the repeated '*heu quod hodie*', with its urgent resonance, and of '*mater in mundum me*'. We may likewise remark the rhyming paring of '*mater*' and '*pater*', the assonance around 'e' as in '*mecum*', '*hodie*', '*de*', etc., 'i' as in '*homines*', '*quid*' or '*proponitis*', 'u' as in '*surrexi*', '*genuit*' and '*produxit*' or similarly the consonance of 'exi' in '*exivi*' and '*surrexi*', and the close repetition of '*ivi*' in '*civitate*' and '*exivi*'. An insistent beat seems to run through the whole passage culminating in the plosive 't', 'p' and 'd' sounds of '*aut quod pater me genuit, seu mater in mundum me produxit*'. This is no happy accident of translation, but rather carefully crafted rhetoric. The force of the words only really works in the language in which they were conceived, namely Latin rather than any Middle English exclamation that the passage purports, but singularly fails convincingly to deliver.

The process by which oral testimony becomes written deposition is complex and somewhat opaque. However, though the actual words spoken are prompted by the questions posed and necessarily obscured by the twin processes of editing and translation, they are neither a parroting back of the questions nor mere repetition of prepared answers, though elements of both, and particularly the latter, are to be found. Clearly the legal counsels employed by the litigants were well versed in the canon law and hence what information or what telling details were needed to prove or break an action. In a revealing pair of depositions made in a suit for legal separation, for example, Joan White and Margery Speight testified to a vicious attack allegedly made by Thomas Nesfeld on his wife, Margery. They included detail of how Thomas used a weapon against his wife, that Margery had consequently sustained a broken arm, that she feared for her life, and that she fled as soon as she was sufficiently recovered from her injury.[32] These details provided elements of physical force and actual injury necessary to make the case in law. Furthermore, by omitting any context for Thomas's alleged attack, they suggested that Thomas was cruel, irrational and a continuing threat to his wife. Finally, two witnesses to the same event constituted the standard minimum yardstick of proof required by the courts.[33]

Compared to the extant thirteenth-century depositions from Canterbury, noted towards the beginning of this chapter, the fourteenth- and fifteenth-century depositions from the Court of York indicate that canon lawyers exercised considerable skill in helping focus witnesses' testimony on the salient points. It may well be, therefore, that considerable incidental detail and information that might be considered prejudicial was pruned even before witnesses testified. The larger picture, however, is that in general lawyers worked with what witnesses had seen, heard or otherwise experienced. Women as well as men testified and hence women's experience is a part of the picture. Thus the Rouclif case women repeatedly testified to their knowledge of and experience of childbirth. Testimony was skilfully shaped prior to appearance in court, but the building blocks were provided by the witnesses. Therefore, though witnesses seem normally to have been 'prepped', their own experience and knowledge still normally formed the basis of what they were required to say. We may see this as a process of negotiation in which the witness was at least an equal partner to the lawyer. Alice de Beleby's testimony may have been cleverly crafted, but it is not invented. It plays upon the gendered model of the devout woman that may well be a model that helped shape Alice's life, but which also lent real authority to her words. Her remembrance of the Black Death and of her son's admission to the Carmelite order or her capacity for introspection and her apparent piety are brilliantly deployed, but their effectiveness is predicated on their authenticity. The sound of Alice's voice and her own words may be forever lost to us, but something of Alice and her experience is still available to us. The life her testimony echoes is thus not a mere construct of the needs of the legal process, but rather an active element shaping and determining her testimony. In this sense, however much coached in what she needed to say, Alice enjoyed agency. Much the same may be said of the other women (and men) who testified in the canon law courts.

3 WOMEN, MEMORY AND AGENCY IN THE MEDIEVAL ENGLISH CHURCH COURTS

Bronach Kane

In a late fourteenth-century Anglo-Norman allegorical treatise, the *Mirour de l'Omme*, John Gower seemingly disparaged the memorial authority of women. Characterizing female remembrance as unstable, he complained that 'if you search for the record of their memory, you shall find it written in the wind'.[1] The denigration occurred in his account of Matrimony, the third daughter of Chastity, in an expansive treatment of governance in marriage.[2] Just as the sieve fails to hold a measure of balm, Gower noted, neither do 'women retain the counsel that you give them'.[3] This supposed inability to remember male guidance was attributed to the vagaries of female memory and identified by a peculiarly feminine form of forgetting. In the *Mirour*, women were endowed with the ability to remember, a marker of human rationality, but were unable to master their faint and unruly memories. Maligned for its apparent lack of order, women's memory was reified in gendered tropes of behaviour, as male agency was contrasted with female passivity. This codification of the relation between gender and remembrance embodied broader anxieties concerning female memory, which was depicted as unreliable, uncontrollable and even wilfully recalcitrant. Such treatments crystallized the relationship between memory, agency and formalized records, reflecting the degree of authority afforded to women in representing the past.

The importance of memory in lay society was acknowledged in significant ways. Parishioners contemplated the sacrifice of Christ, whose suffering was re-enacted in the Mass and memorialized in the Crucifixion. Objects in parish churches performed memorial functions, while kin were remembered in testamentary bequests, commemorative masses and chantry prayers. The role of custom in suits concerning tithes and ecclesiastical rights encouraged parties and witnesses to contemplate the antiquity of venerated practices.[4] In learned and scholastic circles, however, remembrance was interpreted more formally as *memoria*, both a method for recalling the past and for devotional contemplation.[5] The art of rhetoric conceived *memoria* as the engine of *inventio*, the necessary antecedent of speech and the site where knowledge was transformed into legal and literary performance.[6] Remembrance operated both through theological *memoria* and through practical bureaucracy as written record, and its interaction with oral memory.[7] Outside scholastic and humanist culture, a more overtly functional version of memory carried different but related meanings, with attitudes towards its veracity correlating to source, form and mode of transmission. As a concept and practice, memory was imbued with a host of symbolic relations, many of which mapped onto ideologies of gender constructed in clerical contexts. The theoretical alignment of female remembrance with orality over the written word, instability over permanence, and domesticity as opposed to public governance, reflected prescriptive ideals of gender and reinforced a perceived opposition between men and women's social roles. First, this study outlines the context of elite and popular conceptions of memory, and their relation to the exercise of agency in later medieval England; second, it foregrounds attitudes towards women's roles in remembrance, using underexplored legal records to identify how these related to judicial practice. Finally, the chapter assesses the implications of expanding the categories for analysing women's agency in remembering, noting informal areas where female memory was afforded particular authority.

Memory, Gender and Authority

Despite critiques of women's memorial power in anti-feminist writing, particular abilities were ascribed to female memory in social practice.[8] The prominence of female kin in preserving family memory was marked in high medieval Europe, not only in transmitting oral traditions but also in shaping narratives of chronicles and histories.[9] Elite women engaged in forms of cultural production, commissioning literary and historical texts that represented the past in hagiographies, romances and *chansons de gestes*. Female perceptions of the past were accorded less value in legal contexts, with women's actions formally circumscribed in many jurisdictions and otherwise constrained by societal attitudes.[10] The legal constriction of women influenced the activities of those from lower status groups in particular, while women of noble and gentle birth could draw on extra-judicial aid or bypass court processes.[11] The ecclesiastical courts, however, offered women myriad opportunities to initiate cases and provide testimony, representing a significant site for female agency in dispute resolution. Although a number of works draw on evidence from ecclesiastical suits, few studies address the relation between memory and agency in women's testimony during this period.[12] This chapter will address the extent of female agency in the English medieval church courts, particularly Canterbury and York, emphasizing the inextricable association of gender, mnemonic discourse and legal authority in ecclesiastical litigation.

Studies of litigation in local communities indicate that the peasantry drew on a range of legal resources.[13] Villagers pursued grievances in jurisdictions whose processes and punitive measures were most suited to specific actions. Paul Hyams suggests that the ecclesiastical court was favoured for 'its expedition, its weapons of spiritual censure and local publicity perhaps, or possibly its wide networks of connections'.[14] By the late twelfth century the ecclesiastical courts were a central forum for the arbitration of disputes among the laity.[15] The Church initiated both moral and spiritual disciplinary proceedings against parishioners, and facilitated the resolution of private grievances between parties, the latter being known as 'instance' cases.[16] The most extensive litigation from this period relates to the church courts of York, which served as the court of first instance for parties in the diocese of York, and as the court of appeal for the northern province in general.[17] More than six hundred private 'instance' cases survive from the fourteenth and fifteenth centuries, relating to a range of issues, such as marriage, defamation and testamentary matters, as well as tithes and ecclesiastical rights.[18] Legal records from the southern province survive, particularly the courts of Canterbury, but in smaller numbers. Suits arbitrated in the Court of Canterbury, the provincial court, as well as the consistory court, relate mainly to the thirteenth century.[19] Sets of act books for the same period contain *ex officio* prosecutions for sexual misbehaviour, such as fornication and bigamy, and for breaches of spiritual orthodoxy.[20] These focused on disciplinary actions rather than private cases and, therefore, seldom generated witness statements, recording instead laconic summaries of the Church's judicial response. Depositions from the ecclesiastical courts hold particular value since few records survive for this period that preserve elements of what might be termed the female legal 'voice'. The exception is the small number of wills left by women, more often widows than married women, and more readily produced by the gentry and bourgeois than the wealthy peasantry.[21]

Placing women who used the church courts in the context of extra-ecclesiastical legal activity situates female agency in a broader nexus of power relations.[22] Below the level of the gentry, women in towns and the countryside dealt with legal issues using a range of jurisdictions and courts, each of which interpreted women's position differently under the law. The concept of coverture placed constraints on the female voice, assigning theoretical ownership of property and goods after marriage to the husband, while circumscribing women's ability to make contracts and undertake legal activities. Yet its application varied in urban liberties, as noted by Cordelia Beattie, and in manorial settings, as Miriam Müller observes.[23] In local communities the peasantry engaged with government and law, as Phillipp R. Schofield notes, through their 'acquaintance with due process, statute, land law, litigation techniques and the possessory assizes'.[24] Although Schofield describes a generalized peasant group, the opportunity to serve as juror was restricted to men. Beyond the formal processes of the manorial and royal courts, the knowledge and skill-sets necessary to pursue grievances through the law were available to male and female parishioners. Female roles in manorial and customary law may have influenced the ways in which women used the ecclesiastical courts, as well as perceptions of their memory.

A number of works examine the teachings of canon law on female parties and deponents, but few consider how perceptions of women's authority and memorial power influenced their engagement with the church courts.[25] In feminist historiography, the imperative to chart women's agency urges historians beyond attempts to 'restore hidden voices to history'.[26] It is important to recognize, then, that the way deponents represented the past conveyed aspects of their identities, however 'unstable, multiple, fluctuating and fragmentary'.[27] The social foundations of memory have similarly been emphasized, with James Fentress and Chris Wickham noting that group identities expressed through shared perceptions of the past underpin the concept of 'social memory'.[28] The social and the subjective intermingled, as 'collectively held ideas' underpinned the organization of groups, as well as perceptions of their identities.[29] Acts of remembering not only reflected the complexities of individual and collective identities, but also served as an area of agency and the cultural production of meaning for witnesses. Parties and deponents could exercise agency through the structures or the 'systems of generative rules and resources' which they relied on in their daily lives.[30] As Jeremy Goldberg argues in this volume, depositions were produced through the discursive coincidence of various ideologies, processes and experiences. Although these resources might assist deponents in their self-presentation, the legal context that fashioned the depositions in their final form could place limits on human agency.

As Cornelia Hughes Dayton notes, however, it should not be assumed that 'expressions of self by subalterns were always subversive or inevitably represented a desire for autonomy'.[31] Female memory was not always an act of resistance against ecclesiastical hegemony, nor were acts of remembering consistently opposed to such concerns. Female deponents searching women's bodies in marriage suits concerning impotence, for example, contributed to the power relations that structured their social and legal experiences as women. In the feminist study of memory, however, remembrance operates as a form of counter-memory, making visible 'the psychological and political structures of forgetting or repression that have disempowered women or allowed them to veil their own painful pasts'.[32] The appearance of female memory in unexpected areas, its articulation in subjective ways, and its absence from predictable places, emphasizes women's attempts at mnemonic autonomy through ruptures of clerical control. Remembrance and its more elusive companion, amnesia, represent interjections of female voices, filtered or otherwise, in judicial process, legal precedent and archival memory.

Clerical and legal discourse shaped perceptions of female remembrance and its representation. The extent to which women were able to exercise agency in the church courts reflected social perceptions of gender, while simultaneously influencing the range of behaviour available to women in legal settings. Notions of femininity shaped 'relations of power and agency' in various ways, but particularly interactions between men and women, as well as those between women.[33] In the ecclesiastical courts, particularly in marriage suits, female deponents were characterized as possessing specific gendered forms of knowledge attributed to their experience of childbirth and sexuality. Confining the study of female memory to these areas risks the artificial reification of essentialist categories.[34] The chapter will therefore analyse memories from female deponents in a broader context of marriage and sexuality, speech and custom, asking how perceptions of women's collective memory influenced depictions of personal memory. Differences in age, social status, local standing and relations with manorial and parish authorities, influenced the way that memory operated for men and women. Analysis of these contexts accounts for variations in acts of remembering and forgetting among female deponents.

Adjudicating in cases of marriage breakdown and defamation, the church courts provided a setting for the formation and reassertion of gender identities, both masculine and feminine. In late medieval England, the ecclesiastical courts arbitrated between men in suits that both challenged and reasserted the validity of manhood.[35] Thus, in a matrimonial case dated 1269, initiated in the Court of Canterbury, the suit concerned the disputed consanguinity of the parties.[36] Philip, son of Richard de Hurterigg, described his sexual encounter with his uncle's wife in graphic detail, with his virility serving as a form of proof. The negotiation of femininities similarly occurred in church court suits, with female gender identities constructed through categories such as occupation, social status, sexuality and marital status.[37] In a matrimonial suit originally brought before the dean of Dover in 1293, William, the defendant, claimed that his union with Dulcia Herdman was invalid because of his sexual relations with Alice, her sister. Witnesses used a collective memory strategy in which Alice had spent the day planting beans and cultivating fields in the company of her family with whom she worked and ate her meals for the entire day.[38] For Dulcia, memory provided a way for her to ensure that her marriage was deemed valid, while Alice's reputation rested on the convincing depiction of her labour with her family. The memorial capacities attributed to women afforded them opportunities to represent their own desires and exercise choice in the construction of narrative accounts.

The ubiquity of the past in later medieval society connoted a 'memorial culture' in which remembrance permeated each social level in related ways. Intellectual understandings of the past in this period drew on two classical traditions. The first emerged from perceptions of the philosophical and spiritual functions of remembrance that interpreted memory as the pathway to true knowledge. According to this system, memory operated through introspection, providing a means to reflect on prior behaviour.[39] Memory was the fourth canon of rhetoric, accompanied by invention, arrangement, style and delivery.[40] The *ars memoria*, on the other hand, offered a technical way of training human memory by associating images with specific places in an ordered system. Both traditions influenced the development and interpretation of the learned law. From the classical period, students of the law relied on the *ars memoria* in oratorical training. In the schools, legists encouraged the memorization of central legal texts among students of canon law, while technical lectures containing citations and references were often delivered from memory.[41] The remembrance of past events steered learned treatises on canon law and underpinned its juridical application in the delivery of arguments, the memorization of legal arguments and, most importantly, as the pathway to true knowledge.[42]

The significance of memory in ecclesiastical litigation was evident both in general techniques of inquiry and in suits which emphasized the remembrance of past events. In 'instance' cases that generated written depositions, the outcome depended on the proficiency with which witnesses remembered past events. In the early thirteenth century, Tancred, a noted canonist and archdeacon of Bologna, composed his *Ordo iudiciorum* that stipulated the central requirements of proof, along with methods used to examine witnesses.[43] The examination of deponents was to occur in private, with evidence from two witnesses in order to discharge proof.[44] The memories of witnesses needed to concur, and examiners established veracity through a series of questions, many of which conformed to formulaic instructions. Tancred urged that examiners should interrogate deponents in many areas in order to 'better elicit the truth, inquiring prudently about each circumstance, namely about the persons, place, and time, sight, hearing, knowledge and belief, fame and certainty'.[45] Deponents were questioned on the weather at the time of the event, whether parties were sitting or standing, as well as the clothing they had worn.[46] In depositions at Canterbury and York, witnesses were examined on how they remembered the events described in their testimony, 'on the peril of their soul', and as they would swear 'on the final day of Judgement'.[47]

Remembering past events in depositions, therefore, occurred in the judicial context of ecclesiastical authority, whereby witnesses were required to engage in a process of self-examination. A moral framework of conscience guided the analysis and revision of individual memory, through the self-policing of past behaviour. The doctrine of circumstances promoted by Tancred and other theologians in examining canonical witnesses was similarly deployed in the confession of the laity. In confession or in the church court, conscience determined the role of intention in sin, determining the degree of penance required in order to gain satisfaction.[48] The religious verse, *The Prick of Conscience*, of northern English, perhaps Yorkshire provenance, urged the reader as pentitent to 'ransak alle his lyf / And knawe whar of he sale hym schryf'.[49] In pastoral and judicial contexts, the process of self-examination entailed 'the peculiar turning of a subject against itself ... in acts of self-reproach, conscience, and melancholia that worked in tandem with processes of social regulation'.[50] As the Church inquired into memories of past events, deponents examined their behaviour, producing themselves as subjects of judicial authority.[51]

The function of memory in learned and legal settings was implicated in the generation of speech and authority. In scholastic circles where rhetoric was studied, the relation of *memoria* to oratorical delivery concerned male discourse, obscuring the production of women's speech. The denial of memorial abilities to women typified a broader misogynistic literary tradition, in which learning, speech and agency were male concerns. Rationality was similarly associated with *memoria*, such that femininity was deemed incompatible with proper remembrance on account of woman's inherent lack of reason. When acknowledged in clerical-authored works, female memory was depicted as unruly and disobedient emblematizing an essential feminine nature. The author of the late thirteenth-century *La Poissance d'amours* thus commented: 'it often happens that when man bids woman to yield to his will, her memory and reason do not agree'.[52] Female remembrance could therefore be interpreted as a 'source of recalcitrance, rebelliousness, lack of discipline, and failure to submit'.[53] The feminine tendency towards selective amnesia was essentialized in this context, reflecting the mnemonic lapses supposedly inherent in female nature.

Female Memory, Authority and Agency

In social practice, however, the preservation of local histories often depended on female remembrance. The authority of women's memory was founded in part on the association of female family members with the safeguarding of family history.[54] Female perceptions of the past were aligned with orality, domestic traditions and specifically feminine life events, particularly childbirth. Goldberg argues that female deponents in the church courts were used 'to locate past events by reference to childbirth', perhaps reflecting lay attitudes towards female expertise.[55] In a series of cases from both English provinces, female deponents testified to the births of parties where uncertainty obscured their ages.[56] The correlation of female remembrance with oral rather than written memory formed another perception of gendered recollection. The theoretical alienation of women from writing formed only one element of a wider clerical culture in which large sections of the laity were regarded as illiterate. In a similar vein, the alignment of illiteracy with the rural peasantry was embodied in the term '*rustici*' that performed a comparable ideological task, denying rationality to large sections of the laity. During the revolt of 1381, numbers of rebels demonstrated their awareness of the symbolic power invested in official writing by burning records; female rebels similarly detected these linguistic differences, with at least one woman actively destroying the 'learning of clerks'.[57] Latin learning was thus contrasted with vernacular speech and writing, as women formed a particular subset of the laity entirely excluded from clerical status and alienated from its educational practices. In social practice, however, various literate practices were prevalent among lay non-elites, developed and expressed in the bureaucratic context of the village, manor and parish.[58] Thus, in a 1390 testamentary suit from York, the executors of William Awne's testament pursued a debt of thirteen shillings.[59] Avice de Awne, William's wife, testified that 'she had often seen his testament and heard it read' before his death.[60]

The types of cases in which female parties predominated indicate the most visible areas of mnemonic agency for women in the ecclesiastical courts. Female deponents were enlisted to provide evidence in a range of suits, but particularly those concerning marriage, defamation and breach of promise. While the church courts facilitated the legal participation of female plaintiffs and deponents, compilers of legal commentaries were divided on the matter. Canonists proffered different arguments on the legal position of women, with little learned consensus as late as the mid-thirteenth century.[61] Gratian held that female testimony was permitted in theory, though allowed for specific laws forbidding their evidence and ruled against women initiating criminal proceedings outside 'instance' cases. Elsewhere in the *Decretum*, Gratian contradicted this position, citing St Augustine's teaching that women 'are not able to teach, nor to witness, nor to judge'.[62] Tancred urged that judgements should depend on the credibility of deponents, which was established in relative terms. Thus, older witnesses were regarded as more reliable than their younger counterparts, while male deponents were favoured over female.[63] Despite the reservations of several canonists, the application of canon law in England permitted the testimony of female deponents.

Social attitudes, however, influenced both the selection of witnesses and perceptions of their functions. In a matrimonial suit from York initiated in 1430, one deponent remembered the female plaintiff requesting that her putative husband contract with her a second time in front of witnesses as the marriage was initially made before two deponents described as 'only women'.[64] The compulsion to secure male testimony indicates the lack of authority accorded to women's voices in a legal capacity. The position of female parties and witnesses influenced the tenor of women's testimony, shaping expectations of how women should use the church courts. That two female deponents witnessed the initial marriage contract indicates that women understood the force of canon law, while appreciating how social attitudes rendered women's words and reputations more vulnerable to challenges. Similarly, in a statistical analysis of matrimonial suits, Goldberg observes that rural parties, both male and female, selected women as witnesses with less frequency than their urban counterparts.[65]

Despite the preference for male deponents and the restriction of women's participation in specific types of suits, pastoral literature nevertheless provided instruction to female parishioners on canon law, particularly regarding sexual behaviour and marriage. Lay knowledge of canon law, however selective and incomplete, provided parties and defendants of both sexes with the skill-set necessary to exercise agency in the ecclesiastical courts. Teachings on canon law were disseminated beyond scholastic and clerical circles in a number of ways, with parishioners receiving basic instruction in sermons and in confession. Peter Biller notes that female parishioners may have confessed in greater numbers than their male neighbours, while *exempla* concerning confession often featured lay-women.[66] Female penitents were routinely associated with sexual misdemeanours, particularly the sin of lechery, indicating the 'confinement of women to sexual matters'.[67] Laywomen were given particular advice on canon law concerning marriage in the *Memoriale presbiterorum*, a mid-fourteenth-century pastoral manual advising parish priests on how to administer confession.[68] Interrogatories were provided for the confessor in the form of questions for penitents, reflecting sins regarded as particularly common among sections of the laity. The majority of the manual is thus comprised of estates-interrogatories, aimed at parishioners of various kinds, with each group treated according to their status or occupation. Only one section concerns the treatment of female parishioners, addressing the moral condition of 'married women, widows and other sexually-experienced women'.[69] Following admonitions against hypocrisy, female penitents were questioned on wrongdoings in marital matters. Examiners were urged to inquire into several areas, including the making of marriage contracts, as well as bigamy, adultery and illicit unions made after espousals with another. Female penitents were asked if they ever contracted marriage by words of present or future consent, only to contract openly or secretly with another.[70] In this context, the clergy used confession in order to disseminate matrimonial canon law to laywomen, with sets of questions reflecting the estates that categorized women according to marital status.

Clerical depictions of women's sexual immorality formed part of a confessional discourse that aimed to extract memories of sins from penitents. In Chaucer's 'Friar's Tale', a critique of ecclesiastical court personnel suggests more varied attitudes towards laywomen's engagement with judicial process. Accompanied by a devil, a summoner attempts to extort payments from an old woman with the vague charge that she must appear before the archdeacon 't'answere to the court of certeyn thynges'.[71] Instead of bribing the summoner, the old woman requests that he give her the written libel, so she could answer 'swich thing as men wol oppesen me' through a proctor rather than in person.[72] Altering his tactics, the summoner informs the woman that she had been cited for adultery, for which he had settled the fine and she owed him payment. The old woman denies his charge, responding that she had never received a citation from the church court. Although the summoner identifies the old woman as vulnerable, she counters the charges supposedly made by the Church authorities.

The gendering of the most vulnerable parishioner as female might allude to women's alienation from the legal activities of the Church. Yet the only figure surprised by the old woman's pragmatic knowledge of the ecclesiastical court is the summoner. Her apparent defencelessness was marked by her age and gender, which in turn formed the basis for her memorial power. Not only does she respond appropriately to the request to appear before the court, reflecting reasonable expectations of lay knowledge concerning citation, but she also challenges representations of the past inscribed in ecclesiastical records. Written records represent the summoner's 'official' armoury, tangible items that served to prove his legitimacy as court summoner in an inversion of judicial methods of proof. The denial of her presence in the Church's judicial archive suggests the ways in which women's memories provided counter-memories to ecclesiastical interests. Illustrating the significance of female memory, her oppositional narrative is based on the remembrance of sexual activities throughout her life, mimicking women's supposed ability to recall more licit life events. The force of the old woman's memory acted as a corrective to clerical stereotypes of women's immorality, reasserting her sexual probity through her absence from the Church's judicial memory.

The instruction of female parishioners on the formation of canonical marriages underscored the importance of memory in confession or the church court. Female deponents understood the need to provide witnesses to marriages. In 1269, one Agnes de Clopton, deponent in a matrimonial case from the Court of Canterbury, remembered that she had been called to witness the union should she need to offer testimony in the future.[73] When questioned on how she recalled the marriage, Agnes remembered that she was pregnant at the time, a physical state that may have privileged her as a witness to the union. In a matrimonial dispute from York initiated in 1418, Margaret Carow, aunt of Isabel, daughter of Richard Foxholes, remembered her concern that John Littester would later try to annul his marriage to her niece. Margaret deposed that 'she recalls the time because she often brought the said contract back to her memory lest by chance the said John should want to be false in the future by denying the contract in this way'.[74] Memories of past events in the form of testimony became more urgent in contracts where one partner might attempt to dissolve the union. In the suit between Isabel and John, Isabel's aunt was able to manipulate canon legal associations between memory and testimony in order to characterize John as a reluctant groom. Since female deponents were often aligned with the preservation of family memory, including marriages and life cycle events, the memory of female kin was regarded as authoritative.

The patterns evident in the ecclesiastical courts hold broader significance for the function of women's memory. Female parties were particularly common in matrimonial suits, which included a wide range of cases, from marital annulment to dissolution of the bond. Suits to enforce contracts comprised the highest proportion of cases, with plaintiffs seeking the court to confirm the validity of their marriage. In the later medieval English church courts, cases to enforce marriage contracts occurred in greater numbers than suits to dissolve the marital bond.[75] Helmholz notes that in the consistory court of Canterbury between 1372 and 1375 suits to enforce marriage contracts made up seventy-eight out of ninety-eight cases.[76] Gender and status influenced marriage patterns and rates of litigation in the courts. Non-elite women may have exercised greater control over their choice of marriage partner at different points. After the labour market became less welcoming for women in the fifteenth century, marriage was a more frequent choice, a development reflected in the increasing use of marital status in naming patterns for women.[77] Declining numbers of female plaintiffs in this period were concentrated in the late fifteenth century, after which fewer urban women brought suit for disparate reasons. Goldberg observes the concurrence of lower ages of marriage for women with the contraction of economic opportunities in the later fifteenth century.[78]

Although the selection of women as witnesses depended on canon law and on social attitudes, the testimony of female deponents was privileged in a number of areas. Women witnesses predominated in matrimonial suits that required testimony of the ages of parties, and cases requesting annulment on the grounds of spousal impotence. Gratian thus emphasized the particular expertise of female witnesses in matrimonial cases relating to impotence, with evidence from the wife deemed most significant.[79] In practice, however, after proceedings were initiated in suits of this kind, the more visible women were female deponents selected to secure evidence of the husband's physical state.[80] A number of methods were advocated by canonists apart from physical inspection, namely the use of oath-helpers, and trial cohabitation for the couple in question.[81] The procedure that developed in England, with isolated use in Venice, involved the appointment of women, often prostitutes, whose expertise in sexual matters were respected by clerical authorities.[82]

This perceived expertise of female deponents in this kind of case could be challenged. In 1432, Katherine, daughter of Henry Barlay, initiated a matrimonial suit against her husband, William Barton, on the grounds of impotence in the Court of York.[83] In contrast to several other cases concerning spousal impotence, the female deponents in this suit were not sex workers, and were accompanied by male witnesses whose examinations were also recorded. A number of female deponents performed a physical examination of the husband, but the court simultaneously ordered the inspection of Katherine's body, which was conducted by the same set of female witnesses. After her breasts were palpated, the panel of women judged her to be corrupt based on their 'broken' appearance during their examination. While Katherine consented to the inspection of her breasts, the women intended to examine her further but were met with resistance. One deponent, Matilda, wife of John Leek, noted that they wished to perform an inspection of Katherine's 'secret members', but she refused.

Although female deponents exercised particular agency in marriage cases concerning impotence, their evidence could be challenged in a number of ways. In the same suit, conflicting memories in a couple's testimony indicates the tensions that might develop when spouses gave evidence for opposing parties. Despite his wife's position as expert deponent, recognized in her involvement in the physical examination, John Mycholson complained about her testimony to another witness. His wife's evidence on the husband's impotence, given on behalf of the female plaintiff, contradicted his statement supporting the male defendant's virility. In response to his wife's actions in testifying, John commented that once he returned home he would 'make his wife confess to the priest and receive penance for the perjury that she had incurred on her part'.[84] While his wife exercised agency in performing the test, and reporting its supposed findings to the court, her husband critiqued these actions and sought to undo them through her confession and penance.

Female deponents were preferred in suits that required testimony on the births of either party, usually in cases that related to the ages of putative spouses upon their marriage. In 1270, a matrimonial case was transmitted on appeal to Canterbury from the archdeaconry of Huntingdon, relating to the alleged marriage of Cecilia, daughter of Bartholomew, to one Thomas de Walengfeld.[85] The argument concerned the validity of the marriage rather than the existence of a marriage contract. Canon law regulated the minimum marital age of spouses, stipulating the age of twelve for girls, while boys should reach fourteen prior to the contract.[86] Marriage contracts between the ages of seven and puberty were not invalid, but the couple was required to have the union validated once the minimum age was reached. The case between Cecilia, daughter of Bartholomew, and Thomas de Walengfeld thus attempted to discern the contract's validity by evaluating the couple's consent. If the contract was formed after both parties reached the age of 'incomplete puberty', then the union was approved according to canon law, provided consent was voluntary and mutual.

Over seventy-six witnesses from a cluster of villages in north Hertfordshire testified on Cecilia's age at the time of the marriage, around a third of whom were men, but the majority were women. The deponents established this uncertain detail by remembering when the girl was born, with incidental memories of other events operating as temporal markers.[87] Since parochial record-keeping was confined to administrative and fiscal matters, the births of children in the later Middle Ages were seldom noted in written form. The gentry and nobility made use of documents to record the arrival of potential heirs, with parents requesting the entry of births in monastic chronicles.[88] Written records generated a theoretically stable form of physical evidence, while creating an official memory that would underpin rights over lands and estates, anticipating future challenges to inheritance. After the death of feudal tenants, in cases concerning underage heirs, writs *de etate probanda* were produced in order to determine their age and to prove the age of majority had been reached so that seisin of estates could be granted.[89] In form and content, the depositions in this suit resemble the responses of jurors in proof of age inquiries, which constituted part of the apparatus in the common law inquisitions *post mortem*.[90] In common with marriage suits concerning nonage, proof of age statements recorded memories of the births of feudal heirs and heiresses. Unlike cases concerning age in the ecclesiastical courts, however, only male jurors presented evidence in inquisitions *post mortem*, many of whom were drawn from the peasantry in the late thirteenth century but, by the fifteenth century, were selected increasingly from the 'middling sort'.[91]

While cases involving large numbers of women witnesses relied on recognizably female life events, such as pregnancy, lying-in and childbirth, the experience of testifying in this kind of group may have encouraged deponents to introduce subjective experiences into their testimony. In the suit between Cecilia and Thomas, evidence from female deponents indicates gendered experiences of the law that centred on female bodies as sites of memory and trauma. In her deposition, one Sibilla de Hinteworth informed the archdeacon's clerical examiner that she remembered when Cecilia, daughter of Bartholomew, was born, because 'she was [herself] deflowered in the Lent that followed'.[92] Despite the candour of her statement, indicating a sexual encounter in which Sibilla was the passive partner, interpretations of the term 'deflorata' are nevertheless multiple. Sexual activity in the later Middle Ages reflected gendered epistemologies in which men were active partners, while women were passive recipients. In addition, the memory strategy deployed by Sibilla lay at the centre of several jurisdictions, such that these discursive meanings were transferred into the judicial context of the church courts.

Payments could be rendered in recompense for taking female virginity before marriage, with rape often settled outside of the common law courts through private reparations.[93] The 'deflowering' recalled by Sibilla may have been rape, which was settled either through the law or by payment for loss of virginity. Manorial authorities, however, policed the sexual behaviour of unmarried female tenants until the late fourteenth century, such that Sibilla may have remembered a payment of leyrwite, a fiscal punishment for the loss of her virginity before she had married.[94] Judith Bennett detects a considerable degree of agency in women paying their own fines on the manor.[95]

Ecclesiastical authorities themselves policed pre- and extra-marital sexual activity, whether consensual or through rape, judging each through a hierarchy of sinfulness.[96] Despite the Church's moral perspective on virginity as the preferred sexual state, lay sexual behaviour often only became a concern when this resulted in disciplinary action, such as *ex officio* charges of fornication. In addition, private suits relating to spousal impotence only attracted the incidental attention of Church authorities, for whom the virginity of female plaintiffs represented an invalid marriage.[97] In England, manorial authorities fined female tenants exclusively for sexual activity, extracting payments from women while seldom troubling their male partners. Whether representing the trauma of sexual violence or the intrusion of the manorial or Church authorities, Sibilla's account situated the event in judicial terms once more, achieving this reinsertion through her own agency.

The significance of Sibilla's memory lies in the narrative representing her traumatic experience from her own perspective, albeit in mediated and, once again, judicial discourse. Although her words were probably reshaped to fit clerical interpretations of her experience, her examination permitted her to articulate the event, recovering it from her memory and perhaps reinterpreting its implications. This narration worked to realign meanings construed from the objectification of Sibilla's body. From a judicial perspective, her body formed a physical site of memory that was legible to manorial and Church authorities, representing anew the violent assault enacted on her person. Violent acts, at the level of rhetoric, were therefore memorable events. Scholastic writers imbued violent acts with mnemonic qualities, having the capacity to leave impressions on the memory. In the *Rhetorica novissima*, an early thirteenth-century tract, Boncompagno da Signa commented that 'women, of course, remember those who beat them and afflict them through mistreatment, and forget those others who cherish them and honor them'.[98] The anti-feminist culture from which such expositions emerged could align female remembrance with faithlessness, while women failed to nurture memory in acts of neglect. While violence was a powerful mnemonic, providing incontrovertible evidence, Sibilla's memory also represented her trauma, bodily intrusion and potentially, her sexual shame. The act of testifying, rather than repressing and eliding the event, suggests an agency that resisted the imposition of judicial and cultural categories of gender, dishonour and shame.

Matrimonial cases concerning nonage required evidence of the circumstances of children's births, comparable to ecclesiastical inquiries over bastardy. These concentrated similarly on memories of the events surrounding parties' births as well as parental marriage. Although inquiries of this kind were initiated in the royal courts in the course of disputes over land, instances of bastardy fell under the jurisdiction of the Church in its role as arbiter of the validity of marriage contracts.[99] The outcome of such suits rested on proof of marriage contracts pursued in the ecclesiastical fora. The royal courts were not responsible for gathering this evidence, but the relation between ecclesiastical and royal jurisdictions allowed deponents to participate in decisions concerning the inheritance of land. In contrast with matrimonial cases of nonage, deponents in suits relating to bastardy were usually male. From the southern province, three cases survive in which the validity of marriage was investigated, but the examinations concentrate on when the relevant marriages occurred rather than the birth dates of the couples' children.[100]

The ability to exercise agency through memory in the church courts depended on social status as much as gender, with variations between court systems and types of cases influencing the extent of female authority and participation. Ecclesiastical authorities acknowledged the local memory of laywomen, with female expertise in communal relations afforded particular value. In 1291, an *ex officio* action initiated by the office of the bishop of Lincoln inquired into claims that John de Arden, rector of the church of Steane in Northamptonshire, had married Elizabeth de Wade prior to his acceptance of the benefice.[101] Intended to establish John's marital status, the actions against him may have preceded a matrimonial suit. Under canon law, members of the clergy were prohibited from holding benefices until after the death of a spouse. An 'instance' suit was brought in the Court of Canterbury by Ralph, clerk of the earl of Warwick against John de Arden, rector of Steane in Northamptonshire, concerning possession of the church of Ratley (Warwickshire), which lay in the diocese of Coventry and Lichfield.[102]

Focused on the marital status of John de Arden, the bishop of Lincoln's official gathered testimony from substantial inhabitants of the parish of Weston-by-Welland and neighbouring areas. Two deponents were members of the clergy, namely Ralph, vicar of the church of Weston, and Hugh de Weston, vicar of nearby Canons Ashby. Anxieties surrounding the financial integrity of John's household reflected the concerns of canonists that married clergy used the goods of the Church improperly, supporting clerical wives and children rather than God's work.[103] A third witness, whose evidence was recorded last, was Lady Eleanor Bassett, wife of Sir Ralph Bassett, and sister of Elizabeth, John de Arden's alleged wife.

Solemnization of the couple's marriage preoccupied Lady Eleanor rather more than her sister, who is absent from the apparatus of both suits. Born into the de la Wade family, Lady Eleanor was descended from servants of the king, with Henry de la Wade, Eleanor's father, acting as 'King's Cook', for which he received the serjeanty of Bletchington.[104] She later married into a branch of the Bassetts, a prominent Midlands family of noble birth, many of whom were tenants-in-chief of the king.[105]

In her examination, Lady Eleanor was questioned on how she remembered when John de Arden had received the benefice, since twenty-six years had passed, recalling that 'the said John received the said church before the battle of Evesham, and such time had passed after that battle'.[106] While the Bassetts of Weldon were the eldest branch of the line, a prominent kinsman at Evesham (Worcestershire) was Ralph Bassett of Drayton, who fought with the Montfortian opposition. Lady Eleanor's memory strategy emphasized the Bassett family's powerful political connections, while providing an event enshrined both in family history and in national memory. Social status may have influenced her interest in legitimating her sister's marriage and any children from the union.

A number of potential activities were available to laywomen outside the formal court setting. Prominent in the *ex officio* case against John de Arden, Lady Eleanor Bassett became involved again in another suit concerning her sister's alleged husband, on this occasion, a private case relating to the chapel of Ratley. One deponent, William Brun of Weldon, described as *illiteratus*, remembered that the official sent a letter to Lady Eleanor requesting that 'she should send the deponents who knew best about this matter'.[107] William noted that in response to the official's request, Lady Eleanor had selected and sent him and other witnesses to provide the most knowledgeable evidence. This level of consultation by church court authorities appears to have occurred only with aristocratic and gentry women, who were higher in social and economic status than most female litigants in the church courts. The legal agency exercised by Lady Eleanor resembles the 'extra-curial' practices that Hawkes detects among gentry women engaged in common law disputes.[108] By the time the 'instance' case was initiated against John de Arden, however, Lady Eleanor's marital status had changed, as her husband, Sir Ralph Bassett, died in 1292, the year after the initial *ex officio* case. When the bishop's official wrote to Lady Eleanor, he addressed a widow, head of household and manorial lord of the chief messuage of Weston, left to her in dower. In the context of manorial law, at least as it interacted with church court litigation, women of elite status might therefore control the representation of male memories.

Custom and Female Memory

The expansion of categories for considering female remembrance to include areas hitherto aligned with male memory emphasizes the gendered relation between speech, authority and customary knowledge. The extent of female agency in contributing reliable memories to defamation suits depended on the treatment of women's speech beyond the ecclesiastical courts. Until the late fourteenth century, communal policing relied on local inhabitants identifying and publicizing criminal behaviour by raising the hue and cry. Hue-raising provided female villagers with considerable authority, a form of empowerment that confirmed women's perceptions of the law both in recognizing the worth of their judgement, and later confirming it in the courts.[109] From the early fourteenth century, perceived cases of speech crime were pursued increasingly in the ecclesiastical courts. Sandy Bardsley observes changing attitudes towards women's speech in both jurisdictions, while increasing numbers of women were charged with raising the hue and cry unjustly.[110]

By the fifteenth century, female defendants outnumbered men in defamation suits initiated in the church courts, indicating a feminization of cases concerning insult or, at least, greater anxieties over women's reputations. Suits concerning defamation thus often involved female plaintiffs, pursuing formal legal redress in order to restore the purity of their reputations. While the behaviour of wives reflected on their husbands' masculinity, married women participated in defamation suits in the church courts as parties and deponents.[111] As Derek Neal argues, the 'moral substance' of men as husbands and householders was settled in defamation cases. Many suits concerning women's sexual reputations impinged on their husbands' manliness, while cases impugning male honesty in financial matters inflicted almost irreparable damage on male honour.[112]

Female parties and deponents, of course, engaged with speech in other ways. In a tuitorial appeal from the diocese of Salisbury and Exeter in 1291, Joan, widow of William Holeput, was accused of defaming the local vicar of stealing tithes.[113] Despite customary practice that favoured male evidence in cases concerning tithes, Joan formed part of a larger group, and her words seem to have carried as much weight as those of her co-defendants. While ostensibly concerned with theft of goods, the ownership of particular tithes was established in popular ideas of custom, and depended on memories of boundaries, the collection of grain and the longevity of rights.

In a suit initiated in York in 1464, John Dowse complained that Ellen Thomson had accused him of the theft of grain from the tithe barn of the Augustinian priory of Newburgh.[114] In the tithe barn at Brafferton, Ellen Thomson had supposedly accused John, confronting him:

> You conceal and have hidden in your house at Helperby a thief, with whom you have stolen three sacks of grain from the tithe barn of Brafferton, belonging to the priory of Newburgh, and you have turned these to your own use.[115]

The regulatory force of Ellen's words was regarded as powerful enough to underpin John Dowse's complaint in the Court of York. Numerous bequests show how pious women left domestic goods to the Church for sacramental use. As custodians of household goods, women's responsibilities for the domestic economy could thus extend to the parish church.[116] The decline of the hue and cry as a mechanism of social policing evidently did not deter female parishioners from detecting crimes, perhaps reflecting an extended role in social policing.

Litigation over marriage and insult represented the spheres of reproduction and speech in which female legal activity was permitted but less formal arenas evidently allowed women to comment on customs and rights. Local custom represented a central element of communal memory, underpinning less rarefied forms of knowledge that related to the built and natural landscape, parochial and manorial history, and disputes concerning these customs. Communities often possessed groups of inhabitants whose knowledge of the law was particularly respected, many of whom were engaged in related activities, from fiscal administration in the manor and parish to the legal role of juror. The networks of influence maintained by local jurisdictions of various kinds 'mobilized social groups in order to establish, safeguard, and alter local social memories about legal transactions'.[117] Groups of this kind were comprised of male inhabitants whose experiences constituted a form of social memory, yet female deponents contributed to the development and construction of local custom.[118] The position of women as parties and deponents in the ecclesiastical courts depended on perceptions of legal expertise as much as the extent of local knowledge. Laura Gowing notes for early modern London that 'women drew on a set of other powers from the realms of custom, tradition and law'.[119] The extent to which women were able to contribute to local memory related to their position in the community, particularly in parochial organization. Despite the predominance of male parishioners in leadership roles, laywomen were able to exercise agency in a number of fiscal, spiritual and administrative areas, raising funds, organizing events and through 'church keeping'.[120]

Few women witnesses, however, offered evidence in cases concerning tithes and the rather more capacious category of ecclesiastical rights. The majority of suits relating to tithes and parochial rights were initiated by groups of male parishioners, often listed as parties by name but occasionally purporting to represent the parish. The degree of agency permitted to female deponents was therefore restricted in formal terms, but female kin, neighbours and elderly inhabitants may have contributed to the 'social memory' of local communities as memorial guardians whose expertise was respected. Decisions in the ecclesiastical courts often relied on 'common fame', evidence regarded as more reliable than 'hearsay' but less credible than eyewitness testimony.[121] Female deponents in ecclesiastical cases therefore contributed to the evidence used in deliberating judicial sentences. The epistemological force of 'common fame' drew on notions of communal belief and knowledge circulating in the local area. In addition, the communal memory that male deponents deployed often included the perspectives of female inhabitants, occasionally explicitly. In a suit initiated in York in 1496, the male witnesses testified on the repairs to the conventual church of Kirkham; Robert Bringham remembered that his mother, then aged eighty, had told him of the customs surrounding the church, while Robert Turnay recalled them with reference to where his aunt had lived and was buried.[122]

Female parishioners contributed to the development of local custom, despite the alienation of laywomen from suits concerning customary rights. Since custom purported to reflect long-established practice, altering such uses was best accomplished through challenging their existence. In a case initiated in 1293, John St John, prior of Andover and rector of the church of Andover

(Hampshire), brought suit against the executors of Edmund Paty in the consistory court of Winchester for failing to render a mortuary payment after his death.[123] Emma, his widow, was named first as co-defendant with Robert Randulf. As prior of Andover, John St John, and his witnesses, including the rector of Faccombe, argued that mortuaries were owed to him 'by old and approved custom'.[124] While the payment of tithes possessed a scriptural basis, reinforced by canon law, the justification for rendering mortuary fees was more tenuous and depended on local custom rather than learned law.[125] Since female memory was aligned with family remembrance, laywomen exerted authority in memories concerning kin, including customs that informed domestic life. Widows rendering a mortuary fee to the parish priest and a heriot to the manorial lord not only concerned female relatives in their role as carers for the sick and dead, but also emphasized women's roles in the management of the household economy. Although Emma, Edmund's widow and executor, exercised agency in challenging the payment of mortuary in the parish's memory, her resistance depended on another strand of local politics. When the rectors of the parish approached Emma, issuing cautions of excommunication, she admitted the obligation to render payment, but stated that she could not pay it 'for fear of her lady of Foxcote who opposes payments of this kind'.[126] Although no sentence survives, Lady Isabella de Foxcott became an additional named defendant in the case. The suit may reflect local power relations between manorial authorities and parish clergy, but it nevertheless demonstrates the extent of female action in defending and amending customary practices.

Cases concerning tithes and parish rights evidently articulated forms of social memory, in defence of supposedly customary practices, simultaneously eliding alternative histories of local communities. Although lay deponents in such cases were usually male, examples of groups of women providing group testimony to rights did occur, albeit as members of religious houses. In 1440, for example, the female religious of the convent of Thicket in the East Riding of Yorkshire declared their immunity from paying tithes to the prior and convent of Ellerton.[127] Alongside male lay deponents, several nuns of Thicket also testified, citing the appropriation of goods by the house of Ellerton, and, most significantly, their incorporation into the Cistercian order. The female religious of Thicket constructed and defended their social memory, with the same methods of proof required in other cases concerning tithes.

From the emergence of witness testimony in the twelfth century as the standard means of ecclesiastical proof, parties and deponents of both sexes developed novel ways to negotiate the moral and spiritual expectations of the Church. The thirteenth and fourteenth centuries witnessed related attempts by ecclesiastical authorities to determine the most appropriate forms of proof. Yet female engagement with the church courts contended with a range of contradictory perceptions of women's ability to represent the past. Many of these positions drew on contemporary assumptions relating to female speech, reliability and authority. Clerical perceptions of female nature were founded on intellectual categories concerning sinfulness that regarded women as 'a marked category, a signal of difference, exception or emphasis'.[128] Jacqueline Murray observes that, although female testimony was accorded less value than men's evidence, and women were suspected of false accusations against male defendants, in cases concerning spousal impotence 'women's bodies did not lie'.[129] From a clerical perspective, the memory of women's sexual activity was thus inscribed on the female body, a belief that prevailed in sections of lay society. This somatic form of evidence was regarded as legible only to women with accumulated experience of sexual relations and childbirth. In lay society, however, a broader range of memorial roles were available to women and this influenced the types of events that female deponents could relate in court settings.

4 'UTTERLY AND UNTRULY HE HATH DECEIVED ME': WOMEN'S INHERITANCE IN LATE MEDIEVAL ENGLAND

Rosemary Horrox

This essay reconstructs a story, of which the starting point is the woman's voice quoted in the title. The words are not, as might immediately be supposed, those of a woman betrayed by a lover, but of a woman defrauded by her son – and a son of her blood rather than a stepson. The voice we are hearing is that of Jane (or Joan) Stapleton who, on 18 April 1518, began to make her will in her chamber in the monastery of Hailes in Gloucestershire and set out the story in the hope that her executors might be able to correct the wrong done to her. In one respect, therefore, her story runs against the theme of this collection: Jane did not turn to the law for redress.

Late medieval England was a notoriously litigious society, at least among the land-owning classes.[1] The complexity of tenure, particularly when entail and enfeoffment to use entered the equation, meant that title to land could often be open to challenge. The sons of the gentry found it worth spending time at the Inns of Court, not with the intention of becoming practising lawyers but to acquire the knowledge (and the social contacts) that might come in useful if they needed to face or mount such challenges. Resort to the courts, and hence, in the case of the common law, to expensive legal professionals, was, however, only one way (and arguably the minority way) of dealing with disputes. At the other extreme was violent self-help, but in between lay a range of paralegal methods. Arbitration was the most formal of these and was often considered preferable to a court case. It offered the prospect of a settlement that gave something to both parties in place of the 'winner-take-all' outcome at law. The non-adversarial approach also suited collegial bodies such as guilds, which preferred the internal resolution of disputes between members and saw a conflict fought out in the courts as an admission of failure.[2] Some individuals for whom the common law offered no redress took their case into Chancery, a court of equity, by petitioning the Chancellor. By far the most common expedient, however, was for individuals to resort to less formal means of seeking redress and appeal for help to a well-informed (or well-connected) associate.

This was not a matter of finding someone to act for them within a legal process. Issues of law might indeed be involved, but characteristically such petitioners simply presented themselves as having been wronged in some way or as at risk of being so. Their appeal was to a more general sense of 'right': to fairness, in effect, although that usage was not yet current. The hope was that someone with more influence than they would tackle the wrongdoer on their behalf and would be listened to. The recipient of the appeal, if they took action, might in turn invoke the claims of 'right, law and conscience', but in their case this generic plea was backed by awareness that their good will was valuable and that the offender would do well to listen.[3] At the upper levels of late medieval society this is the familiar, and well-studied, deployment of 'good lordship'. But it clearly operated across a wider social spectrum and could utilize a broader range of relationships than that of lord/man. Inevitably the appeals of humbler figures are less likely to survive, and may indeed never have been written down in the first place, but it was a tactic applicable to all but the very lowliest social groups: that a small person asks a bigger person for protection is an almost universal option.

This was the context in which Jane Stapleton sought justice against her son, who had wronged her in a way that the common law could not touch. The trouble, as so often, had arisen over an inheritance, in this case from an attempt to divert land from the children of a first marriage to benefit the child of a second marriage. Jane was an heiress and the land in question was her own. It had come to her, and to her elder sister Elizabeth, because of the death of their father, Sir Miles Stapleton of Ingham (Norfolk), without male heirs. The failure of a family in the male line, and the consequent transmission of its estates through the marriage of heiresses to bolster the fortunes of other families, was not uncommon and contributed significantly to the shifting composition of local elites. The Stapletons themselves had become established in East Anglia through the marriage of an earlier Miles to the Ingham heiress in the mid-fourteenth century. Their origins were in Yorkshire, and in the fifteenth century the Norfolk branch still held land there, which was in due course to fall to Joan's share, but Ingham became their main residence, and its parish church their family mausoleum.[4]

Jane's own story begins with her marriage but, as is usual in family histories, this had roots further back. Since their arrival in Norfolk, the Stapletons had mainly sought their marriage partners among the East Anglian gentry, tying them into a complex network of local relationships. By the mid-fifteenth century they had been drawn into the orbit of William de la Pole, Earl and later Duke of Suffolk, whose influence at court had given him a significant role in the region until his murder in 1450, and from whom they held their Suffolk manor of Weybread. Miles Stapleton, Jane's father, has been described as one of 'the leading lights of the de la Pole connection' and the alliances forged under Suffolk's aegis were to outlive the duke himself.[5] Miles's second marriage, contracted in 1438 after a childless first marriage to Elizabeth Felbrigg, was to Earl William's cousin Katherine, the niece of Michael the second earl who had died at Harfleur.[6] The marriage was evidently considered something of a *coup* for the Stapletons, and the settlement reflects the de la Poles' superior bargaining power.

From the time of the family's acquisition of Ingham, their land had been entailed in the male line. Now, evidently for the sake of the de la Pole match, Miles's father Brian, just a month before his death in July 1438, barred the entail and settled his land in Norfolk, Suffolk and Berkshire on Miles and Katherine for her life, and on her death to their children of either sex.[7] It was this move that was ultimately to make Elizabeth (b. 1441) and Jane (b. 1444) their father's heiresses, although this could not have been predicted and the outcome was probably still not obvious when the time came to find husbands for them. Both marriages were again made within the de la Pole connection. Elizabeth, the eldest, married William Calthorpe in 1458.[8] The price of the marriage for the Stapletons was the manor of South Cove (Suffolk) which Miles bought in 1457 to settle on the couple.[9]

Jane's marriage, five years later in 1463, took her away from East Anglia, while remaining within the de la Pole circle. Her husband was Christopher, eldest son of Sir Richard Harcourt of Wytham (Berks) by his first wife, Edith St Clair. The indenture between the two fathers, mentioned in Miles's will, was dated 20 July 1463.[10] The terms of the settlement are unrecorded but it looks as if Miles may have settled Bainton (East Riding) on the couple; it is not mentioned in Miles's inquisition *post mortem*.[11] Less than five years later the alliance between the Stapletons and Harcourts was reinforced by a second marriage. Miles died on 1 October 1466 and by the beginning of 1468 his widow Katherine had married Sir Richard Harcourt as his second wife.[12] She brought him her life interest in what seems to have been most, if not all, of the Stapleton lands, leaving her daughters to wait until her death in 1488 for a final division of their inheritance. It was to be largely on the strength of Katherine's control of the Stapleton lands in Norfolk that Richard Harcourt became prominent in East Anglian affairs from the 1470s.

Elizabeth and William Calthorpe, too, became figures of note in the region. Calthorpe was the head of his family, with his own connections, and the couple also took immediate possession of Ingham, initially as Katherine's tenants at an annual rent of £40. Jane and Christopher, by contrast, remain largely invisible. In part this must be because Christopher had not yet inherited his family's land – and indeed was never to do so, predeceasing his father and dying in the summer of 1482.[13] By September 1486 Jane had married a second time. The earliest reference to this marriage comes in Richard Harcourt's will of that month, which described her as the wife of John Huddleston and settled lands in Lye beside Asthall (Oxon) on her with remainder to her second son Richard and then to his brother Simon. Her eldest son Miles, evidently named for his Stapleton grandfather and now his Harcourt grandfather's heir, was placed in the custody of Richard Lewkenore during his minority. Harcourt's inquisition *post mortem* suggests that there were doubts about whether Miles would submit to this guardianship, unsurprisingly, perhaps, as he must have been very nearly of age.[14]

It is likely that Jane's second marriage had been made some time before autumn 1486. The Huddlestons were a Cumberland family, established at Millom on the Duddon estuary.[15] In the 1470s they had risen fast in the service of Richard, Duke of Gloucester – an ascent that reached its peak after their patron's accession as Richard III in 1483. Assuming that the marriage was made in 1483–5 it would have been a 'good' marriage for Jane, but at first sight a slightly surprising one, taking her far out of her former geographical orbit. There were, however, advantages for both parties. The husband, although flourishing in Richard's service, was a younger son, not his father's heir. That was his elder brother Richard, who predeceased his father, leaving a son (also called Richard) who died childless in 1503. At that point Jane's husband inherited the family lands. But this outcome could not have been foreseen at the time of their marriage. The rewards of service were proverbially ephemeral – as the Huddlestons themselves had found after Bosworth. But even in their heyday, their reward had taken the form of annuities and office rather than land: money and influence rather than power. Their obvious strategy was to deploy such gains in securing a good marriage. Jane was an heiress. Although Jane's heirs at law were her Harcourt children, were John to have children by her (as he did) he would have a life interest in her land, which would at least be a step on the ladder.

The marriage thus benefited the Huddlestons. But it also arguably benefited Jane. Her own inheritance was to be the northern Stapleton lands. Bainton she perhaps already had. The remainder, notably Cotherstone and the moiety of Bedale and Askham Brian, were taken by Katherine de la Pole into her second marriage to Richard Harcourt. These had initially been entailed in the male line, and under that settlement should have returned to the Stapletons of Carlton (Yorks) at Miles's death without sons in 1466. In 1470 Brian Stapleton had sued Richard Harcourt and Katherine for the land on the basis of the entail made by Miles Stapleton in 1355.[16] Jane may well have welcomed the prospect of a powerful patron to maintain her claim when, in due course, she came to inherit. The disputed land lay within Gloucester's sphere of influence: Bedale was about seven miles as the crow flies from Gloucester's castle of Middleham; Cotherstone less than three miles from Barnard Castle (co. Durham); Askham Brian not far from York. In addition, the holder of the other moiety of Cotherstone and Askham Brian was Gloucester's close associate Francis, Viscount Lovell.[17]

If this was part of the thinking behind the marriage, it was to be overtaken by events. In 1485, with the death of their patron Richard III at Bosworth, the Huddlestons' prospects took a sharp turn for the worse. The family only narrowly managed to escape attainder. Jane's husband, John II, received a royal pardon in February 1486. His father, John I, whose links with Gloucester had been longer and closer than his son's, may have sympathized with the abortive rebellion of that year – at least to the extent of withholding support from Henry VII – but he too was pardoned in August. Both, however, lost the rewards they had enjoyed under the Yorkists, as well as the less tangible benefits that came with being known as men close to power; men, as was said of another northerner, 'that my lord of Gloucester will do for'.[18] John I never recouped that lost influence, but John II did work himself back into the new king's favour. As a younger son, with only a life interest in his wife's land, it was important for him to rebuild his career in royal service.

That career, however, was to be built in Gloucestershire, not the north, and even when the Millom inheritance came into John's hands in 1503, it seems not to have supplanted these newer associations. Huddleston probably owed them originally to Richard, Duke of Gloucester, who was to further strengthen them as king. In November 1469, when Gloucester's future role was still seen as lying in the west rather than the north, Edward IV's feoffees transferred the castle and manor of Sudeley to the duke and his heir's male.[19] They had been surrendered to the Crown by Ralph Boteler, their lord, to escape attainder. In the words of the Tudor antiquary John Leland:

> Kynge Edward the fourthe bare no good will to the Lorde Sudeley, as a man suspected to be in hart Henry the 6. man; whereapon by complaynts he was attachid, and goinge up to London he lokyd from the hill to Sudeley and sayd, 'Sudeley castelle thou art a traytor, not I'. After he made an honest declaration and sould his castle of Sudeley to Kynge Edward.[20]

Gloucester surrendered the property to the Crown in 1478, and the royal grant made in the same year to John II of the constableship of the castle is likely to be a confirmation of a role he had previously filled under the duke.[21] The family connection with Sudeley was underlined by the appointment of Christopher Huddleston as vicar two years later.[22]

John II's career retained its Gloucestershire focus thereafter.[23] He lost his Yorkist grants under the act of resumption in Henry VII's first parliament, but was described as 'of Gloucester' in his 1486 pardon which, although in part a reflection of his earlier office-holding in the county, may also indicate a continuing presence there. Certainly any hiatus in his involvement in the county was brief. He was returned to the commission of the peace in 1488, was knighted the following year, and made constable of Gloucester castle in 1492, by which time he was a knight of the king's body. He was made sheriff of the county in 1500. This implies a landed presence in the county, and that was provided by the lordship of Sudeley (as distinct from the castle) which he was farming from the abbot of Winchcombe at the time of his death.[24] By then he had also purchased the nearby manor of Temple Guiting, but it is likely that this was a late acquisition and that until the Millom inheritance fell to him he still had no significant landed estate of his own. This is the most likely context in which to understand the first stage in Jane's story, which was the diversion of a share of her inheritance to provide a marriage settlement for their son, John III. The marriage cannot be securely dated. Given the likely date of his parents' marriage, it was presumably sometime in the late 1490s, after Jane had finally come into possession of her share of the Stapleton lands, and before the Millom windfall in 1503.[25] The bride is said to have been Jane, the youngest daughter of Henry, Lord Clifford, who was restored to favour and his barony under Henry VII.[26] If so, given Clifford's status, the Huddlestons would have been expected to settle land on the couple to secure the match.

What happened is revealed in outline by John II. He made his testament on 5 November 1511.[27] His possession of Millom was recognized by a bequest of £20 to the fabric of the church there and a further £20 to the chantry chapel adjoining it. He also gave his best basin and ewer to the castle. But Gloucestershire was clearly now his home. He hoped to die in or near Hailes Abbey, where he willed burial before Our Lady of Pity (as Jane was later to do) and where he wanted there to 'be leyde upon me a stone of marble with a picture of my self sett therin and writinge theruppon to make mencion of me and my departinge'. After a variety of charitable and other bequests he named his executors: Sir Robert Southwell, Jane, Master Urswyk and John Daston; the abbot of Hailes was to be supervisor. It was only later, on his deathbed, that he expressed his last will concerning his land, 'declared and spoken with his mouth by goode deliberacion' in the presence of the abbot and prior of Hailes, the latter his confessor, and John Daston, gentleman:

> The aforenamed John Huddelston, havinge grete remorse in his conscience that he had enduced the said good lady his wife to geve the londes of her enheritaunce to his and her sonne John Huddelston and to his heires contrary to the intailes made by her noble auncetours ... charged his said sonne upon his blessinge that he shulde take noon avauntage of his said moders gifte, but that he shulde releese his hole interest of the same londes to his said moder and to her heires according to the first intaile therof made by her said auncetours.[28]

Jane's right heirs were her Harcourt descendants.[29] When she came to make her will in April 1518 she made this very clear:

> Item, it is my last will and full mynde that all my landis and tenementes within Yorkshire excepte Baynton goo to the right heires of the Hercourtes after my decease wherin my said husband Sir John Hoddilston dyde me wrong in his lyf as he testefied

and knowleged and also therof had remorsse at his departyng, and of his saying therof
I recorde me to my said lord Antony now abbot of Heiles and the said Thomas Salley now priour of the said monastery with others, whos reports and sayinges therin
be recorded at the Rooles in London the same yere after the departyng of my said
husband.[30]

This does not go much beyond what had been said in John's will. But Jane goes
on to add something not made explicit there:

> Item, whereas my said sonne John Hoddilston had a feoffement within my lordship
> of Coterston of the yerely value of xl li to hym and his first wif and to theire heires
> of the gift of my said husband his fader; that feoffement was made withoute my con-
> cent and advise. And I never dyd aggre therunto but ever denyed hym of such astate
> of my landes and also of occupacion therof at divers and many requisicions as he
> knowith hym self, my said lord Antony abbot of Hayles, Thomas priour and many
> other. Albeit he ever drove me of from tyme to tyme with faire wordis and promises.
> And this is my will, this my saying be shewed after my decease yf he doo not amende it
> in my lif, to thentent to have it refourmed and after my decease retorned and reserved
> to my right heires the Hercourtes for ever.

The two accounts do not quite match. John II's version implies that Jane had
agreed to the diversion of the land but that he now regretted 'inducing' her
to it. Jane is adamant that she had never agreed to it. If Jane wanted the grant
overturned it was necessary to emphasize the initial lack of consent and her continuing protests. But there was probably more to it than this. It is striking that
Jane's bitterness is directed at her son, not her husband – even though the initial
enfeoffment had been made by John II. It is John III who 'ever drove [her] of
from tyme to tyme with faire wordis and promises'. This surely reflects something that happened after John II's death; in fact just ten days before Jane made
her own will on 18 April.

John II's wish that his son release his rights in Jane's land had been duly
'recorded at the Rooles in London' by the witnesses to it. In other words, it had
been copied into the records of Chancery on the dorse of the Close Rolls – the
enrolments of royal letters sent 'close'.[31] Whether that was enough to annul the
enfeoffment is unclear but John III evidently feared that it might. His 'fair words
and promises' sound like delaying tactics adopted after his father's death. What
is clear is that John felt it expedient to construct an alternative, and fraudulent,
title to the land. Jane's will describes what had happened on 8 April 1518:

> Item, whereas my said sonne John Hoddilston ... came unto me and desired me to make
> hym my bailif and receyvour of all my landis and tenementes within Yorkshire, and said
> he wold bynde hym self unto me yerely to paye the rentes and revenues therof at the
> feastes and termes of Seint James and Seint Andree, wherunto I dyd agree. Wherupon
> he brought unto me a faire dede of releas of my title withe a graunte and gift of the rever-
> sion of the same landis and tenementes after my decease to hym and to his heires for
> ever, neyther redyng nor declaryng therof to me then, and so caused me to seale the said

dede, then saying: now by this wrytyng I stond at officer unto yow in the offices of bailif
and receivour and non other wayes. And therin utterly and untruly he hath disceived
me, as therby it may appere, which also I woll be shewid after my decease if he doo not
amende it in my lyf to thentent to adnull that dede so by him forged.

Within ten days Jane had discovered what she had done. Was it John himself
who told her? The phrase 'not declaring to me *then*' could be read in that way.
Jane, like her husband seven years earlier, tackled the issue on two fronts. There
is a tacit appeal to her son's conscience in her hope that he might annul it in her
lifetime, although it is much less explicit than John II's assertion that his blessing
depended on compliance. John II, 'havinge grete remorse in his conscience', had
suggested that his salvation required the righting of this wrong – and deathbed
wishes of this type were immensely powerful. Jane was not in this position. The
wrong had been committed by her son, not by her, and her salvation did not rest
on its resolution. The second front was the hope that, if appeal to conscience
failed, her executors would take legal action. Here, too, her position was weaker
than her husband's. His executors had been headed by Sir Robert Southwell,
who had been chief auditor of Henry VII, and by Christopher Urswick, once the
almoner of Henry VII and later dean of Windsor. The power of both men may
have been waning by 1511, Urswick was effectively in retirement, but they were
well connected and knew the ropes.[32] Neither was named in Jane's will. Urswick
had presumably subsided further into retirement and Southwell had died in
1514.[33] Jane's executors were the abbot of Winchcombe and the Gloucestershire
esquire William Tracy, with the abbot of Hailes again as supervisor.

The story as told here raises a number of issues. One obvious one is whether the
nature of the deception practised on Jane is evidence that she could not read. Her
insistence that John did not 'declare' the tenor of the deed to her shows that she
had simply taken his word for what it said. The likelihood is that a woman of her
status *could* read, but that she could not understand Latin – the language in which
John's 'fair deed' would have been couched. John's stratagem may have hinged on
the possibility that his mother would be able to pick out words – the place names
in particular – and perhaps also to see that this was a grant of some sort, but that
she would not be able to distinguish a release of land from a grant of office within
that land. It was probably also the case that, aged over seventy by now, Jane's eye-
sight was poor; she later required her will to be read back to her for checking.[34]

Jane's intention had been defeated by her misunderstanding or non-under-
standing of the written word. There was an irony in this. Her will, drawn up
after she had discovered the deception, shows her to be a woman well aware of
the power of the written word as the vehicle of her wishes. The emphasis is most
marked in the matter of her bequest of specified pieces of plate to John III:

> Item, it is my last will and mynde that my sonne John Huddilston have and keep hym self content of and with my gift ... delyvered to hym all redy by the willyng gift of me the said Dame Jane in the presence of Anthony abbot of Heilis the day of makyng and sealyng of agreement made bitwene me and my said sonne John Huddilston under bothe our seales remaynyng with my said lord abbot of Heilis, in full contentacion and gyft of this my last will and bequest to hym as the uttermost parte, porcion or percell of eny goodes that is or ever heretofore was myne, shall or may be.

The date of this agreement is not clear. If it post-dated John III's deception, then the tightness of its terms may have owed something to Jane's sense that he was not to be trusted. The grant of plate to her Harcourt heir, Simon, was equally precise about what it comprised, but did not involve him sealing an indenture to remain with the abbot. The will does, however, offer other examples of Jane's emphasis on the letter of agreements. She was equally firm about the good works that would earn her salvation and ensure that she was remembered. Among those itemized in her will is the roofing of the aisles of the abbey church at Hailes.[35] If the work was unfinished at her death her executors were to complete it, at her expense, as she had planned, 'without any altercation or further delay'. Similarly, if she died before the completion of the Lady chapel in Winchcombe Abbey, it was to be completed as specified in indentures between her and the abbot and convent. In a revealing touch, a very lavish gift of furnishings to the chapel of St Nicholas within the abbey church ended with two gowns of black velvet and one of black satin, with their linings, furs and borders, which were to be made into 'ornaments' for the church at their cost, not hers.

The written word gives greater security. But Jane was 'declaring' her will. What we hear is emphatically her spoken voice. That comes through strongly in her account of the wrongs done to her, but it is audible too in the grant that she makes to John, in spite of his deceit, of a life interest in Bainton:

> it is my mynde and saying afore a temporall jugge yt shuld goo and belong to my said sonne John Hoddilston after my decease for terme of his lyf.[36] And after his decease it to retourne and goo to my right heires of the Harcourtes forever; and not oderways I mak graunt therof, so Crist me help at the daye of Juggement. And so it is my will that it shall goo and retourne as abovesaid.[37]

Nuncupative wills rested ultimately on the reliability of the witnesses who heard the words spoken and could testify to the accuracy of the written version. John II's last will concerning his land had been 'declared and spoken with his mouth' on his deathbed, as the witnesses testified in Chancery. Jane, with more time at her disposal, took steps to ensure that the written version was correct, but there remains a very marked emphasis within the will upon the testimony of the witnesses to her *spoken* word. The will was made on 18 April 1518, and her two executors and the supervisor signed her own copy of it – wording that implies the existence of other copies. But this was not the end of the matter. Further additions were made the following spring, and finally, on 14 May 1519, 'beyng of perfyte memorie and good mynde' in her chamber in Hailes, and in the presence of five named witnesses, including her confessor the prior Thomas Salley, she

> declared and affirmed all the premisses to contain hir very true testament and last will and therupon she instantly required the forsaid persones to testifie and bere recorde, and than and there the same Dame Jane in further testimonye to the premisses dyd sett her seale.

Jane had done all she could to ensure her will was 'holy, justely, fully and truely executed and perfourmed in every thing accordyng to this my last willes and bequestes'. She was evidently a woman who knew her own mind and was determined that her wishes should be met. But in spite of – or perhaps because of – Jane's rather obsessive concern that her wishes be faithfully carried out, she was obviously anticipating the possibility of challenge. One of the additions to the April 1518 will was a note that £60 in a casket had been delivered to the abbot and convent of Hailes to meet the costs of her executors and supervisor, and of her servant Christopher Laughlyn and his wife Elizabeth,

> against anythyng that shalbe layd unto theire charges or any of theim by my sonnes Sir Symon Harcourt, knyght, or by John Hoddilston esquire or eyther of theim, by reason of any bequest, will or dede in my lif or after my decease wherby they or any of theim shalbe called to before witnes or recorde. And if they nor neyther of theim any such trouble or busyness shall make nor cause thrugh theire procurement, that then the said lx li to goo and remayne towardes the perfourmance of this my last will and testament.

Safe delivery of the money was recorded by a bill dated 12 March 1519 – yet another example of *written* evidence.

In spite of all her efforts, Jane may not have been confident of the outcome. The deed she had sealed, although described by her as a forgery, was on the face of it valid in law. The common law offered redress for a widow whose husband had parted with her freehold land against her will, but this did not meet her case.[38] Her executors could possibly have taken the case into Chancery on the strength of the testimony in her will, but it would have lacked the force of a case brought by her in her lifetime. Simon Harcourt, who was the individual most concerned, may not have been very interested in joining in a suit. In 1513 he had inherited Stanton Harcourt (Oxfordshire) and the other estates of the senior line of the family.[39] Scattered lands in the north-east may not have seemed worth the fight. In the end, Jane's desired outcome rested on the possibility that her son would submit to moral pressure and there is no sign that he ever did. In 1596 the manor of 'Goderston' [Cotherstone] was still in the possession of the Huddlestons.[40] Jane's resort to informal tactics had failed, but in the process she has left us what seems at times to be her unmediated voice. Had she taken her case formally to law we would not have heard it half so clearly.[41]

5 'SHE HYM FRESSHELY FOLOWED AND PURSUED': WOMEN AND STAR CHAMBER IN EARLY TUDOR WALES

Deborah Youngs

In recent years a growing number of studies have explored the legal experiences of fifteenth- and sixteenth-century women. Drawing on a range of court records, reassessments have been made on women's knowledge of the law, their engagement with legal procedure and their agency in initiating petitions. In considering the varying opportunities offered by different jurisdictions, the material generated by the central law courts at Westminster – notably those of King's Bench, Common Pleas and Chancery – has proved particularly fruitful.[1] Less well-explored for this purpose, however, has been the court of Star Chamber, perhaps because it is considered to have the smallest female participation rate.[2] This is unfortunate, because the documentation produced by the court makes for vivid reading and is important not simply for the stories told, but, as Geoffrey Elton pointed out over half a century ago, because the reported voices belong to people 'who would never ordinarily make the headlines'.[3] The oversight is particularly unhelpful for late medieval Wales where local jurisdiction in the marcher lordships meant its inhabitants were excluded from the central common law courts of King's Bench and Common Pleas. It was the king's claim to offer justice to all his subjects and provide 'common treatment', which gave the Welsh access to prerogative courts such as Star Chamber.[4] Where the records of Star Chamber have been used effectively to explore the roles and agency of women in Wales, the focus has been on the later sixteenth and seventeenth centuries.[5] Very little comment has been made on the cases submitted during the reign of Henry VIII, and nothing on the period prior to the Acts of Union (1536–42).[6]

This chapter focuses on these earlier cases and the female plaintiffs who were among the first to travel from Wales to initiate suits in Star Chamber. It does so through a detailed examination of two bills, submitted in 1530–2, by Denise Williams and Kathryn Robert who resided, respectively, in the lordships of Gower and Glamorgan, South Wales. The essay begins by providing a brief outline of the court's procedures before setting the complainants in the context of the South Welsh marches. In so doing, it considers how the women attempted to negotiate local politics, procedural language and their own legal positions in the search for redress.

Taking its name from the star-painted ceiling of the room at Westminster in which its members sat, Star Chamber grew out of the King's council in the fifteenth century and became an established court of law under Henry VII and Henry VIII. It was during Thomas Wolsey's chancellorship (1515–29) that its judicial function was advanced, areas of jurisdiction were defined and procedures formalized. It dealt with both civil and criminal business, and while it could not prosecute capital offences, like treason, it had a broad jurisdiction, which included breaches of the peace (riot, assault, murder or trespass), debt, slander, perversion of justice (such as perjury or maintenance), the misdemeanours of crown officials and breaches of royal protocol.[7] It had emerged as a response to the limitations of common law and the onus was on the litigant to demonstrate why his or her case deserved special treatment. This meant that allegations of violence, usually in the form of riot, forcible entry or assault, were deemed necessary to secure a hearing, and may well have been included solely to catch the attention of the judge.[8]

The court's main business comprised cases between party and party. A private suit was entered by filing a bill of complaint according to a particular form. It was composed with the advice of counsel, written in English, engrossed on parchment by professional scribes, signed by the plaintiff's counsel and filed by a clerk.[9] Should the case proceed beyond the bill stage, there would be a defendant's answer, the replication of the plaintiff, and the defendant's rejoinder, followed by interrogations and depositions, and the appointment of commissioners. Star Chamber met at Westminster twice weekly during the legal terms, and its regular sittings, combined with its reliance on the written record, generated a considerable amount of documentation. Unfortunately, a significant amount – perhaps as much as a half of the original archive – has been lost and many suits are incomplete.[10] Frustratingly, no decrees, orders or awards are extant, which has meant that in no Welsh suit is there a verdict recorded.

Star Chamber was not necessarily a cheap option and had the potential to be very time-consuming. It was also a risk: if the bill was disproved, the plaintiff and sometimes the council could be punished. This meant it was a court for those with some resources. Nevertheless, while the gentry did form the largest single group in both England and Wales, they did not dominate. J. A. Guy calculated that in Wolsey's chancellorship, the gentry formed 28.7 per cent of litigants, but they were closely followed by yeomen/husbandmen (25.4 per cent), which included those with modest income.[11] In spite of costs, numbers increased during Wolsey's chancellorship and in Henry VIII's reign it was a court viewed favourably by litigant and lawyer alike. Wolsey had promoted Star Chamber as a vehicle for 'indifferent justice' and he convinced contemporaries that it was an effective instrument for checking the abuses of power by great men; it appeared to be less susceptible to bribery and local pressures.[12] It was also a draw to the litigant who had failed to achieve the desired outcome in another court or who used it to gain an advantage in legal cases ongoing in common law or Chancery.[13] By the 1520s, pressure of volume prompted a move to delegate the Chancellor's work to the newly invigorated councils in Wales and in the North, although with largely negligible results. Set up in 1526 as part of Princess Mary's household in Ludlow, the Council in the Marches of Wales, shared many points of procedure with Star Chamber, and the latter was sometimes used as a court of appeal to the Council.[14]

One of the reasons cited for the re-establishment of the Council in 1526 had been the difficulty inhabitants of Wales and the marches had found in taking their cases to the Westminster courts.[15] The number of Welsh suitors at the court of Star Chamber is not high: there is a single (male) bill for Henry VII's reign and just under 190 cases are recorded for the reign of Henry VIII. This is in a context of Guy's estimation that around 5,000 cases were initiated in the latter's reign.[16] Nevertheless, the volume is not insignificant and reflects both the population size of Wales and its distance from the capital: not unexpectedly, those living closer to London went to Star Chamber more frequently.[17] Among the Welsh cases, women appear as complainants in twenty-three instances (12 per cent), nine alongside their husbands and fourteen (7 per cent) on their own (the majority as widows). These are small proportions, but not out of line with the percentage of female cases going to Star Chamber in later periods, or those pleading in other Westminster courts.[18] There is not an even spread across Wales and no female plaintiffs are noted for Anglesey, Brecon, Caernarfon or Carmarthen. The eastern and more densely populous county of Glamorgan (formed from the lordships of Glamorgan and Gower), however, produced the highest number of female litigants: of thirty-three cases, women were sole complainants in five and co-plaintiffs with their husbands in a further four. This was a county where breaches of the peace generated most litigation,[19] and accusations of assault and murder lay behind four of the five sole female complainants, including the two case studies discussed in this essay.

By their very nature, Star Chamber suits tell a particular story about sixteenth-century society, one unlikely to cast its people in a favourable light. When Ifan ab Owen Edwards calendared the Star Chamber proceedings relating to Wales, he saw the court as a positive force for the country because it was a means of bringing 'some show of justice' to an area where a rapacious bunch of local officials were regularly abusing their position; the caseload could be read as 'a record of the misuse of their office'.[20] More recent historians have not demurred from this assessment.[21] The cases under discussion occurred during a period when the judicial practices of the country were coming under scrutiny. The fragmentation of political power in medieval Wales had led to persistent problems in the administering of justice.

The 'marches' comprised a number of lordships, which were separate units of government and justice, where lords exercised royal rights over the inhabitants. An acrimonious Star Chamber case of 1524 endorsed the right of the marcher lord of Gower and Kilvey to hear and decide 'all plees of the crowne as all oder common plees, reall, personall and myxt'.[22] The Crown might only intervene in cases either by approaching the marcher lord directly or by authorizing proceedings when complaints were brought by aggrieved individuals before Chancery, Court of Requests or Star Chamber. There were accusations that felons avoided punishment by moving from one lordship to another, or by purchasing pardons.

In addition, most lords were absent and power was devolved to deputies and officials who 'rarely worked in the best interests of justice or effective administration'.[23] Responsibility for the dispensing of justice fell to the steward who presided over the county courts. In the early sixteenth century, this position in the lordship of Gower was held by two influential men who commanded the allegiance of numerous retainers in South Wales: Sir Matthew Cradock (d. 1531) and Sir George Herbert (d. 1570).[24] During the 1520s and 1530s, the evidence suggests that the administration of justice within the lordship was inefficient, deficient and operated by corrupt officers.[25] Sir George Herbert has been singled out for his 'deplorable' abuse of power, including an act of judicial murder, and for the degree of lawlessness and disorder he allowed to occur during his stewardship.[26] He made no obvious attempts to check misconduct and was embroiled in various legal proceedings.[27] Misconduct in South Wales was also a reflection of the inadequacies of the earl of Worcester, Herbert's principal patron, and described in 1538 as 'young and foolish and of great power in Wales'.[28] Henry Somerset had succeeded his father as earl of Worcester in 1526 and his lands and officers were concentrated in Wales: he exercised regal jurisdiction in the lordship of Gower and was steward of the lordship of Glamorgan. He rarely exercised that lordship, however, and seemed little concerned about his officers' exploits so long as they did not damage his revenues in any way. Offices were a means of rewarding his supporters and Worcester had retained the services of Cradock and Herbert because they were men with some standing in the area and with whom he had close personal ties.[29]

While these malpractices were not new or unusual in the 1520s and 1530s, Glanmor Williams detected an increased awareness and sensitivity to this misrule by the king's government at a time when the emerging King's Matter was moving the realm into crisis.[30] The Council in the Marches had been charged with instituting good order, but had proved largely ineffectual in its early years. In May 1532, Thomas Philips wrote to Thomas Cromwell that Wales was in 'decay' and would remain so until officers in Wales were restrained from taking fines for felony and murder, and from delaying justice.[31] Further letters to Cromwell in 1533 described Wales as being 'far out of order', where murderers and other felons were left unpunished.[32] By this date Cromwell himself was making known his desire for 'justice and quiet to be maintained in Wales'. His proposal that 'murders in Wales and the Marches may be tried in the Star Chamber' reflects both the perceived inadequacies of justice in Wales and Cromwell's confidence in Star Chamber as an impartial court.[33]

Given the problems inherent in the southern lordships of Wales, how did its female inhabitants negotiate these apparent obstacles to justice? Star Chamber cases offer some insight, but the onus on litigants to show violent disorder, abuse of position or perversion of justice inevitably places limits on female involvement. No woman was sole defendant in any case (a contrast to those found in Chancery) and hardly any were called as witnesses. In these records violent direct action is overwhelmingly a male recourse. Where women do occur in the narratives they generally occupy peripheral roles, although these could be interventionist. They may have initiated the hue and cry or tried to calm down an impassioned situation.[34] In a handful of cases, they assume supportive roles on behalf of their husbands and families. Elizabeth Matthew and Felice Gwyn, for example, were among those accused of riotously attacking or defending (depending on one's point of view) the manor of Boverton (Glamorgan) in support of Elizabeth's husband John Matthew; Amy Coke was accused with five others of forcible entry into property at Mathern (Monmouthshire).[35]

Other women offered verbal encouragement to one of the parties. An affray in Caerleon, April 1542, had resulted in the murder of Lewis Lloyd by William ap Richards. In a series of heated exchanges which occurred while the bailiffs were bringing William ap Richards to gaol, Amy Philip, wife of Philip Gunter, was accused of speaking 'menessyng and thretenyng words' to William Jones, the mayor of the town. She is reported to have said:

> I wold ye knew the stretes of this towne shalbe to hotte for Willyam ap Richard your brotherinlaw and the highest pare of his crowne shalbe cutt whosever take his parte when soever he commyth unto the towne or not.

In turn, William's brother, Alexander Jones, replied 'Gett thee home thowe whoore. Were thowe a man as thowe arte a woman I would sett this dagger in thy belly, for he shall come by thy house and through they howse if it be my pleasure'.[36] Gunter swiftly told his wife to get in the house. It would be unwise to take the reported speech at face value; indeed witnesses for Gunter denied his wife had made those remarks. Nevertheless, Amy Philip's alleged outburst fits the pattern of the scold and her actions would have been judged equally as disruptive to the peace of the community as the male violence that resulted in murder. Such is seen in the 1542 ordinances of Neath in 1542, which stated that any women who 'threateneth her neighbors' would be fined and any who 'scoulde or rage' were to be put on the 'cooking stoole'.[37] At least in Amy Philip's case a distinction was made between acceptable violence carried out on men and on women. On other occasions women were not spared: when John ap Llywelyn was set upon leaving St Michael's Church, Carmarthenshire, *c.* 1532, his wife was similarly assaulted.[38]

While women were rarely portrayed in active roles in the narratives of pleadings, there were, as noted above, twenty-three cases from Wales during the reign of Henry VIII where they entered bills as plaintiffs, fourteen as sole litigants. Among the causes for doing so were the two criminal actions where a woman did have a strong legal voice, where she could self-prosecute: an appeal involving the murder of her husband and an appeal against her own rapist. In these cases it is the woman who narrates the events and identifies the perpetrators.[39] In selecting an example from each group, this essay is concerned with two cases bound consecutively within the papers of Star Chamber. This may indicate that they were entered at the same time or that a clerk recognized the connection. It is possible that their positioning was a product of the organizational intentions of the nineteenth-century editors of the collection.[40] Yet, both bills were directed at Chancellor Thomas More, which would date them to a relatively short period of time, from October 1529 to May 1532. Unfortunately, we only have the bills of complaint so there are no alternative versions to the events outlined in them, but they have been chosen to illustrate how these female plaintiffs and their counsel chose to construct their narratives and the voices used. As with all legal complaints, these bills would have been mediated through a scribe, and produced according to the conventions of the elected court. In the case of Star Chamber, claims of riot, forcible entry or assault are to be expected. At the same time, we must be alert to the choices made by the litigants and their counsel concerning what to accentuate and what to omit in order to achieve a favourable outcome.[41]

The first petitioner is Denise Williams of Glynneath (Glamorgan) whose bill related to the murder of her husband Hopkyn ap Dafydd of Ynystawe (lordship of Gower).[42] This had occurred following a long-running dispute between Hopkyn and a kinsman Dafydd ap Gruffudd ap John. Both men had been compelled to attend the king's council in Cardiff and each was bound in 100 marks to keep the peace towards each other. Dafydd, however, had the support of the steward of Gower, Sir Matthew Cradock, and he decided to take direct action: along with seventeen others, he ambushed and murdered Hopkyn.[43] Left a widow with several children to support, Denise's bill outlined her ongoing struggle to bring her husband's attackers to justice.

It is worth looking closer at the accused. We can assume that the number who assaulted Hopkyn is not accurate because it was common to inflate the number of participants in these cases. Denise, however, was careful to name two others as aiders and abetters. These were Dafydd's brothers, William and Owen Gruffudd, whom Denise described as notorious in Gower for their association with 'thefes, murderers and malefactors'. All three were the sons of Gruffudd ap John who resided in Ynys Derw, Rhyndwyglydach (in the parish of Llangyfelach).[44] This lay in the elevated areas of Gower, in the Gower Wallicana (the Welshry) and one of the most sparsely settled of the lordship.[45] The family was of modest means and status, and hovered on the boundary between the yeomanry and lesser gentry. A handful of conveyancing deeds document the brothers granting and quitclaiming lands in Llangiwg in the manor of Supraboscus (Gower Wallicana). Dafydd ap Gruffudd quitclaimed rights to land there in 1532 in a deed witnessed by his brother William ap Gruffudd and Sir George Herbert, steward of Gower.[46] Around the same time, in September 1532, William and Dafydd Gruffudd were among the eight men listed as tenants of the Welshry in an agreement between the earl of Worcester and representatives of the several classes of tenants living in the lordship of Gower; this was to confirm the liberties of Swansea.[47] Their power in the area, however, owed much to their long-term service to the steward of Gower. Gruffudd ap John had been Mathew Cradock's deputy and regularly held the county court of the Englishry in 1499/1500.[48] In the 1530s, William and Dafydd Gruffudd served the earl of Worcester as beadles for the lordship of Supraboscus; part of their duties involved detaining animals and crops due to the lord as heriot or forfeiture.[49] Here they worked under the steward George Herbert and by the mid-sixteenth century William Gruffudd was one of Herbert's main livery servants.[50] The authority of Gruffudd and his sons, therefore, depended entirely on the favour granted them by Cradock and Herbert.

Denise Williams's tale highlighted the protection afforded to the Gruffudd brothers. She had previously sought help from the Council in the Marches and had petitioned the earl of Worcester and Lord Ferrers, steward of the Council, but to no avail.[51] Instead, she complained, Dafydd ap Gruffudd had managed to obtain a pardon, which had been granted at Westminster in July 1528.[52] She was not the only Glamorgan widow to claim that local powers were impeding the successful prosecution of felons. Joanne ap Howell stated that she was unable to secure justice for the murder of husband, the sheriff of Ogmore, by men of Christopher Turberville because the latter 'bereth greate rule in the seid partes of South Wales'.[53] Jane Carne of Sully implicated Sir Walter Herbert and his men in the murder of her husband in Cardiff, 1539/40. She claimed that although the men responsible had been convicted before the coroner of Glamorgan, justice could not be done because Herbert 'had the rule' of Cardiff under the earl of Worcester and had maintained the accused.[54] Katherine verch David of Llandaff, whose bill emphasized her heavy pregnancy, also had a husband murdered in Cardiff. In this account, the accused, which included several gentlemen, were acquitted because the jury at Cardiff was packed with their supporters and an armed group of friends occupied the town. For good measure, Katherine's bill also condemned the bailiffs of Cardiff as ignorant and not learned in the law, and she demanded a *melius inquirendum* be sent to the bailiffs.[55]

Such claims must be considered cautiously, of course, because plaintiffs had to provide reasons why their cases could not be heard satisfactorily in other courts. Yet a particular value of Star Chamber litigation is precisely the characteristic that the parties had been or still were at law against each in alternate jurisdictions: they can alert historians to legal actions commenced by women in courts for which records no longer survive. Jane Carne, like Denise Williams, had first tried to secure redress from the Council in the Marches of Wales. The defendant, Walter Herbert, indignantly drew attention to his successful appearance at the Council on the same charges where nothing had been proven against him.[56] It is possible, therefore, to look at these cases as examples where women had been forced to pursue more than one avenue for redress. Equally, however, they may have been mounting collateral attacks by using one action to shore up a claim or delay a judgement in another court.[57] Either way, they show that women had legal options and were determined and able to select from a wide range of jurisdictions.

They were careful, however, not to present themselves as thinking strategically or promoting their case too vigorously. Denise described herself as a 'pore' victim of the system. In her bill, she attempted to capture the moral high ground, contrasting her persistent attempts to gain justice with the impotence of the king's laws and the liberty of the perpetrators. She was the one wronged.[58] Yet what makes Denise's bill particularly interesting is that she chose to stress the wider consequences beyond her personal sense of injustice: the reluctance of the local and regional powers to stop the Gruffudd brothers had allowed a family to continue its violent behaviour. To drive home the point, Denise's bill explained that 'after the seid pardon' the brothers 'had ravisshed oon Katheryn Robert' and killed and murdered her father Robert ap William of the lordship of Glamorgan.

The case to which Denise refers is my second example and concerns the rape of Kathryn Robert, the daughter of Robert ap William from Cwrt-Rhyd-Hir (Neath, Glamorgan), a minor gentleman.[59] Kathryn introduced her own bill by recounting that she was in her father's house, 31 August 1529, when it was attacked by Owen Gruffudd and several armed men of his affinity. They forcibly entered the property 'and there felonously toke and ravisshed your said oratrice ayenst her wille and sett her upon horsebak and carried her with theym the space of twoo myles'. At once her father and a group of neighbours made 'fresh' suit with the hue and cry, managed to rescue Kathryn and bring her back to her father's house. This was only a temporary reprieve because Owen, along with brothers William and Dafydd and numerous other supporters, 'freshly' returned and pursued Kathryn and 'your oratrice then fledde to a neighbours house for safegarde of her life'. The group attacked and murdered her father before breaking into the house where Kathryn was hiding. She was 'felonously ravisshed' again and this time carried away and kept for three months during which time they 'compelled her to marye with the said Owen ayenst her wille'.

The opening lines of this narrative of rape, abduction and forced marriage follow the format found in other legal accounts of abduction. There are no details of any physical damage to the body, like bleeding, which would have been found in earlier cases, nor is she a passive virgin. Here it is her consent, 'her wille', that is highlighted, reflecting the wording of the 1487 statute that had most recently defined abduction.[60] The emphasis is also on the violence of her attack, not on the sexual nature of rape. Garthine Walker has shown that in most rape narratives the crime was defined in terms of male violence rather than sexual assault. This allowed the plaintiff to direct attention on to male behaviour rather than the (non) actions of the female victim. Had the sex act been prioritized, it would have brought to the fore questions of female desire, resistance and complicity. It may have been particularly acute in traditional Welsh society where it was a woman's obligation to retain her purity.[61] While this might appear to deny the woman agency in the events, rendering her passive, the language of rape was 'heavily circumscribed' and needed to be negotiated.[62] It was precisely in order to create a strong case that the emphasis in Kathryn's bill is on her flight; there was no occasion for physical struggle.[63] Kathryn's continued passivity is also underlined in the first rescue, which was organized entirely by father and friends. When, after a few months, she fled from Owen a second time, Kathryn attributed it to 'the help and power of God'. Escaping by her own efforts may have implied that she was not held captive and had chosen to stay. Kathryn's bill, therefore, was phrased to avoid accusations of collusion, of an elopement turned sour. She clearly saw the marriage as invalid and she is presented as the daughter of Robert ap Williams, and by implication a single woman.

A woman's agency, therefore, was present not so much in what she said had happened during the abduction, but in her actions that followed, specifically in the act of entering a plea and telling her story. As noted above, this could be undertaken more than once. Star Chamber was not the first court in which Kathryn had sought justice, for she had commenced an 'appeale of rape' in the court of Neath against Owen and his affinity. Kathryn's bill carefully outlined that she had acted according to established procedure and in accordance with local custom: Owen was called five times. What was procedurally deficient was the response of the Gruffudd brothers. When the judgment should have been given against Owen in court, William Gruffudd and '500 persons or above', heavily armed, came from neighbouring lordships and surrounded the court, at which point the jury thought better of proceeding to judgement. Again, the number of assembled men will have been an exaggeration, but it may have felt as much. The hearing presumably took place in the building called 'Le Court House' or 'Le Bottehalle', which stood in the middle of Neath's Old Market Street.[64] This was a central position in a small town because Neath had not recovered from economic downturn in the fourteenth and fifteenth century: only seventy-three names were recorded for the town in the lay subsidy of 1542–3 and none of its houses is likely to have been of any substance.[65] The image of a large body of men descending on the court from surrounding hillsides vividly encapsulates the problems petitioners encountered when trying to bring their abductors to a court subject to the political influence of local men.[66]

Nevertheless, the next part of the bill bears out the view that abducted women were often shown as 'strong-willed and independent' in Star Chamber.[67] Kathryn did not stop after the abortive judgement at Neath, but: 'your said oratrice having parfitte knowlege that the said Owen had fledde toward the citie of London she hym fresshely folowed and pursued'. At this point in the narrative Kathryn becomes the pursuer; she is now running towards her attacker. It is tempting to see the third repetition of the adverb 'freshly' (quickly, eagerly) as an echo of Kathryn's own account of her experiences; it is not commonly used in other bills. What can be stated more certainly is that the narrative positions her as having the advantage: she had obtained information and acted on it. She may have gained foreknowledge that Owen would run. Owen was himself a landowner with territory in Llangiwg, and one wonders if there is any significance in the timing of Owen's grant to Hopkyn ap Rees ap Thomas of half a tenement in Ynysmeudwy on 26 November 1529, three months after he had purportedly abducted Kathryn (and when she estimated she had escaped).[68] That he would travel to London is not surprising because significant numbers of Welsh people had based themselves in the capital by the early sixteenth century. They were mainly from modest families, living in the centre of the city, and often retaining family ties.[69] Old acquaintances could be met and old scores settled on its streets. It is possible that Kathryn's abductor was the Owen Griffith residing in Fleet Street who attacked Robert Lewes out of 'old malice' in 1532, prompting Lewes to petition Chancery.[70] It is at least the type of newsworthy incident that would ripple through a Welsh network.

Not only did Kathryn catch up with her attacker, but she 'caused hym in the said citie to be attached for the said rape and felony'. He was committed to the compter in Bread Street, London, where 'he yet remayneth withoute bayle or maynprise'. Bread Street was one of the twenty-five wards of the city of London and the compter or prison lay on its west side; it acted as a holding cell in this instance.[71] Such a bold response was not unique. Kathryn's actions may call to mind the more famous case of Margaret Kebell (d. 1534), the wealthy widow of serjeant Thomas Kebell, who was abducted in 1502 by the retainers of the Vernon of Haddon family (Derbyshire) and forced to marry the heir of the family, Roger. She also escaped, accused the Vernons of abduction, and showed considerable resourcefulness in pursuing her case in the secular courts of King's Bench, Common Pleas and Star Chamber.[72] These examples give lie to the view that abducted women were helpless or lacking in agency.[73] And yet, Kathryn's bill was careful not to focus too long on any character strength. In the final few lines, she switched voice and presented herself as weak: she had no friends or substance to follow the law against Owen, nor did she dare return to South Wales for fear of her life. Gone is the woman who chased her attacker to London, and now there is the lone woman as passive victim, a position that women – and their lawyers – regularly employed.[74] It is as humble plaintiff that she wanted the Chancellor to direct letters to the earl of Worcester as the steward of Glamorgan to convey Owen back into Wales and there to administer the 'due ordre of the kinges laws withoute favour or partialitie to the exsample of all other like offenders'. Such a sentence may seem like a legal cliché, but in common with Denise's bill, Kathryn's considers the impact of her case on the wider community.

At different points in her bill, Kathryn's voice, therefore, alternated between passive victim and active seeker of justice. What remains relatively constant, however, is the singular presence of Kathryn. Her friends are shadowy figures who try, but ultimately fail, to offer assistance. This may well have been what it felt like, but Kathryn could hardly have been without support in pleading her bill; she may even have been emboldened to do so. Most women entering allegations of rape in medieval England were young, unmarried virgins and Caroline Dunn suggests, on the basis of legal commentaries and prosecution rates, that this was because the ravishment of maidens was considered a more heinous crime than the attack on non-virgins, and it was easier to verify.[75] Family and friends were consequently more likely to encourage the pursuit of the case. Where abduction and forced marriage had occurred, families may well have been the driving forces in persuading women to plead, motivated in large part by the need to redress the loss of property. Stress has been placed on the patriarchal response to abduction as a crime against 'male property' rather than against the female body, a view supported by those cases where the complainants were male relatives.[76] Abducting prospective brides to secure an advantageous marriage was not common in the later Middle Ages, but those targeted were usually the wealthy elite with property and goods. It was this group of women who were the concern of the 1487 legislation, which made it a capital felony to abduct and forcibly marry or rape 'women having substances'.[77]

What we know about Kathryn, however, does not fit this profile neatly. She was not the sole heiress, but shared her inheritance with three sisters who all lived long enough to marry and have several children of their own. Nor was her family particularly wealthy. Genealogies list Robert as living in Cwrt-Rhyd-Hir, one of the smaller-sized granges belonging to Neath Abbey, although there is no documentation to indicate when his family first leased the house.[78] Kathryn's bill makes no mention of property or of any goods taken, which is in line with her unmarried status.[79] This was the abduction of a younger daughter by a younger son and Kathryn would not have had the financial resources at the disposal of Margaret Kebell. There are also no obvious male supporters. Kathryn did eventually marry John Cradock of Cheriton (Gower), gentleman, who would himself lease Cwrt-Rhyd-Hir in 1538, but we do not know whether the match was arranged before the abduction.[80] The one person who can be counted among Kathryn's supporters is Denise Williams. Her knowledge of Kathryn's plight would have been first-hand for not only were Denise and Kathryn's mothers closely related, but Denise's son Dafydd married Kathryn's older sister Jenet.[81] Did these two plaintiffs, therefore, plan their pleas to Star Chamber as a collateral attack on the Gruffudds, part of a broader strategy to bring some order to a small part of Gower and Glamorgan? Given that these bills were submitted within a short time frame, both women would have been in London during the same period, perhaps had even travelled down together. With the male heads of their respective families dead, it is not unreasonable to imagine these two women working alongside each other to protect their kin and community.

We do not know the outcome of Kathryn's bill or when Owen was freed from Bread Street. Both ultimately returned west, married and established their own households. Owen still retained land in Llangiwg and in 1549 can be found conveying a tenement to a neighbour. The conveyance and quitclaim documents were both confirmed with Owen's own seal: a stag adjacent to his initials OG.[82] Only perhaps in the fact that Owen became based in Herefordshire is there a suggestion that he was not welcome back in the Neath and Swansea valleys.[83] This is merely speculation, however, and it may well impugn a man against whom no guilty verdict is known. Any analysis of Star Chamber bills must acknowledge their legal fictions and their need to tailor the case for specific purposes. Nevertheless, the identities portrayed in these bills can tell us much about the construction of female plaintiffs and their agency. There are common tropes. The women are poor and lack support despite the allusions to friends at various points in the text. They do not try and fight against any attack, and are either quickly overpowered or they run away. Witness statements in the narratives of Welsh Star Chamber cases do show women intervening for positive or negative effect, but they do not portray women either instigating or physically defending themselves against interpersonal violence. Despite this persona, the female plaintiff employed an active voice and commonly described a series of proactive measures. There is little indication that she felt the need – or had been advised – to construct a timid profile. Kathryn's counsel did not remove the account of her pursuit of Owen. She had named her rapist and it was her responsibility to take him to court or place him in prison. Yet at all times there was a need to modulate the voice to suit the conventions of the court and accepted gender norms.

It is important not to treat these bills purely as texts, however: these women did exist and they had real grievances. Women had to negotiate a legal system not designed in their favour and within local contexts where malpractice and judicial abuses were going unchecked. The evidence, nonetheless, shows them to be informed and proficient in legal procedures. More research is required on why women elected to go to Star Chamber, although at least some abducted women saw it as a better option than common law.[84] The Welsh women who commenced suits in Henry VIII's reign had already tried and were continuing to seek redress in other courts. In so doing they were adding their voices to the complaints of injustice in the marches of Wales that were attracting the attention of the king's government. Denise Williams and Kathryn Robert submitted their cases to Star Chamber at exactly the time that Cromwell had his eye on legal abuses in Wales. Those who have analysed the parliamentary acts of union of 1536–42 often cite the male letter writers who fed Cromwell information on the judicial problems in Wales, but he may well have had an ear to these female petitioners too.

6 WOMEN AND THE HUE AND CRY IN LATE FOURTEENTH-CENTURY GREAT YARMOUTH

Janka Rodziewicz

Traditionally, activities to maintain law and order in medieval society have been considered a masculine preserve. Medieval women were thought subordinate to men due to dominant religious and medical perceptions of women and the female body, and this in turn affected the way they were treated by the law.[1] Medieval law courts were '"gendered" masculine' because they used the male language of law and were sites for the 'negotiation and reinforcement of masculinity'.[2] Thus, the law courts, although available for use by women, were run by men and fostered masculine ideals; 'law and language simply did not co-operate in the same way' for women.[3] This was largely because of women's legal status as dependents, whereby they were subservient to a male head of household, usually a father or husband.[4] Even though it was possible for a single woman to become head of a household, perhaps if she had been widowed, her position as such was more limited than that of a male counterpart.[5] A study of the socio-legal practice of the hue and cry however, reveals that there was a role for women in the realm of the law.

This study explores the hue and cry in the context of fourteenth-century Great Yarmouth. In the early part of that century, Yarmouth had been a prosperous fishing port with a thriving herring trade and considerable merchant fleet but after 1370 a series of bitter trading disputes, economic competition and the silting up of its harbour led to a severe economic decline. This period became one of increasing tension, hardship and contumacy amongst the port's inhabitants at all social levels, as traditional trades floundered. It is thus an interesting period in which to study the workings of customary mechanisms of social policing and also to explore exactly who was involved in them. Great Yarmouth was selected for this investigation into the practice of the hue and cry due to the excellent survival of secular leet court roll evidence for the borough, with an almost complete series of records surviving for the period 1366 and 1381, a timeframe which influences this study.[6] Although the leet court records survive past 1381, this analysis has ended in that year in order to avoid any distortion which might have stemmed from the specific upheavals and aftermath of the

1381 Peasants' Revolt, a movement which affected many parts of East Anglia including the towns of Lynn, Swaffham, Thetford, North Walsham, Yarmouth and the city of Norwich.

The records of 1366 to 1381 provide thirty-five cases of the hue and cry.[7] The sample is therefore rather small, but the number is no less than that which other scholars have considered. Indeed, if averaged out per year, the number of instances of the hue and cry in Great Yarmouth is on a par with those uncovered by Miriam Müller in Brandon and Badbury for that same century.[8] Equally, the Yarmouth sample is not so small as to conceal the several discernible trends and themes that can be related to the study of women and the law.

This essay will therefore explore the evidence for female involvement in the hue and cry in Great Yarmouth between 1366 and 1381, arguing that the practice offered women a positive means of becoming involved in regulating their own community, participating in the formal mechanisms of the law, and providing women with a means of protection for themselves and their families. It will argue that the nature of the hue and cry – as a mechanism dependent on the community – enabled women to be involved in the maintenance of law and order as integral members of their communities. Indeed, as will be demonstrated, women in Great Yarmouth practised the hue and cry nearly as frequently as men. This essay will first discuss the background and context of women's involvement, or lack thereof, in formal methods of community policing in Yarmouth, before moving on to explore the evidence contained within the thirty-five cases of hue and cry for the port town during the period in question.

The hue and cry was a mechanism for officially summoning assistance and witnesses from a community when a criminal incident, such as a robbery or assault, took place.[9] F. Pollock and F. W. Maitland have argued that the unusual name given to this procedure derived from the use of the phrase 'Out! Out!' shouted by the victim of the crime to raise the hue, which was possibly an abbreviation of *hutesium* (meaning hue).[10] Research into the medieval hue and cry is sparse. Dedicated research is restricted to articles by Miriam Müller and Patricia M. Hogan. Hogan, however, is more interested in the hue and cry for what it can tell us about inter-community feuding rather than policing.[11] This lack of interest in the hue as a policing mechanism may be due to the limited amount of surviving evidence for the practice that can normally be only found documented in the records of the medieval leet courts. The survival of the leet court records can be patchy, especially in urban areas, and Great Yarmouth is unusual for the extent of its surviving evidence. Leet records more commonly endure in rural areas, indeed the work of Müller and Hogan was based on such communities. Equally, where leet records survive, instances of raising the hue and cry are rare; even in the Yarmouth evidence there were only thirty-five cases recorded over a period of fifteen years.

There is, however, much more research about other methods of community-based law and order that can inform this study, such as that on the practice of tithing. The tithing was one of the oldest and most basic forms of community self-policing and the requirement that men belong to a tithing can be found in Anglo-Saxon Law codes.[12] In southern England, territorial tithings – where all the men in the geographical district were expected to participate – were the most common form of tithing known, elsewhere, however, personal tithings – groups of ten to twelve men – abounded.[13] The tithing

> provided a regular jury of chief capital pledges to present offences each year, and sometimes fulfil other corporate functions. All men were bound on oath to keep the peace ... this at least implied the imposition of formal responsibility for their misdeeds on all men from adolescence onwards.[14]

It was likely that Great Yarmouth operated a territorial tithing system similar to its nearest large city: Norwich. As Anthony Saul has argued, the port town often emulated the political organization of the nearby regional capital, including for example the adoption of four bailiffs.[15]

The most extensive recent work on the tithing system has been led by Phillipp Schofield and D. A. Crowley on medieval Essex.[16] W. A. Morris's work on the frankpledge system, although written in 1910, is also an important work but one that is now more often considered a general overview rather than a detailed case study.[17] While the work of Crowley and Schofield has been more focused, they are studies of manorial environments. Urban historians have not undertaken studies of the tithing system, although some have used the evidence of tithings for other purposes. Elizabeth Rutledge has, for example, used the Norwich tithing lists to explore immigration into the city, as too did Penny Dunn for population size.[18] L. R. Poos also used tithing lists and tithing-penny lists in the sphere of rural studies to analyse population sizes and mobility.[19] Capital pledges have also received a substantial amount of attention in the rural sphere, including extensive research completed by Sherri Olson and the DeWindts.[20] Work on juries, which in the Great Yarmouth Leet Court were formed by the capital pledges, has been widespread, but again such work has often been focused on manorial and small-town juries, or central court juries, rather than large urban centres such as Great Yarmouth. Maureen Mulholland has, for example, written on trials in manorial courts, Anne Reiber DeWindt on the leet jury of a small town, and Marjorie McIntosh on juries in market centres as well as villages.[21] Other scholars, such as J. G. Bellamy, have worked on the jury in felony trials.[22]

Community policing was concerned as much with setting and maintaining standards as it was with formal mechanisms of the law, however. Much research has been conducted into the role of social pressure in ensuring individual's conformity to a set of moral and behavioural rules that informed the concepts of neighbourliness and community. The anthropologist Simon Roberts has argued that, no matter the geographical area or type of society, people are, or have been, concerned about public opinion and that fear, perhaps of ridicule or criticism, causes them to adhere generally to accepted patterns of behaviour.[23] Pressure from communities and families to live up to social norms and moral codes must have played a considerable part in maintaining order, but have left little trace in the historic record. We do know, however, that in medieval society, a person's good reputation was highly valued and considered a cornerstone of their honour and credit in a community. The loss of a man or woman's honour could irrevocably damage their own reputation and even that of their family, regardless of their social status.[24] This could lead to any number of difficulties, including ostracism from friends and neighbours, or the loss of professional credit.[25] The danger of losing one's reputation was, therefore, a very real influence on individual's conformity. These ideas fed into established legal practices of 'social policing', such as the hue and cry.

The label 'social policing' is used in situations when legal and community mechanisms overlapped and were available to a wide range of inhabitants. Indeed it was this emphasis on social inclusivity that enabled such practices to be most effective. Methods of social policing practised in Great Yarmouth and captured in the leet's records, included the tithing and capital pledge systems. Both, however, were only available to men. The lack of female involvement in the tithing was a result of the convention that membership be restricted to male heads of households.[26] A husband or father thus represented his wife or daughter's interests because he was responsible for them legally, as Bracton declared in his legal treatise *De Legibus Et Consuetudinibus Angliae*: 'Women differ from men in many respects, for their position is inferior to that of men.'[27] A capital pledge was the head of the all-male tithing, thus no woman could hold this influential and formal position for enforcing order. Women could also not become jurors, bailiffs or justices and by the fourteenth century rarely appeared as attorneys.

Women could be involved in court procedure as pledges of prosecution at this time, perhaps when pursuing a plea, although the practice was fairly rare. Olson found a few examples of female pledges in Upwood and Ellington, for example, and Postles, in his wider survey of personal pledging, found five female pledges in Harcourt between 1277–98 and 1320–48. Nevertheless, they were all mothers or kin of the pledgee.[28] Judith M. Bennett did, however, find that wives could act as pledges for their dependents in their role as a substitute head of household.[29] In Yarmouth there were no female pledges during this time period, a convention that was in keeping with the village courts. Indeed it was a specific requirement in Yarmouth that women plaintiffs use only male pledges and it was for this reason that we find, for example, that Joanna Silkwoman's pledges were John and William of Eccles in 1372, or Joanna Cook's pledges of prosecution the following year were Henry and Adam Cook.[30] The convention was likely the result of the court upholding women's legal position as dependents.[31] In this fashion the 'male pledge for female pledgee mirrored a traditional belief that proper gender relations – men controlling women's behaviour – upheld the social order'.[32] Thus, although women could raise and negotiate disputes at court, they did not often play an active role in the formal practices of law enforcement. The hue and cry, then, was the only formal practice of social policing where women were regular participants.

This is because the hue and cry was different. It was an officially recognized method for summoning assistance and witnesses during a serious crime, like robbery or assault, crimes to which any person of any status could fall victim. Medieval legislation would seem to imply that the hue should only have been raised in response to felonies.[33] It was, however, commonly raised in the localities in response to misdemeanours, probably because raising the hue and cry was acceptable if people were in fear of serious harm, even if such harm never actually materialized.[34] Anyone who heard the shout was legally obliged to come to the aid of the individual who had raised the same and there were fines (*hengwite*) issued to those who did not respond, though in reality it was difficult to prove whether an individual had actually heard the summons or not. Anglo-Saxon and Latin dictionaries differ in their definition of *hengwite*, as do translations of the Domesday Book where the offence of ignoring the hue appeared in the Laws of Chester, but the *Leis Willemi* clearly aligns *hengwite* with failure to raise the hue.[35] There is no evidence that *hengwite* fines were issued in Great Yarmouth. This may be because the residents never failed to respond to any raisings of the hue and, given that recordings of the hue and cry at all were rare this is feasible, but it may also simply be that no evidence of such fines survives. Certainly, despite the findings of D. A. Crowley that tithings declined over the course of the fourteenth century, the town appears to have taken its responsibility for policing very seriously, as demonstrated by its vigorous enforcement of enrolment in the same tithings.[36] Therefore the lack of evidence for fines may also result from the problem of proving whether an inhabitant had deliberately refused to respond to the raising of the hue, or simply did not hear the summons.

The limited number of cases overall can be explained by the fact that the hue was a potentially disruptive method of social policing. Calling neighbours out of their beds at night, or pulling them away from their work during the day was not something to be taken lightly. That the hue severely disrupted everyday life was recognized in instances when it had been both correctly, and incorrectly, employed. When a criminal had been apprehended after the hue had been correctly raised, the individual in question was punished for both his (or her) offence and also for causing the raising of the hue.[37] Equally, it was recognized that to raise the hue falsely, or too often for relatively minor offences, would lessen its urgency and impact in serious situations. This meant that its usage was tightly controlled to discourage people from using it too freely.

The hue was nevertheless an important method of enabling communities to help themselves at a time without a standing police force and a way of formalizing and integrating a shout for help into the legal system. It was thus essential in bringing assistance to those in immediate danger, but afterwards, to ensure that there would be witnesses who could later testify to the veracity of events at court.[38] It was also used during post-crime legal proceedings as a method of reinforcing a victim's word. There were, for example, instances where a person claimed to be an innocent party during a violent attack but because they had not raised the hue their word was held in doubt. This was the case in Northamptonshire in 1329 when one John Brayn, who had been witness to the homicide of Richard le Porter of Aynho for example, was imprisoned 'because he was present and did not raise the hue or arrest the perpetrators of the deed'.[39]

Great efforts were made by the community of Great Yarmouth to ensure the integrity of the system and although misuse could not always be avoided, the perpetrators were punished if they were found to have raised the hue without good cause. This was especially the case when individuals had been found guilty of manipulating the system for their own ends. On five occasions in Yarmouth, for instance, the perpetrator of a crime raised the hue and cry against the victim; the intention would seem to have been to reverse the blame and cause the victim to stand liable for the crime. Henry Glover of South Leet, for example, unjustly raised the hue and cry against his victim, William his servant, whom he had wounded in the arm with a knife.[40] William Cobbler also unjustly raised the hue and cry against Kati Tapster, whom he had attacked with a rock.[41] We know of these cases where the raiser of the hue and cry had actually provoked the fight because the court deemed the use of the hue unjust; the raiser had clearly motivated the violence in each instance.[42]

Wives were also, at times, guilty of unjustly raising the hue and cry against the victim of a person attacked by their husband. In 1378, for example, when Rolland Rhys of North Middle Leet drew blood from the face of John, son of William Cooper, with a knife, it was Rolland's wife who had then raised the hue and cry against John. The court judged that the hue had been raised unjustly, realizing that John had been blamed deliberately to avoid Rhys getting into trouble for provoking a fight. Rolland's wife's accusation probably stemmed from a desire to protect her husband, but she erred in that John was the wrong man to accuse. As the son of one of the capital pledges, John was a man of some standing and this likely increased the chances that his word was granted more credit than hers.[43] In a similar manner, the wife of John North of North Middle Leet also raised the hue and cry against the victim of an attack by her own husband.[44] Had the accusation succeeded, she could have protected her husband from prosecution and her family's reputation from dishonour but, unfortunately for them, the raising was deemed unjust. Women also used the same tactic to protect themselves from dishonour. In 1381, for example, Alice Sweyn was fined for unjustly raising the hue and cry against William Tailor, whom she had wounded with a stick.[45]

Overall, women were very active in using the hue and cry, quite obviously understanding how best to use it to their advantage or when it was necessary for their self-protection. Of all the instances where the hue and cry was raised in Great Yarmouth between 1366 and 1381, women raised the hue and cry only marginally less often than men at a ratio of fifteen to eighteen cases.[46] It is perhaps not surprising that the number of men was slightly higher; as Barbara Hanawalt has argued, there was a tendency for men to be more involved in situations that resulted in violence, such as tavern brawls.[47] Nevertheless, the similarity of the figures is quite remarkable in a society where this was the case and where men dominated the majority of local regulatory mechanisms, such as the tithings.

There was, however, a subtle difference in the types of cases that men and women tended to be most associated with. The Yarmouth evidence concurs with the conclusions of A. J. Finch and Barbara Hanawalt whose research on medieval homicides and violent assaults demonstrated that men were more likely to be involved in violent incidents involving knives or staffs, both items more regularly used by men than by women.[48] Women did of course use knives, but were generally less likely to be carrying weapons that might lead to an escalation of violence and the drawing of blood or worse. The items known to have been used by Yarmouth women in misdemeanour attacks indicate that women tended to use objects of opportunity, such as sticks, fists and stones, more often than men. Of the fourteen incidents involving women where a method of attack was noted, four used knives, four sticks, three stones and three used their fists. In the four cases where women were recorded as having used a knife during an attack, two cases both concerned an attack on Alice Goldsmith, her two female assailants having been prosecuted separately. In this case Goldsmith had raised the hue against Ivette and Katherine, two Dutchwomen, who had beaten Alice with both a knife and a stick. Both attackers were fined 24*d.* for their attack *and* for causing the hue to be raised.[49] It seems, however, that the assault was not serious enough to have drawn blood, a common questioning stratagem of the jury in such cases to determine the seriousness of the attack.[50] This seems fairly typical of the level of seriousness of cases in which women were involved though the ever-present threat of violence should not be downplayed. Even fistfights could have serious consequences.

Sandy Bardsley has argued that use of hue and cry was diminishing in the late fourteenth century, a trend that effectively worked to curtail women's role in local law enforcement. Connected to this was an increased distrust of women's voices and a greater linkage between the false raising of the hue and scolding.[51]

In some respects the evidence from Great Yarmouth supports this argument, although the lack of records from before 1366 makes it impossible to look for continuity or change across the whole century. The evidence of the post-1366 period demonstrates that of the fifteen cases of women raising the hue, ten cases were judged unjust claims, two-thirds of the female cases. Six of these unjust claims were raised against men, such as when Alice Stede had unjustly raised the hue against John de Lincoln, and four were raised against women.[52] On the other hand, there were still five other cases where women were judged to have justly raised the hue, three of which were raised against men. This may indicate, in line with Bardsley's argument, that there was suspicion of female speech, especially when it was pitted against men's word.

Nevertheless, it should also be noted here that the court also judged men to have unjustly raised the hue on many occasions. Indeed, of the eighteen male cases, fourteen men were judged to have raised the hue and cry unjustly: five allegations were against men and three against women (while in six no gender was given). This challenges Sandy Bardsley's assertion that women's voices were increasingly distrusted in comparison with male voices.[53] William Cobbler, for example, had raised the hue and cry unjustly on Catherine Tapster as William's wife had drawn blood from Catherine by attacking her with a stone.[54] This indicates that male usage of the hue against women was not automatically justifiable and that women's testimonies were not always considered unreliable. Indeed, the Yarmouth evidence actually suggests that women's word in such cases may have been considered more creditable: whereas men misused the hue on fourteen of eighteen occasions, women did so in only ten of fifteen instances, thus the ratio of unjust cases according to the number of cases per gender overall was no more biased toward women than to men.

Another revealing aspect of the hue cases was that women were often found to have raised the cry on behalf of others, especially their husbands. In one case from Yarmouth, for example, Troye, the wife of Rolland Reyf, had justly raised the hue on behalf of her husband when William Josse drew blood from him with a saw (unfortunately the record provides no further detail about the nature of the assault).[55] Miriam Müller has suggested that it may have been the duty of men to raise the hue rather than the woman when both were present.[56] So why did Rolland not raise the hue himself? The attack does not appear to have been so violent as to prevent him from doing so, as demonstrated by the fact we find it among the Yarmouth misdemeanours and not reserved for the felony courts. The details of the attack that provoked the hue, stating that blood was drawn and that it was done against the peace, are the same terms used in other cases where the victim was the one who raised the hue, or cases where it was deemed unnecessary to raise the hue. This indicates that the attack in this case was no more violent than in these other instances.[57] So the reason that Rolland did not raise the hue himself may have been an issue of masculinity; perhaps he did not want to appear unable to protect himself.[58] In Badbury, for example, Müller found that men were 'rather unlikely' to raise the hue in cases of violence with another man, and it may have been more acceptable for women than men to raise the hue when they were the victims of violence.[59] In the case of Rolland and Troye, then, Troye may have been aiding her husband without him directly losing his own claim to masculinity by shouting for help himself. In so doing there was a contradiction: Troye played the role of a weak woman in calling for aid but she also directly usurped her husband's role as a protector. This case was not an anomaly. Bardsley's research found many similar examples, leading her to argue that women were quite justified in raising the hue on behalf of others, as well as for themselves.[60] This is significant given that women were not allowed any formal law enforcement role, but they were nonetheless trusted to make a judgement call on raising the hue, an act that might lead to a fine and social condemnation if it were judged inappropriate or unjust.

Unfortunately, with much of the context relating to the hue and cry cases in Yarmouth absent from the leet records, it is hard to do more than speculate as to the pressures placed on husbands or their wives by their families, neighbours or themselves in cases like these.[61] Nevertheless it is interesting that, by raising the hue for their husband, women were not only involving themselves in a method of maintaining order, an area traditionally reserved for men, but were knowingly appropriating a role of authority in raising the hue for a man who could have easily raised the hue himself. More than this, these women were assuming the male role of protection, in shielding their husbands from further physical harm. Why this was acceptable seems to be tied up with a much larger question of why women in the Middle Ages were permitted to raise the hue and cry at all, given the male dominance over public authority and official methods of maintaining order, as already mentioned.

Perhaps the most immediately likely reason for female involvement in the hue was the need to protect their personal safety. As has been noted, it was only acceptable for men and women to raise the hue when in immediate danger or fear of immediate danger. Although medieval societies may have seen women as subordinate to men, they never advocated that they should not be protected from violence to any lesser degree than men. As E. Adamson Hoebel argued, in all societies the right to life has been considered a fundamental right.[62] Indeed, medieval literature on women emphasized their weakness and scorned violence against them or enacted by them.[63] If they could not be expected to defend themselves, therefore, then they were even more in need of an effective method by which they could summon assistance. Indeed the cry for help, such as the hue was, bent as much to the idea of the weaker woman in need of protection as it did to the masculine concept of responsibility and protection. For both genders, then, the use of the hue and cry both inverted and reinforced proscribed gender roles.

That women were accorded the right to wield the responsibility of the hue and cry suggests that, ultimately, maintaining a peaceful society was placed above rigidly enforcing proscribed gender roles. The maintenance of law and order has been and always will be essential to even the most rudimentary of societies as the most basic 'ordering of the fundamentals of living together',[64] thus it should perhaps come as no surprise that any potential social discomfort associated with women exercising public authority was set aside at these times in the interest of the safety of the community. Nevertheless, the hue and cry offered a unique power to women. In public life women generally held authority through a husband, a husband's status or through inherited wealth, but with the hue we see women exerting an authority of their own for no other reason than that they were present at the scene of a crime.[65] If, as seems apparent, maintaining the peace was more important to medieval communities than maintaining gender roles, then this raises further questions about women's role in their community and their personal agency more generally.

The hue and cry was a popular mechanism for maintaining law and order. By popular, it is meant that the mechanism involved the participation of the whole community. The hue and cry bridged the boundaries between commonly held methods of community regulation and the official channels that included the law and the criminal courts. Like many forms of community policing, the prosecution of the law using the hue depended on the community's responsiveness and participation both during and following the crime in question. Because crime affected everyone, female involvement in this aspect of the law was natural and acceptable. Women were not only the victims of crime but witnesses to crime. Like the shaming rituals so common in the punishment of criminals in medieval society (such as incarcerating an individual in a pillory or shaving a prostitute and processing her out of the town walls), an audience was required to successfully prosecute crimes in court and women's words were often needed to bring cases to a conclusion.[66] Certainly, women were involved in other forms of the law when it involved the community, arbitration for example. As with shaming or the hue, arbitration needed an audience to legitimate and memorialize the system of process and agreement.[67] The audience for the arbitration included women as witnesses and their memory of events was often called on to resolve certain situations.[68] In such situations, their voices were accorded credit by the law. Just as there was a place for women as witnesses, deponents and compurgators under the law, so too were women afforded a role in policing their communities.

Although these are preliminary findings, the records of the hue and cry in later fourteenth-century Great Yarmouth suggest that further investigation of women's appropriation of customary methods of social policing may add nuance to our understanding of women's role and place in medieval society. This conclusion thus intimates that women's involvement in regulating their immediate community may reveal a more proactive and authoritative role in the law for medieval women than we currently recognize. The ability to exercise this simple, yet effective legal right was an expression of women's agency both in their community and society at large. It afforded a woman the ability to protect herself, her husband or her family, or the right of redress, with the full backing of the law. That such a right, if only infrequently invoked, existed, should be considered a fundamental component of female agency.

7 GENDER AND THE CONTROL OF SACRED SPACE IN EARLY MODERN ENGLAND[1]

Amanda Flather

Recent scholarship on iconoclasm and iconophobia has thoroughly documented acts of despoliation of religious material objects and the disruption of rituals perpetrated by religious radicals in English parish churches in the decades after the Reformation.[2] It is well established that the Elizabethan settlement was not acceptable to zealous Protestants in sixteenth- and seventeenth-century England, and that they consistently called for further reformation, objecting to what they regarded as 'popish' elements that contaminated the services, ceremonies and sacraments of the Book of Common Prayer. Disputes often turned on seemingly small details such as vestments, gestures and the materials or architectural settings of services, but these were far from trivial matters to the people of the time. Each small-scale struggle signified conflicting but deeply held convictions about religious belief and practice.[3] Disagreements intensified and erupted more frequently into violent confrontation during the decades leading up to the Civil War. Abroad, alliances with popish powers and a marriage to a Catholic queen were believed by many to threaten the fate of the immortal soul of the elect Protestant English nation. At home, the resolve of Charles I and his archbishop William Laud to reassert the independence of the Church and the clergy over the laity appeared to corrupt and disrupt the proper ordering of Church and state. Fears were fuelled by a renewed emphasis on ceremony and sacrament and the demand for significant alterations and improvements to church furnishings, most controversially, moving the communion table altarwise and railing it in. These changes appeared to challenge the customary order of worship to a dangerous degree and in some parishes, especially those with a Puritan influence, they became the cause and the context of violent clashes between godly parishioners and established authority.

Women's involvement in this form of popular religious violence has been widely acknowledged in the literature. Yet to date little effort has been made to interpret these actions in gendered terms. Historians who have attempted to explain female participation in this type of religious activism have focused upon three largely complementary explanations. Iconoclastic attacks by women, it is argued, were inspired by the same religious commitment as men, but were also encouraged by the practical advantages of possible legal immunity, the opportunity offered to a repressed minority to resist established patriarchal authority and, in some cases, an emotional dependence on charismatic clergy.[4]

These interpretations seem somewhat limited in the light of recent work by John Walter, who has argued convincingly that to properly understand the purpose of popular religious violence, we should look beyond the constructions of contemporary commentators (and modern historians) to the evidence of motivation provided by the protestors themselves. The actions of iconoclasts were highly theatrical public performances that contained a strong element of ritual and symbol. There were set phrases, actions and gestures which the audience recognized and knew how to interpret. Violence was targeted and deliberately choreographed to communicate religious principle and to distinguish acts of destruction from mere vandalism or political rebellion.[5]

Here it seems that iconoclasm offers an opening for the historian of gender: a context in which we can hear women speak. One of the guiding principles of feminist history is always to ask: how did women see this? When we pose the question of written sources (in our case legal records) nearly always written by men, we often draw a blank. But if we move away from words to actions, we restore women's capacities to make their own meanings. A gendered analysis of religious violence in early modern England has still to be written. We need to find out what kinds of women were involved in iconoclastic attacks, what actions they took and why. What meanings did religious violence hold for women, and were those meanings different for men? This essay aims to address some of these issues through a detailed evaluation of the forms of female iconoclasm in early modern England. It seeks to show that struggles over the symbolic meaning of the fabric of worship were gendered in more complex ways than existing interpretations suggest. Focusing upon female acts of demonstrative violence committed in Essex parishes in Tudor and Stuart England, it aims to show that women's involvement in struggles over the determination of the meaning and use of sacred space in early modern English churches arose out of their traditional religious responsibility as much as their subordination and dependency.

The Reformation had a complicated impact upon gendered patterns of organization, control and use of space within the local parish church. Women were denied access to positions of formal authority within the Church of England. Widowed members of the middling and better sort were very occasionally elected as churchwardens, although being male was a necessary precondition for election in most counties.[6] Several wealthy widows were also patrons of their parish churches and controlled the appointment of the local minister as well as the maintenance and repair of the chancel.[7] But spiritual equality between the sexes was not held to mean that women could hold official positions of power.[8] They were not permitted to preach, teach or to administer the sacraments; men provided the official leadership and control of the Church.[9]

Nonetheless, women dominated several aspects of religious practice in this period. It seems likely that they formed the numerical majority in many early modern congregations and that this large female constituency wielded considerable *informal* influence over parish affairs.[10] Women's prominence in pew disputes, for example, reveals that sacred space was not static or simply structured by the formal and legal initiatives of male parochial parish elites. Many churches in early modern England maintained the custom of seating the congregation in rank order, according to sex, age and status. Women were keenly conscious of the fine social distinctions within their own symbolic social hierarchy, and were prepared, on occasion, to challenge their own place, or that of others, within the system and to impose their own definitions of what constituted 'order' within the female sphere.[11]

Gender also influenced aspects of the organization and patterns of attendance at the major life cycle rituals of baptism, churching, marriage and burial. Women were often the most prominent participants at baptisms, whether as mothers, gossips or as midwives, and churching was a specifically female ceremony performed after a woman had given birth. The deathbed too was, to an extent, a gendered domain. Poor women were paid to nurse the dying and the dressing of a dead body was a female responsibility.[12] Funeral rituals also had a gendered social character. A single woman's coffin would be carried to church by young spinsters and women often dominated the funerals of small children and widows.[13]

Ordinary women who filled the churches week by week also had distinctive responsibilities for the buildings and their contents. Paradoxically, while some ministers in early modern England viewed menstruating women as corrupting of sacred space, almost all clergymen delegated the day-to-day tasks of cleaning the church and maintaining its liturgical equipment to female parishioners.[14] In Thaxted in 1616, for example, the churchwarden's account for 1 May records: 'Item to divers weomen for washeing dresseing up the churche and fetching flaggs and rushes ijs viiid'.[15] Similarly, the Heybridge churchwarden's accounts for 1639 record payment to a Mrs Frith 'for washing ye surplis and ye tablecloth'.[16]

Careful analysis of the forms and occasions of female religious violence shows that women's actions were given structure and meaning by these traditional religious roles and responsibilities. Admittedly almost any religious event could trigger a disturbance and godly men and women often acted together in episodes of ritualistic and symbolic violence, but patterns of protest also seem to have been shaped by gender. Interestingly, only men were recorded in violent attacks on elaborately decorated fonts installed in several parishes in Essex during the 1620s and 1630s.[17] Men also dominated iconoclastic violence against the prayer book, although in Halstead in 1641 a group of men and women struck the prayer book from the curate's hand during divine service, and kicked it about the church, saying that it was a 'popish book'.[18]

But there were a cluster of contexts in which women repeatedly took the initiative and acted, sometimes together and at other times alone, to challenge male and ecclesiastical power. Because childbirth and its ritual aftermath was such a powerfully gendered domain, women were very prominent in local clashes over the meaning and conduct of this body of rituals. Churching provided a frequent occasion of connection but also collision between godly women and local ministers.[19] Ceremonialists believed that the spiritual significance of the ceremony was bound up with the physical location of the service and the garments to be worn, but Puritans regarded these customary arrangements as mere superstition. Men did not participate in the service and so could only oppose authority over the conduct of the ceremony by expressing support for their wives' non-conformity.[20] It was women who engaged in direct action. Some radicals refused to be churched but more often female protest took the form of dissent from established practice by deliberately coming to be churched at the wrong time, in the wrong clothes and positioning themselves in the wrong place. For example, Joanna, wife of Nathanial Whitup of Corringham was presented to the archdeacon in April 1614 for coming to be churched 'in her hatt', for sitting in 'her seate where she cold not be descried' and for saying that 'none but whores did weare vayles and that a harlot or a whore was the inventor of it, or that first wore a vayle'.[21] In similar vein, another godly woman, Ellen, wife of John Brettle, a religious radical, disturbed her more moderate female neighbours and the churchwarden of St Giles Colchester, Robert Osborn, during divine service in 1615, by 'thrusting' herself into 'the stole where women used to be churched'.[22]

Admittedly, for most of this period, such episodes were regarded as minor matters by established authority which tended to turn a blind eye to occasional acts of non-conformity.[23] But policies altered during the 1630s under the direction of Archbishop Laud, when attempts were made to enforce the wearing of veils and the churching of women at the altar. This smacked of superstition and popery even to more moderate parishioners and it contributed to the escalation of opposition to Laudian practice.[24] Women regularly refused to go to the rail to be churched. The wife of Jacob Malden of Woodham Mortimer was presented to court in 1638, for example, for 'not giving thanks in the usuall place for the women after their childbirth but did sitt in the bodie of the church'.[25] In a similar vein, Edward Firmin's wife was punished for 'refusing to come neere the communion table according to the Rubricke in the booke of common prayer to give thanks for her safe deliverance in childbirthe'.[26] Several women were also presented for refusing to wear a veil during the ceremony. Elizabeth Cram was cited 'for being churched without a vaile' in 1638, and in 1637 Mary Judd of Haverstock was brought before the archdeacon's court, for coming to be churched 'without a vaile or kerchief to the ill example of others'.[27]

Performance of the sacrament of baptism also generated conflict between godly women and conformist ministers. Religious radicals were especially exercised by the use of the signing of the cross in the service, which they regarded as a superstitious and contaminated remnant of popery, described by one Radwinter man as 'the mark of the beast'.[28] Men as well as women were involved in ugly confrontations over this issue,[29] but women's prominent presence at baptisms meant that they were the ones, more often than not, who initiated disruption and attempted to prevent the baptism or to thwart the signing of the cross.[30] In Chelmsford in November 1634, Charity, wife of Alexander Knight, was presented to court because 'she did hinder the clerke from signing the childe of one Millowes with the signe of the crosse in baptisme by covering the face there before he could signe it'.[31] Two women also intervened to disrupt a baptism in Radwinter in 1641, and the incident escalated into an assault on the curate. The local rector recorded that on 12 June:

> the wife of Richard Smith at the christening of Giles Albon's child detained the child when by the rubric it should be delivered into the arms of the parson, though he demanded it of her often. She obstinately refusing so to do, the curate repaired to the reading-pew, expecting their recantation or submission to go out of the church. The service and congregation being disturbed too long, the father of the child moved the said Smith's wife to deliver the said child to the curate. Butt being it seems of too intemperate a spirit, immediately after the words 'I baptise thee' etc she made fresh disturbance, labouring to hinder the signing of the child with the Cross; she covered the child's face with the linen and kept it down with her hand. Another woman, reported to be Richard Durden's wife, laid hold on one of the curate's hands, which was kept behind him by the father of the child.[32]

Another memorable scene of irreverence and female disobedience occurred at a baptismal service earlier in 1626. The Lady Lawrence was recommended to the court of High Commission for a 'gross act of indecency' after she presented a child's hinder parts instead of its forehead to the font. Her action was almost certainly a deliberate scatological gesture of inversion commonly deployed by iconoclasts to strip away superstition and to ridicule a sign they regarded as a 'Romanish remnant'.[33]

In a similar way, the gendered quality of burial practices put godly women at the forefront of clashes over the rites and rituals which marked the passage of an individual from this world to the next. Throughout the period, rituals ancillary to interment, as well as the burial service itself, attracted criticism from radicals who rejected the concept of consecrated ground altogether and wanted burial entirely free of established ritual. Until the 1630s confrontation was largely avoided by ecclesiastical authority which acted with broad discretion and permitted a wide variety of practices. Conflict became more common once the Laudian Church attempted to enforce conformity to the funeral service prescribed in the Book of Common Prayer and required the minister to meet the corpse at the gate or stile of the churchyard in his surplice and to conduct the burial in 'decent manner' with prayers and lessons 'for that purpose ordained'.[34] The godly regarded these rituals as yet another sign of the insidious reintroduction of Catholicism and believed that they needed to be repudiated, by force if necessary. Married or widowed women were invariably prominent participants in these confrontations, in particular in clashes over the conduct of the burial services of other women. In 1639, for example, the wife of one Langley, of Chichele St Osyth, was presented to the ecclesiastical court for 'disturbing divine service being at the buriall of the dead, the minister desiring the people to kneel down at their prayers, she cryed out what make us praye to the dead, and so continued so brawlinge along time together'.[35] In another harrowing episode in London in 1636, the wife of Francis Jessop demanded to bury her daughter

> without the observance of the order of church burial, declaring herself that they could bury without a minister; and her friends which accompanied the corpse to the grave, so soon as the minister began the form of church burial, left the corpse and went away.[36]

Women's voices were also prominent in protest over the surplice. Quarrels about clerical costume were central to religious struggles between Anglicans and Puritans over the establishment of Protestantism in England throughout the early modern period. Conforming clergy dismissed vestments as little more than 'comical dress' or 'ridiculous trifles', but the godly regarded them as dangerous vestiges of popery, 'bloody beasts gear', 'rags of Rome' and 'the outward apparel of the Pope's Church'.[37] Confessional conflict between conservatives and radicals during the Elizabethan period focused on the question of the surplice and the square cap and the issue reignited with the rise of Arminianism and its commitment to ceremonialism during the reign of Charles I. Godly parishioners were outraged by the order that the clergy should wear the surplice when ministering.[38] The Root and Branch Petition of 1640 condemned

> the great conformity and likeness both continued and increased of our church to the Church of Rome, in vestures, postures, ceremonies, and administrations, namely ... the four cornered cap, the cope and surplice, the tippet, the hood, and the canonical coat.[39]

Women's experience in caring for the surplice seems to have fed into a certainty that they had a right to intervene directly in debates about its liturgical significance based on their own religious knowledge and conscience. A continuous thread of female activism can be traced from the height of the vestments controversy in

1566, when women in London formed a vocal and highly visible part of the movement of opposition, through to known instances of popular iconoclastic attacks
on the surplice in the early 1640s that were led by female parishioners.[40]

Women were open and unequivocal in expressing their beliefs about the 'polluting' and 'popish' properties of clerical costume and were conscious of their
ability to rally a crowd. In Elizabethan London in 1566, John Stow recalled that
a tinker's wife, who was punished for her irreverence towards the surplice, rev-
elled in 'her lewd behaviour', and so did the crowd that supported her, praising
God 'for crying out against *superstition* as they termed it'.[41] A few days later when
two nonconforming ministers, Gough and Philpot, were sent into exile out of
the capital, a crowd of two or three hundred women greeted them on London
Bridge with provisions, and exhorted the men to 'stand fast' in their doctrine.[42]
An account of an assault on the surplice at Christ Church in London in 1641
records that an old woman rejoiced in her part in the destruction of what she
called the 'babylonish garment'.[43]

But female protests were often the occasion for more than scandalous words.
Women were also capable of using violence or the threat of violence to express
their opposition. In Elizabethan London, a Scottish preacher who provoked
a riot with a sermon against the surplice, but gave in to political pressure and
appeared wearing one in early June 1566, suffered severely at the hands of the
women of the parish, who stoned him, dragged him from his pulpit, ripped his
surplice and scratched his face in what London's conforming Bishop Grindal
described as 'a womanish brabble'.[44] Richard Drake, Arminian rector of Radwinter, suffered several violent assaults by female parishioners against the surplice
in 1641 and was subjected to gestures of humiliation that suggested and/or
threatened emasculation as well as resistance to gendered ecclesiastical power.
According to Drake's autobiography, on 10 March 1641, he was attacked while
wearing the surplice by 'the wives of John Mountford and Thomas Cornel [who]
conveying themselves closely into the chancel cut the surplice about a foot deep
before and behind'. Later in the month a burial provided the occasion for a more
serious and violent attack by women armed with knives. Drake recorded that:

> Widow Seaman, the wives of Richard Smith, Henry Smith, Samuel and Henry
> Reef[?] and Josias Ward, coming impudently upon the curate as he was passing from
> the grave laid violent hands upon him, drew their knives and near his throat cut and
> rent off his surplice and hood in a most barbarous manner before the congregation;
> and so carried away their spoil, triumphing in their victory.[45]

Women also used dramatic demonstrations that expressed their special relationship to the surplice to add to the symbolic power of their protests. In some
instances they intentionally evoked and inverted their role as carers for vestments and ripped, cut or tore the surplice apart in ritual displays of disgrace.[46]

For example, in the early 1640s in Great Waltham in Essex, four women 'tore in pieces the surplice and hood', while in Halstead in 1641 women and men ripped up the surplice after their attack on the prayer book.[47] Other episodes drew on women's role as cleaners of vestments in acts of 'decontamination' which appealed to biblical interpretations of fire as a sacred means of purification. Female iconoclasts in Halstead burnt the surplice after they had ripped it apart.[48] In a similar vein, when the churchwardens of Dedham demanded the surplice of their godly minister in 1589, his wife responded resolutely that 'yf it was not burnt they could have it againe'.[49]

Women's repertoire of actions also included a form of iconoclastic violence that had been established by Lollards in the fifteenth century and which sought to obliterate any association between the surplice and sanctity by mockery, making mundane use of supposedly consecrated cloth.[50] We find, for example, that the wife of one Genery of Goldhangar was prosecuted in 1587 for her provocative behaviour in literally 'dressing down' the surplice. According to the presentment she 'put on a smock over her clothes, and went to the house of Widow Willings of Goldhangar, who kept an alehouse, amongst divers assembled, terming it to be a surplice'.[51] Gender added power to her parody which drew on a deeper festive tradition of sexual inversion and the license accorded to women to censure authority and to express the central values of the godly community.

Some women went further and desecrated the surplice by more disgusting means, deliberately deploying social meanings ascribed to differences of sex to convey contempt. Susan, wife of John Cook of Little Baddow, sought to excise any sacred connotations by comparing the surplice to her 'rags', manipulating ideas about the polluting properties of menstruation and gendered presumptions that a female presence could contaminate sacred space.[52] In 1636 she was presented to court by the churchwardens, 'for hanginge her lynnen in the churche to dry'. When the minister reproached her, she retorted that she 'might hang her raggs there as well as the surplice and bad him doe his worst'.[53]

It also seems likely that the single recorded incident of a female attack on altar rails which took place in Sandon in Essex on the day after Candlemas (2 February) was timed to perform a dramatic inversion of gendered rites of purification.[54] Candlemas was a religious festival especially associated with women.[55] It was the day set aside for them to clean the church after the Christmas festivities and it also had associations with female purification. According to Cressy, Stuart ceremonialists sometimes made reference to the 'stains of childbirth' in their Candlemas sermons, 'invoking comparisons between the purity of Mary under ancient Judaism and the condition of ordinary childbearing women in early modern England'.[56] It is interesting to speculate whether the Laudian minister of Sandon, Brian Walton, spoke to this subject in his sermon that Candlemas day since gendered symbolism seems to have shaped the structure and timing of the female attack.[57] Once the women had cleared away the Christmas greenery, they purged their church of Laudian profanity and took out the altar rails to burn them 'on the green'.[58] Subordinate and 'contaminated' female parishioners took on the role of official authority to preside as purifiers of their parish church and in the process made manifest what they believed to be the true source of 'pollution'.

Ministers as well as rituals and symbols were also sometimes the focus of female protest. Women and men sometimes challenged the power of the clergy if their preaching was believed to be unsound and, occasionally, deliberately disrupted services by arriving late for divine service or leaving before the sermon was delivered. In 1637, for example, a group of sixteen parishioners of Rayleigh, six men and ten women, were presented for 'running unreverentlie out of church in service tyme'.[59] Another strategy was to use bodily gestures of disrespect to undermine the authority of the minister. Men might keep their hats on, for example, or deliberately fall asleep during divine service.[60] Women, it seems, preferred verbal forms of harassment. Of the sixty-two cases of abuse of ministers recorded in the Act Books during the 1630s, twenty-six involved female defendants. In 1633 Elizabeth, wife of Roger Kendall of Great Wakering, for example, was punished, 'for abusing the minister for openlie raylinge and revilinge him from howse to howse givinge most base and filthie language and saying he could make a better sermon in a chimney corner'.[61] Prudence Carter of Great Holland was presented in 1632, 'for using irreverent speeches to Mr Thomas Evans the minister of the said parish and his wife saying she would not heare him for there were ten persons better than he is'.[62]

Other women simply voted with their feet and neglected their own parish to visit other churches. 'Gadding', as the practice was called, was a relatively common strategy adopted by radicals throughout the period if they believed their local minister did not preach effectively or if his teaching was perceived to be of poor quality. The godly also attended additional weekday or evening lectures to supplement the spiritual activities of the established Church.[63] But although these practices were illegal, prosecution was patchy and partial until the 1630s, when 'gadding' began to be interpreted as a political critique of established authority and presentments became more frequent. In 1634, for example, Elizabeth, wife of John Eaton of Great Stambridge, was presented to the archdeacon's court 'for absenting herselfe from sermons and resorting to another place to heare the preachers'.[64] Joan, wife of John Croxton of Larkwell, had also been prosecuted in 1632, 'for ordinary neglect of her owne parishe church and stragling to other churches on the Saboth daye'.[65] The wife of Thomas Howes of Goldhangar was accused in 1637 'for that having a preaching minister she does often absent herselfe from his sermon (and from divine service) and that she resorts to other places to heare the preacher there'. Her reply was that her minister's words were 'as water spilt against the wall'.[66] A total of forty-six presentments for 'gadding' are recorded in the Act Books between 1630 and 1640: twenty-three, that is 50 per cent, of the defendants were women, fourteen of whom were listed as wives and two as widows. Interestingly, only four women were presented with their husbands, suggesting that godly women made their own decisions about when and where they would go to church.

Sometimes women were not content with mere passive resistance and turned to violence against their minister to refute what they believed to be false doctrine. For example, in Sible Hedingham in 1645 three women were indicted for 'disturbing the peace' in one of a series of local initiatives mounted by radicals against the local minister John Jegon because of his support of alehouses, innovations and criticism of 'professors in general'.[67] Christopher Newstead, the Arminian rector of Stisted, was another victim of violent female assault. For some time a group of godly parishioners refused to pay their tithes and to let him officiate and, one Sunday after Michaelmas in 1642, several women 'threw stones' at him to prevent him entering his church.[68]

Evidence of independent action by strong-minded godly women also surfaces in attacks on ministerial reputation. It is increasingly recognized that married women played an important part in the community in defining and enforcing 'honest' behaviour among their neighbours and research has also noticed women's prominent role as brokers of gossip.[69] It seems that this sense of communal authority and responsibility could extend to commentary and judgement of ministerial behaviour. Tension between clergymen and influential matrons was a perennial feature of early modern parochial life, but it became more visible and more political during the early 1640s when godly parishioners began to assist Parliament in rooting out minsters who were 'scandalous' in morals and doctrine, or were 'malignant' in their preaching, conversation or actions. The sources used to explore this form of female political engagement are admittedly problematic. The analysis here is based predominantly on detailed examination of the testimonies given by women to the Committee for Scandalous Ministers, set up in 1644 to interrogate and, if necessary, to eject and replace scandalous or malignant clergy. The committee was permitted to actively canvas for hostile witnesses if evidence against ministers was not forthcoming and this procedure led I. M. Green to argue that these depositions were essentially fabricated accounts, generated as part of an orchestrated campaign against particular ministers by the Puritan, Parliamentarian gentlemen members of the committee and county elite.[70] Clive Holmes agreed; writing in the 1970s, he believed that even when testimony appeared to be given voluntarily, it often represented no more than petty malice or personal pique.[71]

More recently, however, the value of the evidence has been reassessed, in particular by Bill Cliftlands, who conducted a detailed analysis of the local circumstances surrounding sequestrations and concluded that while interference could not always be ruled out, most charges against ministers were generated by local disaffection that could be traced back to incidents which occurred often a decade before the turmoil of the civil war years. Events described can also be corroborated by a wide variety of other evidence, indicating that testimonies were a reasonably accurate account of actions and behaviour. Most importantly, accusations of scandal need to be set against the background of social and economic change in the countryside taking place during the period. New standards of moral discipline were beginning to be imposed by increasingly powerful parish elites composed of the middling and 'better sort' of people, much as new standards of personal morality were expected of the local minister, the 'supreme exemplar' as well as enforcer of godly behaviour.[72] A gendered reading of these testimonies provides interesting insights into those forms of conduct and practice against which women of the 'well-affected' were prepared to depose.

Details of depositions against twenty-seven north Essex clergy survive.[73] Accusations were wide-ranging, including traditional allegations of negligence or general inability, as well as charges of immoral conduct, notably swearing, drunkenness and sexual misbehaviour. To these were added charges related to the political and religious context of the period, including twenty-four charges of doctrinal unsoundness or malignancy towards Parliament. A total of 194 deponents gave evidence related to these allegations. Of these, 157 were men and 37 were women, who therefore comprised around 17 per cent of witnesses called to give evidence on these issues.

If we turn to charges related to moral offences we find that only four of the group were charged with sexual immorality, fifteen were accused of swearing and blasphemy and fourteen of drunkenness. Details about these allegations were given by seventy-five deponents. Of these, fifty-two were men and twenty-three (31 per cent) were women. Female deponents clearly had a larger role to play in the prosecution of moral offences.

Married women of the middling and better sort exhibited a major proportion of the articles against William Frost of Great Middleton, John Lake of Great Saling and Stephen Nettles of Lexden. A long history of sexual impropriety and offence to prominent female parishioners formed the central theme in all these cases. The anger and resentment at indignities inflicted on women is plain. Goodwife Foulsham of Lexden told the committee that Stephen Nettles, 'in his kissing women he putteth his tongue in their mouth as he hath offered to do to [her] more than once'. Margaret, wife of the influential Puritan gentleman Bartholomew Hall, testified on 1 May 1644 that William Frost, minister of Middleton, 'was a man dangerously suspected of incontinencie as may appear by these presumptions ... that he hath offered to put his hand under a woman's clothes in an obscene and uncivill manner'. She made a further submission to the Committee on 11 May, admitting that, 'she was the person ... under whose cotes he offered to put his hand meeting her alone in a strait entrie to her house'.[74] The women of Middleton also deposed that Frost had kept a 'whore' in his house and that he had previously appeared before the court of High Commission 'upon the crime of Bastardy'. All these accusations can be verified from other sources.[75]

Women also criticized clergymen for 'setting an ill-example' by neglect of their family or by behaving in ways which disrupted domestic order in other households in the parish. Joan Osborne deposed that John Jegon of Sible Hedingham, the minister who had been attacked by his female parishioners, had failed to read the scriptures to his family.[76] Frost of Middleton was alleged to have clashed with his wife over his drinking.[77] Daniel Falconer, royalist rector of Aldham, was accused of 'disorderly' drinking with two parishioners to the extent that the wife of one was forced to go into the alehouse 'hirself and brake the Potts' because the constable was too embarrassed to disturb the minister.[78]

More seriously, Elizabeth Smith, Joan Osborne, Elizabeth Carter and Bridget Cant, married women of the middling sort from Great Saling, took the opportunity to testify against their parson, John Lake, who they said was 'notoriously vile in attempting the chastity of his maides and sometimes by violences ... using another by such violences that she by her sickness was brought into a dangerous sicknesse and other conveniences'.[79] Lake had had to purge himself before the Middlesex Archdeaconry Court in 1637 on a presentment of incontinency with two of his accusers, Joan Osborne and Bridget Cant.[80]

Conflict between the minister and prominent women was also a key ingredient in the campaign against the minister of Great Maplestead. In 1644, sixteen women of the parish, 'some of good sort', came to the committee to declare their minister, Edward Shephard, 'altogether unfit'.[81] More detail about the case came to light the following year when Shephard prosecuted his maidservant, Elizabeth Spurgeon, for theft. The maid responded by accusing him of repeated sexual assault and local women came to court to support her story.[82] Elizabeth Neville, wife of a local yeoman and former churchwarden, told the magistrate that Elizabeth Spurgeon had come, 'many times to [her] house much discontented', but had only revealed the reason for her disquiet once she had left Shephard's service when she admitted that, 'she wolde not tarry with him though he gave her never so much mony'.[83] Elizabeth Beare, wife of another prosperous husbandman, claimed that she had seen Shephard 'tooke [Elizabeth] on the mouth with his hande and made it bleed'.[84] Elizabeth Beauwater and Elizabeth Mitchell, two other literate and respectable women who had possibly petitioned against Shephard in 1644, verified the maid's story along with James Male and John Tyndale, son of Deane and heir to the largest estate in the parish, and Spurgeon was acquitted.[85] Beyond that little is known about Shephard's ministry in Great Maplestead until a parochial inquisition of 1650 recorded that Mr William Hicks had been appointed, 'By choice of the parish' as curate in Shephard's place.[86] It is unlikely that gender conflict was the only reason behind the clergyman's departure for he had also been accused of political malignancy in 1644. But we may assume that the hostility of prominent female parishioners was important in undermining his spiritual authority and that women could exert informal influence that helped determine the success or failure of the local religious establishment.

Personal animosity, as well as principled opposition, no doubt motivated some women to testify against their minister. Yet to dismiss the allegations entirely as petty or malicious is to misunderstand their wider social meaning. The presence of a supposedly 'scandalous' clergyman was believed by the godly to pose a serious threat to local moral and social stability. Cultural shifts in the attitudes of middling men and women about what constituted orderly and 'respectable' behaviour, especially in parishes with a Puritan impetus, meant that questions of morality were central to broader issues of social, political and ecclesiastical order in seventeenth-century England. Laura Gowing has rightly emphasized that when the attitudes and values of godly ministers and local matrons were in harmony, they frequently worked together to regulate sexual order.[87] But when the minister failed to measure up to expected moral standards, conflict could occur.

What is interesting about these testimonies is that they are about older, married women setting and controlling limits to *male* ministerial power, in particular power over the female body. Throughout the period, this traditional and informal form of female influence could cause recurrent strains between ministers and older matrons.[88] For example, the right of mothers and midwives to baptize babies in the absence of a minister if the child's life was in danger, was a contentious issue within the established Church until after the Restoration.[89] Women also expressed their opposition to ministers who preached in public about childbirth or the female body. Ambrose Westrupp, minister of Great Totham, for example, found himself in trouble because he preached on 'matters concerning the secrets of women'. According to critics he used his sermons to expound on his belief that normal sexual intercourse and menstruation were sources of pollution, and it seems that his remarks contributed to his sequestration in 1643.[90] Many years before, the archdeacon of Colchester, John Pulleyne, angered and offended many women in the town for similar reasons. The wife of one John Fowle, butcher, was presented to the borough court in 1563, 'for speaking 'very disorderly of Mr Pulleyne and his preaching'. Unrepentant, she appeared before the bailiffs to explain that she had been outraged, 'because of things he spake ... touching things that are known but to women only at the birth of children'.[91] In a similar vein in 1623, Mariam, wife of Joseph Camber of Hadley, was presented to the archdeacon's court for rude behaviour towards members of the parish, including her minister. She argued that, 'Mr Sabridge did putt her child's neck out of joint when he did christen it, and that he did preach of women's matters things which were not fitting'.[92] Women's experiences and roles seem to have convinced them that they had the authority to intervene when a clergyman transgressed traditional and gendered boundaries in order to redefine the limits of ministerial intrusion into the female domain.

The women who were involved in the protests described in this essay were able to act not only because they were women, but also because they spoke with the voice of their local community. Very few of them were marginal figures; most were married and of middling status.[93] Of the four women indicted for ripping the surplice at Great Waltham, one was listed as a yeoman's wife, two others as wives of husbandmen and one as the daughter of a husbandman.[94] Several protesters also had connections with religious radicalism. Lydia Barnard's husband, one of the Great Waltham rioters, was indicted for 'being voluntarily present at conventicles' in 1647. Grace Poole and her husband Jonathan, who took part in the incidents at Halstead, were rendered excommunicate for non-attendance at church in 1641.[95] Charity Knight, the baker's wife, who tried to prevent the curate from baptizing a child in 1634, was married to a radical who was presented before the court of High Commission in 1619 for refusal to take communion in the form 'appointed by the book' and who later left Chelmsford for New England.[96] The impression is of respectable women driven by strong religious conviction to engage in principled direct action.

Thus, in conclusion we see that attention to gender deepens our understanding of the shape, structure and meaning of iconoclastic disturbances. We find that respected and respectable godly female parishioners intervened regularly, but informally, as the voice of the community to defend godly protestant doctrine and/or to rid their church of 'polluting' objects or gestures which they regarded as 'popish'. Some confrontations involved physical violence, while others were symbolic and connected closely in time, form and setting to female religious life. Women expressed their beliefs by drawing on their 'normal' religious experiences and their traditional duties towards liturgical objects to assert a powerful sense of legitimacy and a conviction that they had a right to a voice in debates about their meaning and use. Mary Douglas and others have noted that women were regarded as the guarantors of order in culture, defending social and cultural boundaries against fears of pollution. Casting themselves as cleansers, purifiers and protectors of reformed religion, godly women drew symbolically on this deeper tradition to increase the demonstrative power of their acts. Such interpretations take us some distance from explanations of female iconoclasm in terms of marginality and dependence. Women's interventions had more substantial implications; their actions engaged them in serious struggles for control over local sacred space and the reformed faith. Although excluded from formal avenues of authority, women of the middling sort used the powers they accrued as married women, mothers and Christians to exert informal influence over the meaning and use of space within their local parish church.

8 THE TRAVAILS OF AGNES BEAUMONT

Bernard Capp

Agnes Beaumont, baptized in 1652, was the daughter of a Bedfordshire yeoman farmer, the youngest of his four children to survive infancy.[1] She lived a generally uneventful life, except for one dramatic episode in 1674, which she later recounted in a vivid and highly emotional narrative. First published in 1760, it was to become a popular text within the nonconformist community, and had passed through ten editions by 1842.[2] Agnes had no doubt told her story many times before writing it down. While the language is fresh and immediate, she ends with the throwaway remark, 'I wish I was as well in my soul as I was then' (l. 224), which suggests that the narrative, at least in its present form, was written long after the events it describes.

In the early 1670s, Agnes was still living at home with her father. Her mother had died, and her older siblings had married and left. Agnes remained at home, acting as housekeeper for her father, John. Semi-retired, he had made over much of his estate to his eldest son (also John), who now ran a much larger farm close by, in Edworth, about ten miles south-east of Bedford.[3] Her father still raised cattle, while Agnes ran the house. They employed no servants.

In October 1672 Agnes had joined the nonconformist congregation at Gamlingay, six or seven miles from where she lived, during the brief period of religious toleration under Charles II's Declaration of Indulgence. It was one of the outlying branches of the famous Bedford congregation, founded in 1650.[4] Her brother and sister-in-law were members too, and her father attended for a time, though he soon withdrew and became increasingly hostile, swayed by the malicious stories that circulated about the Dissenters.[5] A communion service was arranged at Gamlingay on Friday, 13 February 1674, to be led by the preacher John Bunyan, who sometimes rode out from Bedford to take services. Agnes's brother was going, with his wife riding pillion behind him. Agnes was desperate to go too, and eventually persuaded her father to consent. She was hoping to be picked up from her brother's farm by John Wilson, a leading member of the congregation, and became distressed when Wilson failed to appear. Then, by luck, Bunyan himself came riding by, and was prevailed upon, with much reluctance, to carry

Agnes behind him (ll. 195–7). That might sound harmless, but it immediately set tongues wagging. As they entered Gamlingay they were spotted by Mr Lane, an Anglican minister from Bedford who sometimes preached at Edworth. Lane knew them both – Bunyan, of course, as a spiritual rival – and glowered 'as if he would have staird his Eyes Out'. He spoke to them harshly, and subsequently 'did scandalise us after a base manner, and did raise a very wicked report of us' (ll. 198, 214).[6] Moreover, her father was furious when he heard that Agnes was riding with Bunyan, for he had heard damaging rumours about the preacher (ll. 197, 209).[7]

When Agnes returned home that night she found the house in darkness and the door locked. Her father, roused from his bed, railed at her from the window and refused to let her in unless she promised never to attend the meeting again. Agnes, equally determined, refused to please him by abandoning her hope of salvation. Instead she crept into the dark, freezing barn, and passed a miserable night huddled in the straw among the cows. Next morning her father remained angry and resolute, and their stand-off continued. Her brother's attempts to mollify him exacerbated the situation, and his wife's efforts proved similarly futile. Agnes made another attempt to appease him that evening, to no avail; he even threatened to push her into the pond. After spending Saturday night at her brother's house she tried again on Sunday evening, but her father now delivered an ultimatum: unless she submitted he vowed to turn her away and leave her not a farthing in his will. Agnes's resistance finally crumbled, and she promised never to go to the meeting again without his consent – which, he told her bluntly, he would never give. She was at last allowed back in the house, consumed with feelings of guilt and betrayal (ll. 199–207).

On Monday morning her brother called to see what had happened, and was appalled to learn she had submitted. He accused her of denying Christ, a terrible sin, and one she had already admitted to herself (ll. 205, 207). A fresh storm arose on Tuesday night, for after Agnes and her father had retired to bed she awoke to hear him crying out in agony. 'I was struck with a pain at my heart', he told her, 'I shall dye presently'. Agnes did her best to help him, and then ran over the snow-covered fields in the dark to her brother's house to summon assistance. But there was nothing they could do, and by morning her father was dead (ll. 211–14).

This shock was bad enough, coming so soon after the bitter confrontation between father and daughter. Worse was to follow. On the day before her father's death, Lane spread the news at Baldock fair that he had seen Agnes riding behind Bunyan, adding a crude sexual smear that they had been 'naught together' (l. 214). When word spread of her father's death, a neighbour named Feery, a country lawyer, immediately spread a still more damaging rumour: that Agnes had poisoned him, as an act of revenge (ll. 215–17). Feery summoned Agnes's brother and demanded an investigation, whereupon the funeral plans had to be put on hold. A surgeon summoned to inspect the body found nothing suspicious, but Feery persisted and on Friday a coroner's inquest was hastily convened at John Beaumont's farm.[8] The coroner and jurors went to view the body, and the coroner then interrogated Agnes on the circumstances surrounding her father's death. She was understandably terrified. If the jury judged it suspicious she would face a criminal trial, and the charge for killing a parent was not murder but petty treason; if convicted, she would be burned at the stake. Feery, the witness against her, was already confidently predicting this outcome. In the event, of course, there was a happier ending. The jury found no evidence of foul play, and the coroner scolded Feery for his malice and cruelty in starting the rumours. The funeral, delayed two days, went ahead on Saturday evening (ll. 215–22).

Agnes's troubles were still not over. Feery now persuaded her brother-in-law to challenge her father's will, made several years earlier, and she reluctantly surrendered £60 'for peace and quietness', to avoid a lawsuit (ll. 222–3). A few weeks later she learned of fresh rumours, 'hotly reported' at Biggleswade, that she had now confessed to the killing and gone mad.[9] She resolved to silence them by going to the town on market day, and passing through the crowd to demonstrate that she had nothing to hide. 'I may say almost all the Eyes of the market was fixt upon me', she wrote later, with people whispering and pointing. Though some laughed, others told her she had confounded her critics, and she felt vindicated (l. 223).

Little is known of Agnes's later life. She did not marry until she was fifty, in 1702. Whether that was from choice or because some of the mud had stuck remains unknown. After her husband, a landed gentleman, died in 1707, she married a second time, this time a prosperous London fishmonger, and it was in London that she died, in 1720. She remained a nonconformist, and asked to be buried not in London, but close to the meeting house at Hitchin, whose pastor, John Wilson, she had known and admired since her early days in the Gamlingay meeting.[10]

What can Agnes's story tell us about women's voices and lives? The voice itself is personal and vivid. The narrative has the flavour of an oral account, and no doubt the text grew out of a tale that had been often repeated. Direct speech features prominently, presented as if verbatim, and the oral flavour is reinforced by numerous conversational phrases such as 'Now to tell you the truth' and 'As I said' (l. 203). Many sentences begin with 'Well,' or 'So'; eight on one page alone in the latest edition start with 'So I see', 'So I went' and similar expressions (l. 202). The original manuscript, possibly written by Agnes herself, is poorly spelled and has no title or paragraphs. Agnes had little education but she knew the Bible intimately; passages that echoed her situation flooded into her mind, and they coloured her dreams. They buttress her story throughout, and she took comfort to find her joys, hopes and fears paralleled in scripture. Her narrative devotes as much space to her emotional and spiritual state as to the story itself, and the mood throughout is intense. The first two pages alone include six exclamatory interjections – 'oh, how great hath the kindness of god been to me', 'oh, how sweet is his presence', 'O the fiery darts from hell', and so on. She relates her thoughts and feelings, hopes and fears, and her terror of being burned alive.

Another key dimension of the narrative is Agnes's battle for autonomy and freedom. Her life on the farm was lonely and constricted. She always faced a prolonged struggle for permission to attend the religious meetings, and sometimes failed. She respected her father, but did not conceal the fact that he was possessive, short-tempered – and snored loudly (ll. 195–6, 210). She had little autonomy, and almost no privacy. She cherished the rare occasions when he went to bed early, giving her a little time to herself by the fireside. The dissenting groups in Gamlingay and Edworth gave her wider horizons and supportive friends, and she was desperate to retain them, despite her father's opposition (ll. 218, 223). Her longing for autonomy is evident throughout the narrative. When her father locked her out, she could have walked to her brother's house and had a hot meal there and a bed for the night. That is what her father expected her to do, and what he assumed she had done (ll. 201, 209). It was her own choice to spend the night in the freezing barn; she would accept suffering in God's cause, and she would fight her battles alone. Those battles were partly in her own mind, as she fended off Satan's assaults. She felt God's presence in the barn, protecting her; she felt Satan there too, and spoke out aloud to defy him (ll. 200–1). Next morning she was still determined to fight her battles alone. When her brother urged her not to endanger her soul by abandoning the Church, she silently brushed his words aside; 'Thought I, *I do not want any of your Cautions, upon that Account*' (ll. 205–6). She would look after her own soul. And finding his attempts to mediate unhelpful, she decided she would do better alone (ll. 202, 206).

The theme of autonomy returns at two later points in the text. The first is at the inquest, where the narrative notes Agnes as the only woman present in a room that was crowded with jurors (some of them gentlemen, far above her in status) and witnesses. She is conscious that her bearing and demeanour will be as important as her words, and puts on a deliberately cheerful and confident performance to underline her innocence (ll. 218). Even after the jury decided there was no case to answer, she tells the coroner she is willing to have her father's body opened, to show she has nothing to hide (ll. 222). Finally, at the end of the narrative, she makes it clear that it was her own decision to go to Biggleswade and walk through the market to face down her detractors (l. 223).

The issue of autonomy takes us back to the key relationship between Agnes and her father. She was his daughter but also his housekeeper, and their relationship resembled in many ways that of husband and wife. Agnes cooked his meals; they sat together in the evenings by the fire, while she span at her wheel; they usually went to bed at the same time, and slept in beds in the same chamber (l. 210). John clearly felt a sense of ownership; Agnes was his daughter, housekeeper and quasi-wife. Her new passionate devotion to God posed a threat that was deeply personal. Agnes sensed it too. When she uses the term 'father' in the narrative, she is usually referring to her biological father, but sometimes to God. She honoured two fathers, both jealous fathers, both in their very different ways loving fathers. She imagined God speaking to her, and sometimes addressing her as his 'beloved'. John Bunyan posed an even more direct threat to her father's emotional and physical ownership. There is nothing to suggest that Bunyan had any feelings for Agnes, or knew her well. Initially he had refused to carry her to the meeting, saying it would make her father angry, as it did; it was only her tears and her brother's pleading that changed his mind. The rumours about Bunyan provoked anger and jealousy in her father, and his jealousy was not wholly misplaced. For Agnes was more than simply grateful to be offered a lift. She was very conscious of Bunyan's stature as a famous man of God. And she admits that as they rode along, with Bunyan talking of the religious matters, 'my heart was pufft up with pride ... proud to thinck I should ride behind such a man as he was; and I was pleasd that any body did look after me as I rode A long' (ll. 197–8). Bunyan reappears briefly later in the narrative. Feery had spread rumours that Bunyan had counselled Agnes to kill her father, and had even supplied her with poison, and she muses that if she was found guilty of the crime, Bunyan would probably be convicted too, and they would die together (l. 217). The second extant manuscript, made after her death, ends with reference to rumours that Bunyan was now a widower and had urged her to poison her father so they could marry, and to subsequent rumours that they had indeed married. 'And truely this did sometimes make me merry', she adds. 'I could not but tell this News to several [people] myself, and it did serve to divert me sometimes' (l. 224). Was she simply diverted? Or flattered to be linked romantically to such a famous man? If her father had any inkling of her feelings, it is easy to imagine how they would have sharpened his fear of losing her emotionally. Agnes may not have been fully aware of this dimension – God rather than Bunyan features as the rival protagonist in the narrative – but her father was certainly conscious of it.

Though the narrative is a tightly constructed domestic drama, we catch occasional glimpses of wider dimensions. In 1673 the king had withdrawn his Declaration of Indulgence, rendering nonconformist meetings once more illegal. Meetings clearly continued in this area, and her brother, who had the largest house in Edworth, was able to serve as parish constable despite being a known Dissenter (l. 215).[11] Local tensions are also evident, however, in the malicious gossip already circulating. The allegation of poisoning owed more to personal spite. Feery, the lawyer, had once thought of Agnes as a possible wife, before turning against her when she joined the nonconformists. It was Feery who started the rumour of poisoning, who insisted on calling in the coroner, and who persuaded her brother-in-law to challenge her father's will. Six months later, when a damaging fire broke out in Biggleswade, Feery spread new rumours that Agnes was responsible for starting it, perhaps hoping to see her arrested and charged (ll. 215–16, 222–4). If so, he was thwarted, but regarding her father's will he had triumphed. Here Feery and Agnes's brother-in-law were engaging in the threat of vexatious litigation, a practice that bedevilled English society in this period.[12] When her father had made his will three years earlier, Feery had persuaded him to allocate Agnes a larger share of the estate than her sister, hoping to reap the benefit himself if they later married. But as soon as her father was buried, he sent for the brother-in-law and told him the will had been changed (because of Agnes's defiance over attending the nonconformist meetings), and that she had been cut off with only a shilling. Moreover, 'he told him he could set him in way to come in for a part, which my brother [-in-law] was glad to hear of'. Agnes was promptly summoned to meet them and told she must promptly agree to surrender part of her inheritance, 'or else he would sue me ... I was threatened at a great rate'. She had no idea whether or not the will had been amended, and with no one to guide her, and no doubt still in a distressed emotional state, she was bullied into giving up the very substantial sum of £60 rather than face litigation. It later emerged that the will had not in fact been changed, but Agnes had already signed away her rights (ll. 222–3). It makes an unedifying story, and was an admission of defeat. In her narrative Agnes reclaims the moral high ground by pointing to another 'great mercy' from the Lord: 'he was pleasd to keep pregudise out of my heart to this man', and she prayed God to forgive the wrongs he had done her, and have mercy on his soul (l. 223).

Agnes's ordeal reflects both the religious divisions of her age and the domestic tensions that recur in every generation as children reach maturity and press for some independence. That combination was replicated in many other family dramas of the period. One poignant case saw the Quaker convert, Anne Upcott, daughter of the vicar of St Austell in Cornwall, arrested in 1658 for mending her waistcoat on the Sabbath and set in the stocks, in the rain – at the instigation of her own brother, the parish constable. He and two more brothers poked fun at her, gathered a crowd to watch and jeer, and supplied beer, bagpipes and tobacco to entertain them. Her own father came to mock her.[13]

Similar conflicts could set fathers against sons. The diary of Isaac Archer records a long and painful struggle with his father William, a rigid Independent minister who wanted no truck with the Restoration Church settlement. In 1660 Isaac was a 19-year-old student at Cambridge, enjoying university life and reluctant to sacrifice his future career prospects. William Archer, another dominant, controlling father, kept his son on a tight financial rein. He also demanded that Isaac should repudiate the Book of Common Prayer, whatever the consequences, and was enraged when he prevaricated. A blazing row ensued, and it rumbled on for months in the bitter letters that passed between them. In his rage, William declared he would rather see his son working in an alehouse, or dead, than wearing a surplice. In calmer moments he begged Isaac not to break his heart. Isaac, raised in a Puritan environment, was desperately torn and very conscious of the Fifth Commandment's direction to honour one's father and mother. For two years he battled with his father and his own conscience. He pored over the writings of William Perkins, William Whately and Lancelot Andrewes on the scope of the Commandment, and even thought of abandoning the clerical career he had planned. In 1662 he finally settled for conformity, was ordained, and secured a small vicarage. Father and son eventually came to an uneasy reconciliation, but Isaac long suffered pangs of conscience over the course he had chosen.[14]

Another domestic drama saw the young Thomas Ellwood similarly pitted against his father, a justice of the peace in south Oxfordshire. In 1659 Thomas came under the influence of local Quakers, and soon became a convert. He adopted their practice of addressing everyone as 'thou', and refused to take off his hat in the presence of social superiors – including his father. His enraged father beat him with both fists, snatched off his hat, threatened to strike his teeth down his throat, and banished him from the dinner table. He too, like Archer's father, oscillated between rage and grief at effectively losing his son. When Thomas walked out of the house one day after an angry clash, his father wailed, 'Oh, my son! I shall never see him more'. But when he returned, a couple of days later, his father flew into a rage and violently assaulted him. During the winter of 1659–60, Thomas was almost confined to the house, much of the time banished to his chamber. Like Agnes Beaumont, he never doubted that his duty to God must take precedence, but like both Agnes and Isaac Archer, he felt deeply troubled by defying his father's authority. He too spent months brooding over the extent of parental authority, and fighting off the temptation to give way and follow the easy path.[15]

Agnes had briefly succumbed to that temptation, and she also continued to feel guilty for having disobeyed her father. When he was taken mortally ill, she worried that she might have been responsible – that he had taken cold round his heart, as she put it, because she had not been in the house to look after him (ll. 211–12).

The narratives of Agnes, Archer and Ellwood are all told from the young person's perspective. We might consider them briefly too from the parental perspective. In each case the father struggling to assert his authority knew that his patriarchal status was already much diminished. Agnes's father, long widowed, had made over most of his wealth to his son, who was now the dominant male in the family. His fear that Agnes would be drawn further into his son's orbit added another layer of tension to their rift. Archer's father, also long widowed, had seen most of his children die, and had retired from the ministry. William Ellwood, who lost his place on the bench at the Restoration, had seen his financial circumstances deteriorating for years; his elder son had attended university, but he could not afford to send Thomas. The family was already shrinking: his wife had died, his elder son and daughter had left home, and most of the servants had been turned away.[16] In each case an ageing father was clinging to the vestiges of his authority, like a humbler King Lear. The clash between father and son triggered the total disintegration of the Ellwood family. In Agnes's case, the family has already shrunk to just two members: father and daughter. If he lost her, emotionally or physically, he would have lost everything.

But preserving authority was not the fathers' only consideration. There was a paternalistic as well as patriarchal dimension to their concern, though their children's narratives understandably pay it little attention. Ellwood's father was genuinely concerned about the likely fate of his son, as a Quaker, once the king was back on the throne. Thomas was indeed arrested, and released only when his father undertook to keep him at home, and prevent him from attending Quaker assemblies: a sort of protective house arrest, under parental supervision.[17] Agnes Beaumont acknowledges that her father was concerned for her reputation when she was seen riding behind Bunyan. Bunyan himself had anticipated problems, and Agnes admits that the malicious gossip proved very hard to dispel. Bunyan's reputation suffered badly too. In later editions of his spiritual autobiography, *Grace Abounding*, he inserted twelve new paragraphs vehemently denying defamatory rumours of bigamy, adultery or any other improper dealings with women.[18] Agnes's father had further concerns, as she also acknowledges. For several months she had been in a state of almost religious mania, swinging between despair and rapture, and alarming both her father and neighbours. She was scarcely eating or sleeping, and he feared she was becoming mentally deranged. Others feared she might be suicidal (ll. 194, 209). It is not hard to see why he saw Agnes's obsession with the nonconformists and their intense religiosity as deeply harmful to her health and welfare. He himself took religion less seriously; he had lived sixty years, he told neighbours, 'and scarce ever thought of my Soul'. But he too had agonizing doubts about whether he was doing the right thing. His manner was blunt, almost brutal, but when she submitted, and he saw the terrible state to which he had reduced her, he broke down 'and wept like a child'. He admitted too that after locking her out of the house he had been too stressed to sleep, and after the heart attack, facing death, he hoped desperately that his behaviour would not be among the sins God counted against him (ll. 208–9, 212).

Many other women in this period suffered emotional and physical hardship when their sense of religious duty led them to defy a spouse or parent. Agnes Beaumont's story is perhaps unique, however, in spelling out so vividly the kaleidoscopic emotions that engulfed her throughout her ordeal. It reveals, in compelling style, the fusion of a spiritual ordeal with a half-conscious personal quest for autonomy within a confined and male-dominated world.

***

Autobiographical writing in the seventeenth century and beyond very often took the form of spiritual autobiography or conversion narrative, with the author recounting his or her struggle against sin, despair and temptation before finally attaining a state of grace. The genre quickly acquired its own conventions, to which writers consciously conformed.[19] Many of these writings found their way into print while the writers were still alive, or soon after their death. But Beaumont's narrative, despite (or perhaps because of) its dramatic, sensational content, was not published until almost a century after the events it describes, and has attracted relatively little critical interest.[20] This may be, in part, because Agnes's voice remains hard to position within the main strands of autobiographical writing of the period, or within other categories of women's writing. Women were largely excluded from the public stage, and those women writers who ventured upon it did so primarily through the prophetic voice. They spoke and wrote as God's mouthpiece, delivering divine warnings over the religious, moral or political sins of the age.[21] Beaumont makes no such claims, and has very different concerns; she is preoccupied with the fate of her own soul (and body), not the fate of the nation.

Agnes's narrative, however, is far from a conventional conversion narrative. John Bunyan had published his influential *Grace Abounding* a few years earlier, in 1666. Agnes was probably familiar with the text. But most spiritual autobiography is primarily concerned with the conversion experience itself, and Agnes, already a born-again Christian, had passed beyond that stage. At the start of her narrative she describes the elation, almost ecstasy, it had brought. As she moved round the house, barns and stable, she was repeatedly overcome by a religious rapture, and tears of joy – 'as if I had been in heaven, and as if my very heart would have Brake in peeces with Joy' (l. 194). Like other nonconformist writers, she records her struggles against temptation and despair, and describes how she finally attained a renewed assurance of grace. In conventional spiritual narratives, these inward experiences provide the central focus, and their value lay in the help they could offer others in the conversion process. Agnes follows convention in stressing human weakness and the power of divine grace, but she gives as much weight to the dramatic external events as to her inward spiritual trials. And despite the insistence on her female frailty and timidity, she repeatedly draws attention to counter-examples of resolution and defiance in the face of adversity. In the farmyard, at the coroner's inquest, in Biggleswade market, Agnes's narrative testified to her moral strength and physical courage.

Women's spiritual autobiographies that found their way into print in this period, by contrast, are far more passive in spirit, and emphasized their conformity to social and gender conventions. Confessing the weakness of their sex, female writers often acknowledged the role of male pastors or preachers as key instruments of divine grace. Many, indeed, carried prefaces or epistles by ministers, husbands or sons to confirm the propriety of the female narrative.[22] Jane Turner's *Choice Experiences* (1653) tells the story of a woman who shared Beaumont's independent spirit, but whose narrative was heavily packaged to make it more acceptable. Brought up within a family that was conventional in its religious outlook, Turner had found her own way first to Puritanism and then to separatism, guided by private biblical study and reflection. The spiritual autobiography she subsequently composed, initially for her personal use, was written without the knowledge of her husband, who was away serving with the army. She recalled her internal struggles against fear, despair and self-doubt, and reflected at some length on the significance of each stage of this spiritual journey. Once he learned of it, her husband urged her to publish it, and their London Baptist pastor approved. Yet those involved recognized that many would judge it improper for a woman to publish such a work, and the narrative appeared in print prefaced by no fewer than five defensive epistles. Two of them were by Jane's husband, who assured readers that the work represented merely 'the labours of one of the weakest Sex', and that its spiritual value lay in the fact that 'strength appears in weakness'. Jane's own preface is an uneasy mixture of assertiveness and apology, reflecting the tension between her independent spirit and the power of gender conventions. She chides other church members for the discouragement she has faced, while expressing her own serious doubt that her work could possess any spiritual value, being written in such 'a broken, scattering way'. Conscious of her own 'weakness and unworthiness', she professes herself willing to submit to superior, male judgements on the issue.[23] Jane Turner's testimony was acceptable in print only with these endorsements from her husband, pastor and another leading church member, and with her own obeisance to gender and family proprieties.

Agnes Beaumont's narrative, by contrast, remained unpublished for almost a century and carried no such male endorsements. Though Beaumont, too, stressed her female weakness, and acknowledged the duty she owed her father, male contemporaries would have found the narrative's gender politics deeply unsettling. She paints unflattering portraits of her father, other male family members and most of the other men who appear in her story, and pointedly prefers to fight her battles alone. And whereas Turner acknowledges that all her battles were inward, Beaumont's are simultaneously internal and external. She is reluctant to ask or receive help from her brother, and there is no indication that she turned for any help to the officers of the Church after her father's death, or in the difficult months following the inquest. Nor, it would seem, did she ask her brother to accompany her to the meeting with Feery over the disputed will, where his advice or moral support might have proved advantageous. This was a spiritual narrative centred on suffering and steadfastness rather than conversion, and with very little attempt to conform to the conventions of the genre.

With its dramatic story of physical threats and dangers, Agnes Beaumont's narrative might appear closer to Quaker accounts of sufferings. Quaker narratives

stress the protagonists' dangers, persecution and imprisonment, and record the
vindictive cruelty of magistrates, gaolers and 'rabble' public. It is very unlikely,
however, that Beaumont had read any such tracts, given the hostility between
the rival denominations; Bunyan himself frequently clashed fiercely with Quaker
leaders. Moreover, the similarities do not go very far. In Quaker narratives, both
male and female protagonists invariably remain undaunted and unshaken in the
face of violence and imprisonment.[24] Agnes, by contrast, makes no attempt to
conceal her doubts, fears and temptations. And while her 'many and great try-
als' (l. 193) include the cruelty of the vindictive lawyer Feery, she presents the
coroner and his jury as kindly and sympathetic. Her actual sufferings are mild
by Quaker standards. The threat of trial and execution brings the narrative to a
dramatic finale, but its central concern is found in the conflict between the duty
Agnes feels she owes to God and the duty she also owes to her father. Both had
a legitimate claim to her love and obedience, and the tension in the narrative is
rooted in her recognition that their demands were mutually exclusive.

The narrative of trials and temptations suggests other possible parallels and
influences. There is a loose resemblance to Bunyan's most famous work, *Pilgrim's
Progress*. Its hero, Christian, similarly sets aside family ties and obligations to
follow the road to salvation. He too meets with sufferings, doubts, dangers and
temptations, and he too briefly falls away from the righteous path. Though Bunyan had not yet published his story, it was largely written during his long years
of imprisonment in the 1660s, and it is at least conceivable that he had aired
some of its themes in his sermons or discourse. Agnes would certainly have been
familiar with the still more dramatic Old Testament story of Job, subjected by
God to horrific torments to test his faith and obedience. Agnes tells how shortly
before her troubles she had premonitions that some terrible ordeal lay ahead;
certain biblical passages came repeatedly into her mind, hinting at terrifying
dangers, but also promising God's presence and comfort (ll. 194–5). She would
have been well aware of the sufferings of the faithful down the centuries, from
biblical times to the Marian martyrs and the sufferings of her own contemporaries, including Bunyan himself. The history and indeed the identity of Restoration
nonconformity was bound up with trials and persecution, which leaders insisted
were to be accepted and even welcomed.[25] That context played a considerable
part in shaping Agnes's behaviour and her narrative. She imagined herself facing
her own ordeal, perhaps even burning at the stake. That was the punishment laid
down for women guilty of petty treason, and it had been the fate of the Marian
martyrs. Knowing herself innocent of parricide, Agnes would have gone to the
stake as a martyr in her own mind, whatever the court had decided. When her
ordeal began, she tells how fear of being burned alive 'would sometimes shake
me all to peeces'; at other times she pictured herself dying calmly and coura-
geously, confident that God would be there to strengthen and comfort her (ll.
217–18). She too would be a brave martyr.

Finally, we may consider Agnes's narrative in the context of the emergence of the novel. Spiritual autobiographies are generally recognized as one of its precursors, in their focus on the inner life and affective relationships of the main protagonists. Both genres give the reader access to the private thoughts and emotions of the subject(s).[26] In this respect Agnes Beaumont's narrative looks forward to the eighteenth-century novel of sentiment, such as Samuel Richardson's *Pamela* (1740). Like Richardson's heroine, she has a moving story to tell. She too is young, female, single, vulnerable and emotionally torn, and she too emphasizes throughout her frailty, danger and distress. Like Pamela, her sexual honour is in danger, albeit in very different circumstances. More dangers soon crowd in, and Agnes, like Pamela, spells out her distress. During her night in the barn she fears she 'might be knokt o the head' by vagrants, and tells how it froze so 'vehemently' that 'the dirt was frosen upon [her] shoues' (l. 200). When her father turns her away, and threatens to cut her off, she pictures a dismal future, begging from door to door, or forced to work for her bread (ll. 203, 205–6). Though at her age many young women would already have been working for years, as domestic or farm servants, Agnes would be forfeiting the status she had enjoyed as *de facto* mistress of the house. When her father is taken ill, and Agnes runs to fetch help, she again imagines robbers lurking outside the door, ready to knock her on the head, and as she runs through the snow she thinks she can hear them chasing after her (l. 213). Like the sentimental novelist, Agnes ratchets up the pathos of her story. She is repeatedly reduced to tears, and later in the narrative tells how her father and brother also shed tears at her plight. The coroner's jurymen are tearful at her ordeal, and even a year later 'they would speak of me with teirs' (ll. 207, 215, 219, 222). The narrative as a whole, with its direct speech and detailed description of Agnes's thoughts, must surely have been in part imagined reconstruction rather than a precisely remembered record.

It is perhaps not very surprising that Agnes Beaumont's story remained unpublished until long after her death, and only then alongside half a dozen other spiritual narratives. It did not appear as a separate publication until 1801.[27] The spiritual autobiography of the seventeenth century had quickly developed a standard form, governed by a tight set of conventions, and Beaumont's narrative conformed neither in content nor style. If even Jane Turner's voice had appeared too strident for some of her Baptist brethren, Agnes Beaumont's self-dramatization and stubborn independence would have made her story uncomfortable reading for the nonconformist brethren. Unlike most spiritual autobiographical writings, the text offers no clue as to its intended audience. Agnes was not writing with an eye to publication nor, emphatically, for her family. It may well have been initially the 'sisters' in her own and other congregations who heard her voice, valued her story, and ensured that it would eventually be written down and finally find its way into print.

9 PARISH POLITICS, URBAN SPACES AND WOMEN'S VOICES IN SEVENTEENTH-CENTURY NORWICH

Fiona Williamson

Introduction

In recent years, gender historians have investigated defamatory speech as a way into the lives, mentalities and identities of ordinary women. By exploring words used by women, or about women, these scholars have argued that female identities were shaped by culturally specific preconceptions about morality and personal honour, in addition to, and linked with, individual circumstances such as credit, marriage and status.[1] What these studies have also shown is how women's words could be potent weapons, illustrating the irony that by defaming other women – attacking their reputation and sexual morality in particular – those women hurling the insults reinforced female stereotypes whilst stepping outside the role of 'meek and subservient' themselves.[2] Words equalled power. Injurious words had the ability to affect a person's place and credit in the local community, although not without risk to the defamer.[3] However, women's words were not always defamatory. Their testimonies as witnesses and compurgators were crucial to the outcome of many court cases and their participation in networks of information was vital.[4] Thus women emerge as central players in early modern parish politics: influencing, guiding, reporting and criticizing the actions of others.[5]

Most recently, close readings of women's words and the places in which those words were spoken, have shown how women's lived experiences challenge our contemporary views of early modern cultural stereotypes.[6] The 'spatial turn' of social history in particular has complimented post-revisionist gender dialogues emerging from a tradition of dichotomies, such as 'public and private' or 'male and female'.[7] As Amanda Flather argues, 'people lived space as social beings, and the way they did so could not be organised in so orderly a pattern'.[8] The term space, however, has not escaped criticism for its sense of abstraction from the society it is intended to describe. Michael Camille, for example, warns that we tend to understand the word in relation to our own modern sociological, geographic and philosophical theories, and it may not always be the most appropriate or relevant word to use in historic contexts. He proposes using instead 'spaces' or 'place', an approach adopted in this study.[9] This evolving scholarship emphasizes the flexibility that early women might have had in negotiating their roles, spheres of movement and personal agency. Certainly there are few historians who would still assume that women's lives were strictly governed by the ideals preached from both pulpit and pamphlet.[10]

This essay thus builds on a literature that has explored defamation and/or spaces of interaction. The first part will argue that although much research has been completed on women's words in urban social settings, it is important to consider how women's words influenced the politics of the parish, governing the twist and turns of men's, as well as women's lives according to the patriarchal ideals that dictated appropriate behaviours and ways of living.[11] Thus defamation suits were a legitimate, and often very effective way of censoring unruly neighbours of any gender and restoring parish harmony. As Bernard Capp has argued, however, defamatory language insinuating sexual deviance more often than not concealed wider problems than a simple preoccupation with sexual morality.[12] Gender is conceptualized here as only one part of a broader narrative of parish relationships which included individual actions and histories, minute differences in social status and, crucially, the strength of individual personalities.

Drawing from the spatial turn of social history, in particular the work of those scholars who have focused on urban spaces, the second, and final, section of this essay, builds from the argument that the spatial paradigm of a unified 'neighbourhood' identity featured prominently in early modern mentalities. Expanding on the work of scholars who have explored the traditions associated with parish boundaries and the concept of belonging to a parish, but not necessarily influenced by the spatial turn,[13] I intend to move the discussion of parish boundaries away from its corporeal limitations to demonstrate how the creation of urban communities adhered to both physical margins and imagined perimeters, neither of which necessarily followed the same course. By aiming a close lens into the networks extant in the politics of one parish in Norwich, this essay explores how rural networks translated into urban relationships, allowing a multilayered sense of identity to emerge from the tight-knit hub of the urban parish, often drawing on connections established many miles away. As Naomi Tadmor states, 'when people moved ... they were only likely to find themselves once more living in local communities, surrounded by new yet structurally similar sets of neighbours and neighbourly relationships'.[14] Translated across time and place, the persistent concept of 'neighbourhood' intimately affected people's lives.

Finally, this essay will explore the spaces of parish politics, those places that can be considered central to the interactions and social relationships of urban dwellers, places that included the streets, domestic thresholds and the church. Following Laura Gowing's claim that thresholds and doorways were important in the construction and deconstruction of personal identities, for example, this essay seeks to re-evaluate this claim in light of the Norwich evidence.[15]

The archival sources utilized for this essay are predominantly, though not exclusively, defamation suits from the court of the Norwich diocese.[16] Defamation cases normally recorded the location of offensive words, the words themselves, the place of residence of each participant in the suit, alongside many other expedient details. They are therefore exemplary sources for piecing together the relationship between people and place, and for understanding the weight, value and meaning of people's words. The depositions reveal remarkable patterns of residential propinquity: protagonists and witnesses were more often than not drawn from the same neighbourhood, yet if we delve deeper, often these relationships had not been formed in that parish.

Moreover, from the way that deponents spoke about their surroundings – how they described where defamatory words had been uttered, for example – the observer can piece together something of an individual's relationship with that place, their spatial memory and the frameworks against which contemporaries conceptualized the landscape around them. The parish emerges as the primary geographic paradigm by which people ordered their physical world, over and above street names or even landmarks. Within a parish certain places lent their gravitas to words uttered within them, a spatial association established through tradition, usage, memory and symbolism. Words uttered in public places, for example, were more damaging than those spoken in private; words uttered against a trader in the market square attacked that individual's economic veracity, and the sanctity of religious places lent extra 'shock' value to a defamatory speech uttered in a place intended for contemplation and prayer. Thus examining the relationship between words and place is also testament to how early modern people perceived their immediate environment and how they actively and knowingly used words (and place) to their best effect.

The focus of this essay is a defamation case that entered the diocesan records during the 1660s. Not only does a close reading of the depositions allow us an intimate glimpse of the lives of two everyday seventeenth-century families, but it illustrates intimate knowledge of the legal system and shows how words could be used to upset the balance of power and alter community dynamics. Drawing from this study, it is possible to explore how speeches and spaces were appropriated in the daily negotiation and regulation of the neighbourhood by ordinary people, how relationships were constructed and deconstructed, and to demonstrate how people's networks crossed and re-crossed the boundaries of the parish, both physically and metaphorically, imposing the past into new places. In the process, ordinary people defined and redefined their own identity and that of their parish.

Defamation and Parish Politics

Late seventeenth-century Norwich was, by contemporary standards, a large city. Its population of some 25,000–30,000 people lived in 34 parishes bounded by medieval flint walls. The task of policing these inhabitants fell to the two sheriffs, twenty-four ward constables, a night watch, an indefinite number of parish householders who performed their duties on a volunteer basis, and the Church. All these parties relied on sets of commonly accepted moral guidelines and inhabitant's cooperation to make the city a peaceful place to live. As Keith Wrightson states, 'neighbourliness' was 'a relationship based on ... a degree of normative consensus as to the nature of proper behaviour amongst neighbours'.[17] Many inhabitants took on this role with gusto, reporting gossipmongers, common 'railers', petty criminals and immoral acts to the appropriate authorities.

In an age when most people knew their neighbours, or at the very least, knew about them, and when moral 'policing' was the duty of good neighbours; private lives were constantly on view. Walking home one evening in 1617, for example, Joanne Mackam of Norwich had seen Mr Williams, her neighbour, acting rather out of character as he loitered suspiciously outside Thomas Tawney's house. Knowing Tawney was away, Mackam went home and fetched a dish, and, on pretence of returning it to Mrs Tawney, boldly strode through the Tawneys' gate. Here 'comeinge by the window [she] saw Mr Williams on the bed with Goodwife Tawney & she would be sworne that they were naught togither & ... gott his wife with child'.[18] Spying at windows was not uncommon, nor was it entirely unacceptable. It was one way a neighbour could protect his or her community from the spiritual and financial consequences of immorality. People were expected, even obliged, to intervene in domestic affairs if immorality was suspected, even if this meant intruding into private space. This incongruity, along with the commonplace of shared living and sleeping spaces, suggests that the meaning of private life for early modern people shares little common ground with our modern preoccupation with privacy.[19]

Neither was spying or gossiping the preserve of the so-called fairer sex. In 1607, for example, John Barnes of St Clement's parish had overheard his neighbour, Thomas Claxton, exclaim at Mr Hardy's door that Albert Ansten had 'had the use of the bodye of Amyes wife, as often as much as his own'.[20] The encounter survives because Amyes subsequently sued Claxton for defamation. In another defamation case from 1680, spying worked in the defendant's favour. Andrew Faireman had been accused of having an affair with the married Anne Bately.

Faireman's neighbours believed that the rumours circulating about him were malicious, so late one night they went to Faireman's house to locate evidence to prove his innocence. Finding a small gap in his bedchamber shutters, they settled in for a long and uneventful night watching Faireman's bedroom. His concerned neighbours were subsequently able to produce statements declaring that Faireman had been on his own all night and 'hath carried himself soberly and civillie amongst his neighbours & was never heard of to be noted or suspected of anie such crime as is said to his charge with anie woman'.[21] It seems Faireman's neighbours had been right to be suspicious of the local gossip. Further investigation proved unambiguously that one Michael Metcalf had deliberately spread the reports of an affair after he had been involved with Faireman in the latter's official capacity as a warden, in a dispute over the sale of some cloth. Metcalf and Faireman's neighbours also testified that Metcalf was a poor man, unable to pay his debts and by implication, untrustworthy.[22] Faireman was absolved.

The records of the Norwich diocese overflow with cases like those above, where neighbours warred against or defended each other. One – the subject of this essay – stands out in particular. The Frogg and the Austin families had lived in St Saviour's parish in Norwich for many years and did not get along. In 1664 their personal animosity was suddenly made public. At least thirty of their friends, relatives and neighbours became involved in a prolonged suit raised at the church court which ran on over two years. Their conflict was acted out publically on the streets and lanes of their parish, in their church, and in the courtroom.

The story of the two families can be traced back as early as the 1640s. As civil war ravaged many parts of England, life in rural Norfolk went on much as normal. Leaving the security of her family home in Salthouse on the north Norfolk coast, a young woman named Mary Roberts became a maidservant to the wealthy dyer William Mitchell of Norwich. During her time at Mitchell's, she met and was courted by the young William Austin, and somewhere between 1646 and 1647 they married in the parish church of Arminghall in Norfolk. They set up house in Norwich permanently and over the next fifteen years or so had five children in the parish of St Saviour. During her early marriage Mary Robert's father died. As was so often the case for early modern women after the death of the family breadwinner, Mary's younger sister Anne (as yet unmarried and living at home) and their mother, Elizabeth, fell on hard times. Mary sent for Anne with the intention of finding her a job in service in Norwich, similar to the one she herself had had before her marriage. Anne, also known as Amy, was placed in the service of their cousin, Katherine Goodwin, who had married a tailor living in the same parish as the Austins in Norwich.[23] After a few years in Norwich, Anne returned to north Norfolk (possibly to be nearer her mother) to work in service for Mr Charles Davell, who was at that time minister of the small parish of Morston near her old family home. It was during her stay here that she heard the news of her sister Mary's untimely death.

William Austin, now a widower with five children, sent for Anne, asking her to become his housekeeper and care for his children. The arrangement made perfect sense. William was not rich and trusted his sister-in-law, also godmother to one of his children, to take far better care of his family than a paid servant. We might also assume that William and Anne, suffering from the loss of their close relative, offered one another comfort and support at that difficult point in their lives. However, it was this simple move that began all their troubles.

Neighbours and acquaintances began to comment on their relationship. 'What? Will you sweep to bed your sister ere long?' quipped one when he passed William in the street, provoking an angry outburst, 'God, doe you think I am mad to marry her sister?'[24] With the benefit of hindsight, William's passionate rejoinder concealed a guilty conscience as, only six weeks after Mary's death, he had married Anne in secret. Mary Frogg swore that he had confessed to her that Anne 'wilbe a kind mother to my children and several tymes deserving of it' but William had also made a point of telling others that Anne and Mary were not related.[25] Certainly, it seems strange that he would have confided to Mary Frogg his secret intentions when he told virtually nobody else.

William Austin knew that his marriage would be controversial. Troubled by his conscience, he had spoken 'with Mr Carter and some other Devines whether hee might lawfully marry two sisters and some of them dissuaded him from it and others told him that as the tymes then were hee might doe it'.[26] Without a conclusive answer, it appears Austin had decided to take the plunge but keep it quiet. He arranged for the ceremony to take place outside the city and away from prying eyes, and to the casual observer it was impossible to tell the difference between housekeeper and master, or husband and wife. However, Austin had not taken into account the importunity of parish gossip.

Mary Frogg had a history as a contentious and cantankerous neighbour, and was well versed in how to use defamatory words to bully others. John Morton and Katherine Goodwin (Anne Austin's former Norwich employer) were neighbours of both parties. They first heard about Frogg's accusations on Goodwin's doorstep in November 1664. Austin had walked past the pair, furious, stopping to tell them that Mary Frogg had defamed him, his wife and his children,[27] adding that Mary Frogg should be hanged 'for a dirty whore'.[28] A month later, the church court heard how Mary Frogg had accused Austin of bearing five 'bastard' children and had defamed them for the same, calling them 'whore and Rogue'.[29] Frogg's accusation that the Austins had married illegally fell on deaf ears, however. The Austin family was universally liked; the Froggs had next to no evidence, and the court case entered its second year simply because Mary Frogg refused to back down. Frogg, in desperation, decided to take matters into her own hands. The Austins had a servant, William Bell, one of only four people who could claim to have known the Austins since Mary Roberts and William Austin had courted. Bell's testimony was heard but subsequently discredited by the Austins' neighbours.

Elizabeth Goodwin had overheard Mary Frogg boasting 'that although she had heard the chancellor say that two witnesses were sufficient ... she should produce forty to putt ... Austin to charge' adding that 'shee ... would use her meanes to pack her beyond ... and that this case should not bee bought of for money and that if shee should dye her husband had promised her to prosecute'.[30] Likewise, Katherine March said she had overheard Mary Frogg planning to ruin the Austin family, regardless of the personal cost.[31] Katherine March also added that Bell had come to her house in a panic, informing her of how he had just come from Edmund Witherley, the attorney, to whom he confessed that Mary and Nicholas Frogg had bribed him to testify against his master, William Austin. Bell had gone to Witherley worried that he would be found out, hoping that he might persuade Witherley to talk to Austin and persuade him not to prosecute in light of their long acquaintance. Witherley's response however – according to Samuel March, Katherine's husband – was to tell Bell that if Austin went to the law he 'might take away his eares' and that Bell should confess all to the Chancellor before it was too late.[32] Bell duly acknowledged that he had been paid by the Froggs to give false evidence and was turned over to the civic magistrates. He was turned out of service, sent to prison, and his reputation in the parish as 'a person of very lewd life and conversation' was secured. In Bell's own words, he 'was undone and ruined through Froggs persuasion'.[33]

The Bell incident was not the only suspicious episode to occur over the course of the suit. The only other significant witness against the Austins – aside from the Froggs and Bell – was Mary Cotwin. Cotwin lived in St Saviour's parish with her husband Robert, a blacksmith, but had previously lived for many years in Cley-Next-The-Sea. The coastal village of Cley was only around two miles from Salthouse where Mary and Anne Roberts had been born. Cotwin had been Mary Robert's wet nurse. In her first court examination Cotwin claimed she had no knowledge of the two women's familial relationship, but she later changed her story, confessing to James Denew (one of the Austins' compurgators) that she had only said that William Austin's two wives were sisters after she had been threatened by the Chancellor of the court. The circumstances surrounding the threats are very unclear. As Mary Robert's wet nurse, she was in a good position to have known the family well. If she had been close to them, she may have tried to protect them and then later cracked under the pressure. Equally, her original statement may actually have been true, if the two girls had been apart in age Anne may not have been born when Mary was being nursed. We do not know the women's ages, but Mary had certainly been married for a few years before Anne went into service. The threatening behaviour of the Chancellor adds a twist to the tale but may not have had any sinister motivation. Cotwin, an old woman from a small, rural village, may simply have been intimidated by the Chancellor, the imposing surroundings of the courtroom and the formality of the proceedings. What is clear is that none of the main witnesses against Austin – the Froggs, a lying servant and an aged wet nurse who changed her story – were credible and it is interesting that the Froggs were seemingly unable to find any other witnesses.

However, Mary Frogg was not the only person who suspected the truth. John Morton had lived in St Saviour's parish for twenty-three years and as a 'neare neighbour' had known both wives. Having 'taken [them] to be lawful sisters' he 'hath divers tymes heard severall of the neighbours say in the late tymes that if the tymes should turne speaking of the said William marrying of two sisters that hee would bee troubled about it'.[34] Thomas Smith, the minister who had married Anne and William at Lakenham, had also married Mary and William seventeen or eighteen years earlier at Arminghall. Nonetheless, he claimed he could not remember any details about either woman, although he could remember a surprising amount of detail about the Robert's family from Cley-Next-The-Sea, so much so that one has to question whether he was trying to protect his own reputation having knowingly performed an illegal marriage. The connections here are also important. Austin had clearly known Smith for years, perhaps deliberately choosing his services again in the knowledge that he could be discreet.

But a key question remains: how did the Froggs have so much information about the Austins? The main witnesses, including Anne's mother, Elizabeth Roberts, the late Mary's wet nurse, Mary Cotwin, and William Bell, all hailed from villages in the same area, linked by their proximity to one of the main old roads from Norwich to the north Norfolk coast, including Cley, Edgefield and Stratton Strawless. It is at this point that the links between the Froggs and Austins become clear. Nicholas Frogg had been born in Edgefield, moving to Norwich to serve an apprenticeship as a worsted shearman under Thomas Warnes. It was here that Frogg met Mr Mitchell the dyer, working closely with him because of his job. Mitchell, of course, was the same man who employed Mary Roberts as a domestic servant and Frogg would have seen Mary at Mitchell's house on a regular basis. Frogg probably also met Austin here too, as it was during the period of Frogg's apprenticeship (1642–9) that Mary and William Austin courted and married.[35] As first-hand witnesses to both courtship and, first marriage, the Froggs' statements offered the most comprehensive retelling of the Austins' story to the court. It is no great leap to see why the Froggs were keen to reveal the truth about Austin's second marriage. They, above anyone else, were party to the intimate details of their past, and although some people may have preferred to turn a blind eye, in theory marriage to kin was not permitted.[36] But Mary Frogg's reasons for naming and shaming William Austin went deeper than we might think at first glance. Mary Frogg had a very personal grudge against the family, stemming from the fact that she felt slighted by a lesser family in her local community.

Nicholas Frogg and his family can be considered to have been of the 'middling' or 'better' sort of St Saviour's inhabitants. He was a freeman, rated in the 1666 hearth tax assessment on six hearths, and together Mary and Nicholas ran the Golden Dog Inn on a lane that still bears its name today.[37] He may also have held a minor civic office as a collector in 1659. Austin was not a freeman, was not assessed for the hearth tax, and the only possible civic office he may have held was as a constable, also in 1659.[38] At a time when status determined one's lot in life and could be as quickly lost as it was gained, social standing was the lynchpin of parish politics. When the case first entered the courts, in September 1664, the church court was acting on information received about Austin at the visitation. Mary and Nicholas Frogg had been called as witnesses to testify because of their long-standing association with the family (and it is possible that it was they who fed the visitation officers the rumours in the first instance). In November of the same year, the first personal defamation suits reached the court, where Frogg (it is not stated whether Mary or Nicholas) sued William Austin. One month later, Anne Austin sued Mary Frogg for defamation. Clearly, Mary Frogg was offended after William, being presented at court and knowing Mary to have been instrumental in giving evidence, had been angry, shouting and defaming Mary Frogg in the street. Mary Frogg herself was not blameless; according to witnesses she had been spreading rumours about Anne and William Austin for some time. But this brings us to a new chapter in the case. At the same time as Mary Frogg and William Austin had been at each other's throats, Mary Frogg was involved in another defamation suit with Susan Denew, also of St Saviour's parish. Mary had attacked Susan in St Saviour's Parish Church on 17 July 1664, pushing Susan out of her seat, calling her a 'brazen faced and bold faced slutt' and insulting her father's reputation.[39] However, it is unlikely that Susan Denew's morality was actually at issue.

Church seating arrangements were frequently a source of contention, leading to violent outbursts and, ultimately, many legal disputes. This was due to the fact that where one sat in church was a direct, symbolic reflection of your place in the parish hierarchy.[40] The wealthiest inhabitants traditionally paid for their own, often very elaborate, pews at the front of the church that were passed down from one generation to the next. The further from the altar, the poorer the congregation became and the less likely it was that they could afford their own seat. Some churches provided benches for the very poor along the back wall or in a gallery, paid for from donations from the richer inhabitants.[41] The seating plan was a microcosm of the social sphere put into practice by the churchwardens. Sitting in the wrong seat therefore could be taken as an assault on the fundamental elements of an individual's or family's status, credit and honour.

It was thus no surprise when people reacted strongly to the misallocation or deliberate seizure of a seat. In 1638, for example, between prayers and the sermon in the parish church of Diss, John Hunt had pushed and hit Alice Martyn 'on her body with such violence as she was inforced to lay hould upon the end of the said stoole to save herselfe from falling'. Hunt refused to desist, and in front of horrified onlookers hit Martyn with his elbow 'in a very furious and violent manner' declaring 'here I have stood & here I will stand'.[42] Hunt's attack on Martyn, though unusual in its level of violence towards a woman, was by no means unique. In 1696, for instance, Phillipa Kett had defamed Susan Nicholls in front of all their neighbours gathered for services in their church after Nicholls had sat in Kett's seat. Shouting that Nicholls was a 'foole and silly whore for going into the seate and a bitch for doing it',[43] Kett's words were not actually a reflection of Nicholls's sexual reputation, but were a critique of Nicholls's claim to higher social status by the appropriation of another person's pew. Nicholls responded with similarly inflammatory language, claiming Kett knew 'noe more what belonged to a gentlewoman than their dog, Plunder'.[44] The conflict was a powerful example of how social politics and social status were managed in practice.[45] By exploiting these same recognized conventions of social space and social place, Mary Frogg could belittle Denew's status publically and symbolically. But why was this relevant to Mary's quarrel with William Austin?

James Denew, Susan's husband, was one of William Austin's most prominent supporters. It is tempting to read more into his involvement, as the suit between Mary Frogg and his wife ran concurrent to the Frogg and Austin suits. A fellow inhabitant of St Saviour's parish, James Denew had know Austin for many years and spoke in his defence. Denew's first statement told how he had known both of Austin's wives and, although he had heard the rumours that Mary and Nicholas Frogg had spread, he had paid them no attention. His words against the Frogg family's evidence were damning. He maligned William Bell and said that Mary Cotwin was ignorant, 'knew nothing of the business she was examined on' and only confirmed the rumours about Austin and his wife after she had been threatened. James Denew had given his occupation as merchant, but he does not appear in Norwich's freeman's lists and he was only assessed on three hearths in the 1666 hearth tax assessment.[46] In both the Austin and the Denew case, Mary and Nicholas Frogg were positioned against people who were, if Mary's words are to be believed, of a lower social standing. No doubt Mary felt slighted by Susan Denew's usurpation of her pew, and later by being spoken about in a derogatory manner by a lesser family at court. This could well explain Mary's vehemence in pursuing the case at court, refusing to let it drop even if, she threatened, she died before the case was seen through in her favour.

Nevertheless, by 1665 this situation did not look positive for the Frogg family. Their underhand dealings with Bell had been exposed to the whole community and they now had defamation suits raised against them by Anne Austin, William Austin, and James and Susan Denew. To try and regain some face, they made careful choices as to who should act as their compurgators. Compurgators were expected to provide evidence of the good name and character of a defendant, and were generally chosen from the better sort of the defendant's neighbours and peers. The words of peers were judged on recognized indicators of good standing within the community, such as office holding, credit and self-sufficiency. William Pepys for example,[47] grocer, former constable and resident of St Saviour's parish, told the court how Nicholas Frogg (and by association his wife) was 'honest in his dealings' and Christian Langley,[48] a merchant, said that Frogg was known to be of 'good credit and reputation', a tradesman by occupation by which he 'maintains himself and his family [and is] credited for one hundred pounds'.[49] Robert Thurrold and John Todd also swore that

> Frogg and Mary his wife are persons of good condition and reputation and soe are taken and reputed by their neighbours ... and that Nicolas Frogg hath borne some offices within the parish of Saint Saviours and ... has in good fashion by his trade ... payeth any taxes or rate imposed.[50]

Some also added negative comments about William Austin, referencing in particular his lower social status.[51]

After October 1665, the two families ceased to appear in the church court depositions. Sadly, the corresponding Act Books do not survive for these dates and neither do the recognizances for this particular case. The only verdict to survive relates to Mary Frogg's suit with Susan Denew, from which we learn that Mary was dismissed and absolved in 1665.[52] It is possible to make a cautious assumption that the sudden absence of proceedings meant that Mary Frogg had won her suit against the Austin family, as she had sworn not to drop the case until she had achieved victory. Equally, it is also possible that the strife was brought to an end because of the advancing age or incapacity of the lead players. William Austin died intestate in 1672, only seven years later, and the records suggest that his wife, Anne, was not living to inherit.[53] However, the Froggs do not disappear from the records completely.

Eleven years later there is an interesting note in the probate records for the parish that might also shed more light on Mary Frogg's relationship with her neighbours. In 1676, Nicholas Frogg passed on.[54] He died intestate and his estate passed to the Probate administrators until his daughter, also called Mary, became twenty-one. This strongly suggests that by 1676, Mary Frogg senior had also passed away, indeed, Mary junior was placed into an apprenticeship with Robert Ducker, also a Norwich innkeeper, the month following her father's death to learn the skills of 'houswifery', strongly suggesting that she no longer had a parental figure to look after her.[55] The significance of this tale lies not in their daughter's situation but in the names given in Nicholas Frogg's records. Frogg was in fact an alias. Nicholas Frogg's original name had in fact been Frohock, a name that his daughter, Mary, adopted. The name Frohock was one of a kind in Norwich and suggested roots in the Low Countries. Although the conclusions to be drawn from this are tentative, the suggestion that the family may have been second or third generation strangers may well provide an underlying reason as to why Mary Frogg was so determined to prove her case against the Austins. Possibly she or her family had struggled against prejudice, or had been considered as outsiders by the local community. Perhaps by pursuing the Austin family she had hoped to appear community-minded, guarding the reputation of her parish. Indeed, this avenue of reasoning suggests a compelling argument as to why Mary Frogg may have been so insecure about her seat (and by association her status) in St Saviour's Parish Church, explaining her determination to match, or better, her neighbour's position. Interestingly, the surname Denew is also equated with the stranger congregation. The Lay Subsidy records relating to the strangers recorded in Norwich in 1624, for example, and the parish poor rate for 1634, both cite Denews living in Norwich, the latter in St Saviour's parish.[56] Again, the connection can only be tentative given the lack of other evidence but if it were indeed the same Denew family, a mutual connection to the immigrant congregation may suggest why Mary Frogg singled out Susan Denew in their parish church.

Putting Parish Politics in its Place

Seventeenth-century cities presented a unique set of circumstances that worked to channel and exacerbate social tension. Thin walls, shutters instead of glass, shared alleys and courtyards, the constant propinquity of neighbours, homes that doubled as trading places and workshops, the common use of domestic thresholds as social and working spaces, shared bedrooms, sleeping quarters in workshops, and so on, all worked to enhance public knowledge of private lives and vice versa. Domestic properties were neither truly public, nor were they truly private, especially for the average inhabitant. The household was open to public scrutiny and the occasional desire for privacy might easily be misconstrued; locked doors and shutters demanded investigation in the name of the public good.[57] In most cases private life spilled out onto the streets and it was there that we gain an insight into the social and spatial dynamics that governed people's lives.

    The seventeenth-century street was a 'public' place in the most conventional sense of the word. The urban street, however, differed from the country road. Urban streets were multifunctional, providing close linkages across and through public and private properties via sight, sound and physical proximity.[58] Small domestic properties opened onto the street, often without a hall to separate interior rooms from the public gaze. This was often purposeful, allowing the occupant to connect his private business with the public consumer, providing a space for workshops and shelves of wares, where business often spilled out on the street itself. The street was also the place of work for the travelling tradesman, tinker or street seller. Streets were integrally linked to the civic and religious life of the city; the setting for progressions, pageants, ceremonial walks and public festivities,[59] they were also an important social space for people of all social levels, where they shared news and gossip, watched entertainments or walked for pleasure.[60] At the bottom end of the scale, the street even functioned as a 'home' for the itinerant and wandering poor. The street was a site of negotiation and communication: between neighbours, between public and private interests, civic regulation and individual freedoms. News was passed on as people traversed the street, providing vital links in the communication of rumours and gossip. By spreading rumours amongst the 'better and greater sort of the inhabitants' or even anyone who might listen, bad news travelled fast. The street therefore emerges as one of the most important 'lived' spaces of the period. In the set of suits relating to the Frogg and Austin families, we see the street emerging, and re-emerging as a normative site of social interaction, at the same time as we witness just how private life was considered to be public property. The public setting of the street added the edge to Frogg's defamatory words and provided her with an audience and public jury.[61]

Thresholds also emerged time and time again during the suit, usually as the vantage point from which defamatory words were overheard, or the place at which people had become the target of verbal abuse.[62] From the safety of her own doorway, for example, Katherine Brotherhood had observed William and Anne Austin walking along the street whilst Mary Frogg, standing at her own gate, had shouted to the nearest passer-by to 'bid him stare and see a whore and a rogue come by together'.[63] On another occasion Brotherhood had witnessed a row between Mary Frogg and Anne Austin where each was standing at their own door.[64] Likewise, Elizabeth Harris,

> standing at the gate of [Mary Frogg's] howse being the signe of the Golden Dog ... observed ... William Austin to follow ... Mary Frogg comeing to her owne howse and heard him say ... thou arte a whore ... with an intention to defame.[65]

The combination of public speech and neighbourly scrutiny was a powerful one.

However, the street was not the only public place that featured in this series of depositions. Before long, St Saviour's Church was drawn into the dispute, although this should perhaps come as no surprise because the parish church was the centre of the neighbourhood, literally and figuratively. St Saviour's Church was within view of Austin and Frogg's houses and it played an important role in the suits, albeit erring more towards the symbolic, than the spiritual. Certainly, its function as a hub of spiritual education and sustenance for the parish was not being carried out effectively as 'for these seven or eight years last past ... there hath not ben a constant minister of the parish'.[66] The lack of a regular minister had led to some parishioners, like Katherine Brotherhood, complaining that they had not been able to receive the Holy Communion for some years. Regardless, the place of the church as an important symbol of hierarchy and community persisted. Services, however irregular, brought people of all social backgrounds together under one roof and made them feel part of a parish community. No wonder then that the parish church was often the setting for very public disputes, such as that which occurred between Susan Denew and Mary Frogg.

With the church at its centre, the parish was one of the many available frameworks inhabitants had to conceptualize the urban landscape around them. A potent symbolic division, parish boundaries were well known to inhabitants responsible for looking after their own interests, collecting taxes and providing for the poor. Each parish had its own civic and ecclesiastical jurisdiction within the city as a whole and had its own churchwardens, surveyor, overseers and constables.[67] Moreover, the parish was the focal point of local news, gossip and rumours. In 1608, for example, John Skott had described the wife of Mr Thull as 'with childe by an honest man of the parishe', an accusation to which Elizabeth Dynsdale responded by saying 'Ay marry that is by her husband is not he an honest man of the parishe?'[68] Likewise, in 1635, a couple were presented for 'the fame of incontinency' by their fellow parishioners of St Andrew's,[69] and five years on, in the parish of St Peter Mancroft, there was a common rumour and knowledge that Anne Inman was of 'lewd life ... and hath suffered her body to be knowne in scandalous adultery'.[70] Reputations were thus defined by local knowledge on a parish-to-parish basis and it was for this very reason that neighbours were the first port of call to provide information about an inhabitant's character at court. It was for this reason that William Kempe, for instance, was asked by the church court about neighbour Frances Gothan's reputation in 1682. Kempe had been able to undermine Gothan's reliability as a witness by stating that she 'is of noe credit or estimacion & soe is looked upon' by the parish and 'about 8 or 9 years ago questioned for feloniouslie taken away of some goods & ... hath heard was found guilty'.[71] Such was also the case for Thomas Browne who kept an alehouse that attracted 'Rogues, whores, vagabonds & beggars' and who was known locally in the parish as a man 'lately pressed for a seaman and afterwards ran away'.[72] Local knowledge could be long-lived and inescapable.

Certainly, the Frogg and Austin case study demonstrates how inhabitants constructed a personal frame of reference and thought about the world around them, viewing the city as a series of parishes in which they located themselves and others, despite the fact that other frames of reference were available. Wards, for instance, were civic jurisdictions that were never referred to colloquially in church court depositions. The linguistic convention of referring to a parish offers clues as to how people envisaged their world and defined, bounded and attached importance to certain places. Thus an individual's concept of their immediate environment was based on subjective visual and mental cues, symbolism, common experience and memory in a largely visual culture, over and above the available tools of reference like maps or street names.[73] More than this, the parish was an essential part of their identity as much as it was a way of locating people and events.

We see the importance of the parish at first hand in the limited geographical boundaries of the defamation suit between the Frogg and Austin families in St Saviour's parish. The events and defamatory words reported by their witnesses all took place in the parish itself, mostly in and around the streets adjacent to the church. Such corporeal boundaries were reinforced by the disinclination to accept strangers or marginal people into the closed world of the parish. In Norwich, the unusually high number of parishes (commented on by contemporary travellers such as Daniel Defoe and Celia Fiennes) may even have enhanced Norwich residents' responsiveness to this aspect of their environment, as they sought to lay claim to familiarity in the face of continual population movement and growth. Parishes, at the centre of inhabitants' lives, were an obvious, familiar and habitual framework from which to build individual and community identities.

It could be argued that the bias towards obvious parish identification in diocesan records was simply a product of the questions and responses requested during court proceedings; defamation suits were after all religious records, couched in a language which adhered to that particular frame of reference. However, on closer examination, this argument does not stand up. Witnesses were predominantly drawn from the same parish, or were connected to the area by familial networks, but this sense of self-identification with a particular parish occurred in secular records as well.[74] Indeed, it appears that ordinary people more often identified with religious, rather than civic divisions of city spaces. This association is perhaps not unsurprising. Parish boundaries had been established from time out of mind, and even the shake-ups of the Reformation had not unduly changed the basic layout of Norwich's parishes. By the seventeenth century, although the pre-Reformation Church would have been beyond the living memory of the city's inhabitants, many ritualistic traditions relating to its calendar persisted, such as Rogation, a practice habitualized within popular consciousness.

Settlement boundaries held a symbolic place in early modern mentalities, yet at no point were they impervious. Social networks stretched across county and city, often emulating the prior connections and networks of rural parishioners. This is particularly striking in the Frogg and Austin case, which reveals the extent of kinship and communication networks between rural parishes, and demonstrates how these relationships were later translated into the urban parish. Linking Cley-Next-The-Sea, Salthouse, Edgefield, Stratton Strawless, Lakenham and finally St Saviour's parish in Norwich, the suit illustrates the movement of people and information across a geographic frame. Rumours and reputations travelled across city and county by 'piggy-backing' on networks of transportation and communication. John Utting, to give another example, was a scandalous minister well-known for his open affairs with other men's wives and he was known in at least seven different parishes across south-east Norfolk, as was Thomas Wilding, who was 'generally accompted in this parish and other parishes where he is best knowne to be a fellowe which will sweare to anything' and was subsequently discredited as a witness in a defamation suit against John Broome and Susan Hills.[75] Pre-determined reputations were also a hurdle for newcomers to the city, such as the young, single Anna Horne, who 'came out of the country' supposedly after having 'had a little one', a rumour that city dweller Esther Warren promptly spread around Horne's new neighbourhood.[76] Moving to the city was not necessarily a guarantee of anonymity.

Conclusion: Women's Words, Agency and the Law

Words, voices and places surface clearly in the politics of St Saviour's parish. Public speech, even defamatory speech, offered some women power over others (including men), and the ability to alter the course of their neighbourhood's dynamics. In this case it was Mary Frogg, not her husband, who emerged as the most memorable personality in the series of depositions pertaining to the defamation suits between the Frogg and Austin families. It was Mary who was responsible for bribing the domestic servant, William Bell, and it was also she who had provided the case with continuing momentum, even when the tide of opinion had turned against her. Mary Frogg was a woman who knew how to use the legal system and with a little money behind her, she was able to bend it to her will. By deliberately appropriating moral and gender conventions to wage war against others, she demonstrated a contemporary awareness of these stereotypes. By acting in this aggressive manner, however, she proved that she herself did not live by the same gendered rules. Her case demonstrates how, in the everyday politics of the parish, social relationships were negotiated and contested on a variety of grounds, ones that included reputation, honour, status, belonging, power and strength of personality. Social mobility in both directions was a fact of life for everyone, but was most keenly felt below the level of the nobility. Thus negotiating and maintaining status was an essential part of securing one's place at a local level and achieving inclusion within a community. Indeed, it may be that for the rising middling sorts, struggling to assert their new place in society, honour was an especially contested issue however it might have been expressed.[77] However, place emerged as the means by which these negotiations were grounded, articulated and enforced. Thus this essay interprets parish social relations as not only reflecting notions of honour, morality or gender, but as broader expressions of what it meant to belong to a community and contemporary senses of urban space. In so doing, it reveals how contemporaries were able to harness abstract notions of place and use them to their best advantage.

10 'WITH A SWORD DRAWNE IN HER HANDE': DEFENDING THE BOUNDARIES OF HOUSEHOLD SPACE IN SEVENTEENTH-CENTURY WALES

Nicola Whyte

Introduction

Recent explorations of gender and household space have convincingly demonstrated that domestic space cannot easily be separated into feminine and masculine spheres. Research on masculinity and the political conceptualization of early modern households has highlighted the importance of dwellings as signifiers of identity for both men and women.[1] Protestant writers employed the male body as a metaphor for the house. Invasions of household space were analogous to an attack upon patriarchal order and dominance, and the honour and reputation of the husband and father. Just as the dwelling house informed and signified manliness, female honour and reputation was also bound up with cultural discourses concerning the moral worth of the household, nourished and sustained by the 'good housewife'.[2] Women, especially married women, assumed a significant role in demarcating and reinforcing the physical and conceptual boundaries of the home.[3] The expanding body of research in this field invites a more nuanced approach to understanding married relations based upon patterns of integration rather than separation. An assault on the material and moral worth of the household amounted to a violation of the reputation and authority of both husband and wife.[4]

Metaphors of household and dwelling in patriarchal discourse suggest stability, rootedness and a deep temporal attachment to place. But while late sixteenth- and seventeenth-century prescriptive literature drew upon a figurative language of spatial and temporal fixity, the power invoked in such imagery was achieved through the threat, real and imagined, of economic uncertainty, destitution and displacement.[5] For many families living in rural villages, dwelling was not a given but a hotly contested issue. The destruction of cottages built by poor migrants upon common land is a well-attested example of the politics of dwelling and the enforcement of the boundaries of inclusion and exclusion within local societies.[6] Such concerns were not merely a matter for the poor but middling and gentry families also. The right to occupy property, to enclose and cultivate the land was in no way foregone but was, to borrow Craig Muldrew's phrase, 'a process of continual achievement'.[7] For contemporaries, this achievement was not simply founded upon shrewd business transactions; it was deeply implicated in moral judgement and good reputation based upon thrift and creditworthiness. A time of grave economic uncertainty for many, a fine balance existed between self-sufficiency and a slide towards debt and impoverishment. Important insights have been made in capturing the meanings of honour, reputation, credit and worth in the construction of self-identity, and how these attributes and aspirations were judged and mediated though social relationships in early modern England.[8] Of interest here are the ways in which Welsh households expressed their identity and agency through, in particular, a material language of dwelling.

Within the disciplines of archaeology and anthropology material culture is viewed as having agency; objects, monuments, buildings and landscapes are given meaning through the actions of individuals and social groups.[9] Apotropaic objects provide a useful example of the ways material things are afforded power. For example, the interment of objects believed to ward off witchcraft at access points to the home, especially the hearth, an activity often attributed to the mis-tress of the household, suggests an important spatial and gendered dynamic to understanding the ways material culture came to manifest cultural values, beliefs and power.[10] Phenomenological approaches are also useful in realizing the potential insights studies of material culture and landscape can offer to our under-standing of agency and identity in the early modern past.[11] Following Bourdieu, phenomenological studies are concerned with bodily movement and embod-ied practices, and thus break down the distinction between mind and body.[12] In this essay, an appreciation of the landscape as embodied and performed not just during prescribed ritual events or during moments of popular protest and resistance, but in everyday contexts, is especially important. Movement through the landscape was part of the process of memory formation, evident for instance in the making and remaking of household and community knowledge of rights and jurisdictional boundaries.[13] Household identities were mediated by drawing upon commonly held meanings prompted by the material culture of dwelling, including buildings, fields and enclosures. Quotidian features such as these were nevertheless social constructs; they carried meanings derived from past actions, memories and experiences, while simultaneously looking towards the future.

The following discussion is concerned with the material contexts and spatial boundaries of the household, stretching beyond the doorstep and encompassing a physical and moral landscape beyond the dwelling house. In this an under-standing of landscape, embodied practices and materiality in the formation of household identities is central. The scope of recent writing has tended, however, to be circumscribed by restricted notions of what constituted household space in rural settlements in this period.[14] This is in part a consequence of the geographical setting of the majority of research which has been concerned with nucleated settlements and urban localities, especially London. Evidence of women working and gossiping with neighbours in their doorways and in the street, has highlighted female agency in negotiating and articulating personal, familial and neighbourhood identities, and has blurred the boundaries of public and private spaces.[15] In densely crowded urban centres the subdivision of tenements provoked tensions and conflict between neighbours over property divisions and boundary maintenance, and the physical, visual and imagined encroachment of living spaces.[16] The physical and conceptual boundaries between public and private were porous and open to neighbourhood scrutiny and inspection. Indeed, recent research has thrown light on contemporary notions of privacy and secrecy, which brings into question the historical validity of space as public and private.[17] Yet while this level of social proximity may shed light on the interactions of women living in densely nucleated settlements, with the exception of Amanda Flather's study of Essex, far less attention has been paid to elucidating the everyday experiences of women and men living in dispersed villages, hamlets and isolated farmsteads which characterized a large portion of England and Wales.[18] In rural villages houses generally stood alone or in small clusters, often environed by a network of enclosures, which made up the tenement.[19] In Wales, outside the strongly nucleated villages of Glamorgan and Pembrokeshire, settlements were characterized by varying levels of dispersal. Some historians have posited that in these sprawling and scattered settlements there may have been a tendency towards more separate social and spatial interaction, but this has yet to be fully investigated.[20]

This essay is an attempt to thread these ideas together by tracing the movements and experiences of women from the small-scale domestic arena of the household into the wider, external landscape of messuage and tenement. In so doing, it brings together two distinct strands of historical research and debate concerning contemporary meanings of enclosure, boundary breaking and household space. The perspective developed here differs from the majority of studies which tend to conceive both women's participation in preserving or attacking property, and the activity of boundary breaking as a form of protest, in overly narrow terms. Historians have long noted collective female action in large-scale riots and protests against the infringement and loss of customary rights.[21] But the extent to which boundary breaking occurred during other forms of protest has received relatively little attention. Given the vast number of litigation proceedings heard before the Quarter Sessions and central equity courts, featuring attacks upon property and in particular the physical borders of house and field, this is a remarkable omission.[22] As we shall see, rich insights can be gleaned from court records into the nature and meaning of boundary breaking employed during inter-household and neighbourhood disputes and, importantly, the complex demarcations of household space in upland settlements. Just as the conceptual boundaries of female honour might be expanded beyond sexual reputation to incorporate cultural discourses extolling the virtues of the diligent housewife, as Garthine Walker has argued, so the spatial parameters of honour and reputation might also be expanded for women living in rural settlements.[23]

The sources drawn upon are predominantly cases of forcible entry and disseisin heard before the court of Star Chamber during the reign of James I. A relatively common category of offence in England and Wales in the sixteenth and early seventeenth centuries, as revealed in the Quarter Session and Great Session records as well as equity courts, they have been surprisingly neglected by historians.[24] More usually considered the domain of historians of crime and disorder and approached from a different angle, cases of forcible entry can reveal the meanings contemporaries gave to household spaces and the physical and conceptual boundaries that shaped daily movements and social interactions. Of particular interest are the ways in which evidence from the law courts can be used to reveal contemporary notions of household space not as a distinct and separate locale but as a sequence of interconnecting spaces and boundaries presided over, maintained and at other times transgressed by both women and men. Whether criminal intent such as theft or the legitimate disseisin of property, the records reveal the prominence of women both in defending and, at other times, contravening the material and symbolic boundaries of their places of dwelling.[25] The following discussion commences with an exploration of the borders of dwelling houses before moving on to consider their broader landscape context. Both spatial scales are related through the physical and symbolic acts of boundary making and breaking. The final section explores the ways in which people interwove their personal and familial experiences of injury and injustice into a moral narrative of landscape and place, revealing contemporary anxieties about the continuing self-sufficiency and agency of the household unit.

Entrances

We begin with a case involving forcible entry on a messuage in St Woollos (Monmouthshire). Husbandman Roger Thomas told the court that he was in lawful possession as tenant of the tenement called Tir Pen y Lan, having paid his entry fine and a rent of ten pounds, and having lived there for three years. He recounted how in January he had left his family in the morning, accompanied by his neighbour Jenkin John Morris and his workman David Edmund, to 'helpe anie of his neighbors for the savinge of their cattle & people from being drowned in the late great overflowinge of the sea in those parts'.[26] He was absent from the premises all day, returning home 'aboute an houre before night ... thinking there to have founde his famely', instead Katherine Herbert came out of his house 'with a sword drawne in her hande' and prevented him from entering 'striking at [him] ... with the said sworde & saieing that [he] ... should not come into the said house'. His wife Margaret confirmed that Katherine had entered the messuage and lands 'and finding noe man within' succeeded in putting the family from the premises. Two hours later, and after Katherine had departed, Roger returned to search for his wife and children, finding them in a room at the lower end of the house and three of Katherine's retinue at the upper end, where his bedding and household goods were located. He told the court that he requested to be allowed access to his goods, and being refused, how he thrust open the door with just his hand 'by putting backe a barre of that dore'. According to Roger he talked with the complainant's accomplices and ate and drank with them, after which they apparently left of their own accord 'perceiving that there was a wronge done unto [him]'. Roger since learned of Katherine's intentions. At the last assizes held in March in Monmouthshire, Katherine had procured an injunction against him; his wife; William Rosser, his 12-year-old son; and John Rosser, another of his sons, an infant of eleven years, for forcible entry and forcible keeping of Tir Pen y Lan.[27]

The case is clearly interesting on a number of accounts. It demonstrates the contested nature of dwelling and the right and title to property, and shows how ordinary tenants became caught up in much larger and complex disputes between elite families over the right and title to property. Roger Thomas maintained that he was neither kin nor servant in wages nor retainer to his landlord Sir Edward Herbert. Roger and his family had been in occupation of the tenement for three years, which apparently counted for little in the complex web of inheritance rights and customs claimed by widows and male kin from wealthy landowning families.[28] Margaret's words to the court that Katherine succeeded in putting her family out of Tir Pen y Lan due to the absence of her husband, suggests both the everyday proximity of Roger (and his labourer David Edmund) as he worked on the tenement and perhaps opportunism on the part of Katherine, who took advantage of the knowledge that Roger was some distance away. Importantly, the case illustrates the role of women on both sides of the dispute and the fine line that was drawn between perpetrator and victim.[29] Katherine Herbert evidently considered her actions to be legitimate and necessary in reclaiming property that was rightfully hers. In occupying the threshold of the dwelling house, her conduct was at once a physical and symbolic transgression of household boundaries claimed by Roger Thomas and his family. The case also reveals the intersection between gender and class identities. Tenant and husbandman Roger Thomas's fervent appeal to the court combined nonviolence with restraint. His passivity contrasted with Katherine's alleged violence towards him and his family. In wielding a sword, Katherine employed the apparatus of power and status more usually preserved for men of her rank and status.[30] Unsurprisingly, a common theme of the court records concerns the abuses of power among elite landowning families, achieved through violence and intimidation and narrated by evoking the weakness of victims, a consequence of their age, gender, socio-economic status and also their material environment.

The dispute over Tir Pen y Lan encapsulates the ways in which physical sites of dwelling, epitomized in religious treatises and prescriptive literature as places of security, were also sites of conflict. Access points, entrances to tenements, thresholds, porches and doorsteps were all tightly regulated and guarded spaces. Entry into Mr Panton's dwelling in Henllan (Denbighshire) was barred to John Lloyd and his retinue, including his wife Anne, 'by goddes providence' and importantly 'by shutting the doores'.[31] To date, much discussion has focused on the malleability of domestic spaces and the inferred meaning of closed spaces, doors and windows, as indicating misconduct often of a sexual nature. In the rural settlements of Wales the closed door, barred and bolted, signified the sanctuary, security and strength of households. Both husbands and mistresses played important roles in controlling access to their homes.[32] Many dwellings were clearly well protected from violent attack by the robustness of building materials and strength of locks and bolts. Retreat behind closed and bolted doors was often a necessary course of action during altercations in the highway as people journeyed to church, as in the case from Henllan, or travelled on day-to-day social and economic business. Katherine verch Hugh, the 48-year-old wife of Sir Richard Brown, related to the court how she encountered the defendant in the high way where he 'railed her with filthy terms' and would not let her pass quietly. When her husband, who was in 'his garden', intervened and the altercation appeared to worsen, it was Katherine who apparently stepped in to diffuse the situation. Drawing her husband into the house she 'shutte the doore & soe lefte the defendant there alone'.[33] For wealthy families at least, the refuge and safety of the house was signified by shutting the door and, in this case, it was the mistress of the house who claimed and reinforced the threshold. Open or barred, entrances were important places of negotiation and carried strong cultural and legal meanings.[34] As a political unit the house, and in this case the garden, was gendered male. Yet women like Katherine asserted their responsibility and role in safeguarding the boundaries of their home.

The autonomy of women in protecting household goods and property is corroborated in the actions taken against constables and bailiffs in distraining goods or making arrests.[35] In one such case, concerning an attempt to arrest Mary David of Llanllawddog (Carmarthenshire) at the local mill, the bailiffs were met with adroit resistance. While Mary apparently yielded to the warrant for her arrest, she nevertheless insisted upon certain terms that were to be met before she would agree to be taken to the sheriff. She demanded that one of the bailiffs fetch her a horse, 'for that she wolde not travell on foote because she would not shew the defendant John David that pleasure'. She also persuaded them to accompany her home so 'that she might there putt on her better clothes'. According to the bailiffs, upon returning home Mary provided them with drink – a token of hospitality expected of a person of social means and status - but then 'shutt the dore' and 'so did rescue & keepe herself' from them.[36] Apparently the bailiffs attempted to forcibly enter the property in order to carry out their arrest. Having succeeded in breaking the latch of the outer door, their attempts were foiled by the strength of the inner door 'having gotten three powles or stakes & putt the ends thereof under the doore would have opened the same but could not & in seeking to open the same the said stakes broke'.[37] These words proffered by the bailiffs offer insight into the construction of feminine identity and, outside routine everyday activities, the importance of both apparel and mode of transport for a woman of high social standing. It also suggests the weaving together of a narrative based upon embodied experience and practice substantiated and embellished through the reimagining of the materiality of the building. The alleged breaking of the wooden poles, which presumably occurred when the bailiffs attempted to lift the door off its hinges, served to corroborate the self-determination of Mary David.

In other cases, however, the nature of building materials and construction, such as timber-framed wattle and daub and thatched dwellings, coupled with the determination and ingenuity of alleged rioters, ensured entry was gained.[38] John Bodvell of Gwydry Esq (Caernarvonshire), for example, told the court how rioters broke open 'a verie strong doore' into his messuage.[39] Assailants broke in through the doors, windows and walls of less substantial buildings. In a case from Yale (Denbighshire), the riotous assembly 'did breake and pull downe the rooffe and walles ... and did teare downe the doores and wyndowes and rafters' of Thomas Roger's house.[40] Harassment, intimidation and physical attacks upon property often occurred at night, when the household was together under one roof, and when doors were barred and bolted.[41] As others have shown, women were particularly vulnerable to attack and sexual assault when they were found at home alone.[42] The cases discussed here also suggest this vulnerability, but by no means were the circumstances gendered in a straightforward sense of men intimidating or assaulting women. Women's names frequently appear alongside men in lists of identified rioters. In Yale (Denbighshire), husbandman Thomas Rogers described how in January 1623 his daughter Elizabeth Rogers and two of his sisters, being alone in the house, were attacked and beaten by twelve named rioters including Margaret Harris and Jane the wife of John Kenricke.[43]

The prevention of families from accessing the main living quarters of their homes cut deep into their subsistence capacity and threatened their future livelihoods. In another case from Ysceifiog, not only were the family barred from accessing the living rooms of their house, they were also deprived of their household goods and provisions, while in the case of Tir Pen y Lan the offenders allegedly helped themselves to ale and food. Elsewhere in Dinley (Caernarvonshire), the court heard how the group of rioters forcibly entered the messuage belonging to John David ap Howell ap Lewis and in the possession of Humfrey ap Humfrey, his undertenant. They

> did beate punch and breake open the doores of the said messuage and house beinge locked and barred fast and then expulsed the said Humfrey Humffreys his familie and servants and contynued in breakinge the wales of the said house and enterringe into the chambers thereof.[44]

Complainants often reported the wilful breakage of household goods and the tearing and staining of clothes, bedding and furnishings. In one such case from Yale (Denbighshire), for example, the riotous assembly 'did breake and pull downe the rooffe and walles ... and did teare downe the doores and wyndowes and rafters' of the house. Upon entering the inner rooms, they tore open 'chestes, coffers and cubberds' and threw out the complainant's 'bedding and household stuffe into the streetes' and with the 'highe waies being in the tyme of a great snowe' most was lost and 'utterly spoyled with snow and wett weather'.[45]

The waste and spoil of household goods clearly caused consternation for the entire family. Yet the systematic defilement of moveable goods and chattels carried particular meaning for mistresses of the household. As Amy Erickson writes, for early modern people their wealth was founded not upon wages but from inheritance. Inheritance of 'a single cottage and garden, or even of a cow, a kettle, a brass pan and a bed' was as important as the inheritance of a landed estate.[46] For Welshwomen moveable goods – 'household chattels, livestock, clothing, ornaments and cash' – formed the greater part of their wealth.[47] Walker argues that women's identities were measured and defined in terms of material possessions, thus their defence of property was an act of material and symbolic self-definition.[48] In an in-depth study of Cheshire court records, Walker found that married women had a high profile in court cases concerning land and buildings.[49] Insight into the jurisdiction of women's interest and entitlements to the moveable goods of the household is further suggested in a case of marital breakdown from Flintshire. Edward Piers's wife Marie apparently 'had the household stuffe and corne that was within the house towards the mayntenance of her and her children'.[50] In view of the importance given to the construction of identity through the material possessions a woman brought to her marriage as part of her dower and inheritance, the alleged wilful consumption, defilement and damage of those goods struck at the core of her identity.

For both men and women their status and worth was bound up with the right and title to hold property and to farm the land. Not only were household goods allegedly ruined, but written records, deeds and leases were sought out by rioters. Secured within chests and cupboards, locks were broken and documents rifled through. In a case from Usk, intruders into the house of Maurice Davies gent, 'ransacked and rifled all the chests closetts and coffers ... and searched every corner of the said howse and did take away diverse evidences and writings'.[51] Widow Anne verch Richard described the forcible entry made by her son on her property and how with axes and hammers the company broke open chests and coffers and took deeds and evidence concerning the lands and tenement in which Ann claimed lawful estate.[52] One of the key recurring features of the cases heard before the court of Star Chamber is the way in which the external boundaries of dwelling related to the inner rooms and spaces of the household.

Boundary Breaking

For men and women living in rural villages setting up a household, securing a place of dwelling with land for pasture and tillage, appurtenances and common rights were social as well as economic aspirations. For middle ranking tenant and gentry households, their place, in both a material and social sense, was articulated through the material practices of dwelling in the landscape, the occupation and maintenance of houses, tenement, land for pasture and tillage, common resources and, increasingly in the seventeenth century, the right to sit in allocated seats or pews in church.[53] Houses need to be viewed not in isolation as separate entities but as a constituent element of a series of interconnected spaces. Thus for example, Oliver Curteys of Trevelyne told the court how he was lawfully seized in his demesne of one messuage with appurtenances and twenty acres of land, including arable, meadow, pasture and wood in Trevelyne, in a place called Carue y Thiffithe.[54] Networks of boundaries made up the external parameters of messuage and tenement, encompassing folds, closes and fields and stretching further beyond, following rights of way to common land, church and neighbouring houses and tenements. Biographical narratives related to the court offer an insight into the connectivity between dwelling, embodied experience and the outside world. Johanne ap Howell, a 69-year-old widow of Istradevoduck, for example, spoke about her identity as the legitimate holder of lands left to her by her husband 'as in her owne right' by recounting the journeys she made through the landscape. She described to the court how she travelled on foot to Landaff, about fourteen miles from her home in order to prove her husband's last will and testament. Two weeks later, on Easter Monday, she made another journey, this time of eight miles to Lantissent to be sworn tenant of the lands her husband had bequeathed to her for life.[55] Johanne interwove her experiences into a journey narrative of physical exertion and potential danger, which instilled a sense of place and belonging within a broader landscape of movement and practice.

Occasionally the court records reveal women's voices and conversation about property rights.[56]Anne verch Robert of Llangower, a 71-year-old spinster, recalled the origins of a dispute concerning the location and rents owed from Ffrith Comin. When dwelling with her uncle in Llangower parish some forty-eight or fifty years previously, Evan ap Humffrey, a tenant, fisherman and agent of Mr Vaughan of Gelyllyn, had visited their house on a Friday or Saturday evening to read to them. She remembered how afterwards they turned to the fire to take tobacco and it was then that Evan ap Humffrey informed her uncle that he had been ordered by Mr Vaughan to gather rent due from all commoners who grazed upon Ffrith Comin, including one particular place that her uncle was uncertain of its whereabouts. Her aunt reasoned 'that is impossible for you to knowe for a man may leadinge his horse along bite or cutt some of the grasse' to which Evan ap Humffrey replied 'that [it] is very true'.[57] Evidence that women conversed with their husbands and male neighbours about agrarian matters suggests a more integrated understanding of landscape beyond the boundaries of house and yard.

Just as women took part in large-scale collective protests against enclosure, by breaking down boundaries and physically occupying common land, in everyday contexts they played a prominent role in protecting the material boundaries and goods belonging to the household. Conversely, they also took part in destroying the boundaries maintained by other households. For example, in Yssa (Caernarvonshire) Richard Bulkley the elder brought a bill of complaint against John Owen, William Lloyd, Margaret verch John, Gwen verch Jeffrey and others, on behalf of his tenant Andrew ap Hughe and his wife Ann. It was reported that in the previous July of 1622, twelve rioters from Denbigh and Merioneth cut down and broke open the hedges and fences encompassing an arable close held by Andrew ap Hughe. With their feet and weapons, they 'did treade spoyle and distorye' the corn growing, which being high summer was 'near ripe'. Andrew and Ann were at home at the time and went together to confront the rioters, but were forced to turn back when the rioters threw stones at them.[58] In the reimagining of the riot, based upon an account given by his tenants, Bulkley drew upon commonly recognized motifs to define the rioters. Rioters were frequently envisaged as gathering at an alehouse, armed with weapons, marching in 'warlike manner' to their victim's tenement, throwing stones, assaulting family and servants and destroying the material substance of the household. Forcible entry was an orchestrated performance that drew upon tropes of ritualized violence common in the ways contemporaries thought about riot and disorderly behaviour more generally.[59]

The evidence reveals that women were active participants in committing forcible entry and were clearly not considered to be different from their male counterparts in executing attacks on the bodies, property and goods belonging to their victims.[60] In the records for Dinley (Caernarvonshire), out of the ten named rioters five were women, three of whom were identified as wives. While, as others have pointed out, women rarely acted alone in carrying out assaults, there are indicators that women, including Katherine Herbert, instigated the repossession of property. Similarly Jane, wife of William Walter yeoman, mobilized an attack upon property owned by Sara Fletcher. Together with Thomas Harrie and Alice his wife, David Poyer, George Waden and Elizabeth his wife, John Harries, Jennett Coale, Joan Younge, Margaret Phillips, Annas Witham and Richard Evans (yeoman), Jane was accused of breaking down hedges and forcibly entering and driving away cattle belonging to the tenants of Sara Fletcher.[61] In the evidence discussed here, both men and women cast stones as a means of physically occupying the external spaces of the tenement. Hurling missiles was a convenient and efficient means of ensuring the withdrawal of rivals behind closed doors, and thus the abandonment of exterior spaces, and was one of the many gestures and actions employed to intimidate victims. In his Bill of Complaint, John Hawkyne of Lancedell (Glamorganshire) yeoman, confirmed he was lawfully possessed of the messuage and tenement called the Wood held in the parish of Penmarke, containing forty-five acres held in several closes. On 20 July 1613 the defendants entered his premises and began cutting down timber trees growing close to his house. When he and others from his household, including his sister Anne Hawkins, went to ascertain their reason for so doing, the rioters threw stones at them, one hitting him which 'sore breake his head'; as a result they were forced to turn back.[62] Similarly there are instances of assailants using firearms to prevent families re-entering their property. Thomas ap Thomas, his wife and family were prevented from approaching their house, being forced to remain out of the reach of the shots fired by rioters.[63]

Levelling field boundaries by pulling down hedges and walls and filling in ditches, followed by the trampling, grazing and flattening of crops, the chasing and wounding of livestock, and physical assault upon the bodies of victims, were all highly charged acts of intimidation accompanying forcible entry, detainer and disseisin. Attacks upon servants, for example, or animals (dogs, horses, livestock) were carried out as a substitute for their masters and mistresses. Of particular interest here is how the attacks upon the exterior landscape were viewed in relation to the dwelling. Assaults upon physical boundaries and household commodities, including livestock and corn growing in the fields, often culminated in attacks upon the dwelling house itself. Evidently the aim of the rioters was to deface, level and appropriate the network of boundaries and spaces constituting messuage and tenement. In another example, Oliver Curteys told the court how in the month of May rioters moved across his land destroying field boundaries and crops, and when they reached his dwelling house assaulted and battered his doors.[64] Levelling boundaries was at once a material and symbolic act of opposition against the right and title to the produce of the soil, and not necessarily the reversion of the legal status of common land. The behaviour of those involved gained momentum as the perpetrators crossed the landscape, moving from exterior to interior spaces, and traversing the material and symbolic borders of household space.

A Moral Landscape

When taken together, the evidence displays common elements in the way forcible entry was performed and its impact upon the subsistence capacity of the household unit. Violence, real or imagined, was meted out upon a sequence of related boundaries, connecting field, house, locked cupboards and chests, and the physical bodies of the victims. In this the victims of forcible entry constructed morally charged narratives about themselves, and the social order of the society in which they lived.[65] Alexandra Shepard has shown how violence, especially male violence, was an accepted means of reinforcing moral boundaries and was sanctioned by law.[66] Violence was part of a repertoire of actions, gestures and language used by men in order to maintain hierarchy and reputation; yet a fine line was drawn between acceptable violence and the violation of social norms. Shepard reveals the relationship between violence, territorial authority and masculinity: 'male honour was closely bound up with such assertions of territorial authority and dominance; violence was as intrinsic to the policing of territorial boundaries as it was central to maintaining social hierarchies'.[67] It is well attested how marriage, setting up home and family were compelling achievements for men in this period. Patriarchal space and meanings of manhood extended from the borders of the home into the exterior landscape where ideals of good husbandry, improvement and enclosure were physically enacted.[68] Yet, as we have seen, the regulation of territory was not an exclusively male prerogative.[69] As widows and mistresses of households, women stood alongside their husbands, male kin and servants in asserting territorial authority.

In order to offset and perhaps exaggerate the alleged violent excesses of the perpetrators, complainants frequently drew upon an idealized vision of the household as a harmonious and stable unit. In Usk Maurice Davies, high constable of the hundred of Usk, described how, on 31 August 1608, he, together with his family, and John and William Richard, was sat in his messauge or tenement, at ten or eleven o'clock at night, all in a peaceable and harmless manner. The court heard how the rioters arrived with 'great polls, loggs of wood, yron barrs' which they used to 'thrust and burst asonder the outter doores' of his dwelling 'being then stronglie barred and fast locked and did breake and enter into all the inner roomes'.[70] Elsewhere a disagreement over the payment of tithes culminated in an attack on the house of Morgan Bleythyn, parson of St Fagan's (Glamorgan). Bleythen related to the court how he was awakened about midnight by the defendant, who beat and broke down the doors, walls and windows of the parsonage house, while he and his servants were taking their 'quiet rest' in their beds.[71] Quietness within family and neighbourhood conveyed important moral messages about the well-ordered household and society.[72]

Narratives of complaint thus reveal insights into the passivity and suggested non-agency of victims, and were employed to signify the social and moral reputation of the household. Some men were certainly careful to indicate to the court their nonviolence and diplomacy, and reluctance to inflame already highly volatile situations. Humfrey ap Humfrey of Dinley, for example, appears to have genuinely feared for his life and played down his role in the dispute, leaving his wife to act as intermediary. As discussed earlier, Humfrey's family and household were driven from their tenement and were forced to leave behind all their household goods, including livestock and the corn ricks standing by the dwelling house. Humfrey downplayed any intervention on his part, describing how he was in 'bodily feare' of the rioters and how he 'durst not come' to the house. However, he had yet to thresh his corn which was needed for his and his family's sustenance over the winter months. Not venturing to retrieve the corn himself nor wanting to send any of his servants, he asked Humffrey Gruffith to go with his wife Grace who was 'to see the same performed and done accordinglie'. Both were prevented from reaching the premises by rioters who, 'soddenlie rising out of secret places where they then before hid themselves', did 'sett upon beate wound and dangerouslie hurt yor subiects said wief and the said Humffrey'.[73] Perhaps Grace was perceived to be a less provocative presence than her husband. Nonetheless, the case demonstrates that women had a defined and significant role in delimiting the physical and moral boundaries of the household. When presented to the court the narrative construction of the bill drew upon the mutual needs of the diligent and respectable family and household faced with impoverishment.

While the exercise of power was gendered, the extent and nature of that power was modified and shaped by a number of other influential factors, including age, physical strength, rank and status, which were frequently drawn upon by complainants. Elite women were sometimes perceived as provoking and orchestrating property disputes.[74] Randle Hammer of Braden (Flintshire) gentleman, described himself as 'beinge nowe growne verie aged neare threescore and ten yeares old and verie poore haveinge a wief and manie children', in contrast to Dame Marie Cholmondley, who was in his opinion 'a woman of great power and wealth and of highe and willfull speritt'.[75] Knowing that he had a 'good' lease, the validity of which she would never question before the law, he accused her of seeking to oppress him 'with daily disturbances' and by that means to draw him into trouble and suits.[76] Elsewhere, Morgan ap Howell, yeoman from Aberedw (Radnorshire), described the defendant Sara Baskervill as

a woeman of a haughtie and turbulent spiritt and presuming ever much upon her title
wealth and frindes And desirors to raise dissention and differnces not only betweene
her selfe and her neighboures but alsoe betweene other neighboures one with an other.

In other cases, alliances between women and men were deemed to be a formida-
ble force.[77] Among the allegations of deception and covetousness in obtaining a
lease of the manor or township of Dolbenmaen (Caernarvonshire), deponents
judged the defendant Eleanor Williams to have been manipulative and uncom-
promising, and the cause of friction between her late husband and tenants.
Regarding the couple's 'breach of trust', John ap Richard, yeoman of forty-six
years, commented that 'allwaies when there was any speeches betweene her said
husband and the tenants he [the defendant's late husband] would never yeld
answere to any thing without her privity and assent'. According to the plaintiffs, in her widowhood Eleanor Williams remained determined to displace the
ancient tenants by exacting excessive rents and fines they could ill afford.[78]

Conclusion

Recent writing on early modern households has emphasized the organization of interior spaces and the authority of women as mistresses in controlling
boundaries, rooms, cupboards and keys, yet also their vulnerability to physical
and sexual attack. In contrast, this study has explored the material and conceptual boundaries of households situated in their broader landscape contexts. It
has been argued that contemporary understandings of dwelling related not just
to the physical structure of the house but to the dwelling as part of a series of
interlinked and meaningful spaces. Household identities were mediated and
contested through the preservation, or deliberate defacement, of material culture and property, whether enclosures, land, moveable goods including crops
and livestock, as well as household goods. In the conflict over the right and title
to dwell in the landscape, women were both agents and victims of forcible entry
and disseisin. The perspective developed here differs from the majority of studies
which tend to conceive both women's participation in attacking property, and
the activity of enclosure breaking as a form of protest, in overly narrow terms.
In this chapter, enclosure breaking has been viewed as relational. Breaking the
boundaries of house, field, locked chests and cupboards where written deeds
and records were kept, as well as assaulting the bodies of victims, were deeply
meaningful precisely because of the materiality and symbolism of such actions.
From this perspective we gain an insight into the ways complainants experienced
and imagined the exercise of power. Threats of impoverishment and dislocation,
physically enacted through the destruction of property, had a potentially desta-
bilizing impact upon the material and spatial agency of the victim's household.
By incapacitating servants and disabling oxen the land went untilled, by tram-

pling and destroying crops, maiming and slaughtering livestock, and preventing families from retrieving their household goods, including provisions such as grain and ale, the self-sufficiency of the household was seriously undermined. Perpetrators were envisaged as powerful, yet immoral agents, whose actions were fostered by cultural values and practices abhorrent to the diligent tenant farmer and landowner. The court records offer by design extreme accounts of violence and suffering and, as others have emphasized, were embellished and contrived in order to strengthen the complainant's charge.[79] Nonetheless, they are revealing of patterns of everyday intimidation and power between households. While descriptions of passivity, indeed the non-agency of victims, were undoubtedly employed to provoke an empathetic response from the court, the binary construction of power relations suggests the articulation of heightened concerns and anxieties among contemporaries, revealing the spectre of dispossession and poverty. The repercussions, real and imagined, of forcible entry and attacks upon the boundaries and goods belonging to the household shed light on the contested nature of dwelling in the Welsh landscape at the turn of the seventeenth century.

APPENDIX

Petition of Humfrey Bawde and Johanne his wife v.
SHERIFFS OF LONDON (*c.* 1480)

To the right reuerent ffader in god the Archebishop of York and Chaunceller of England

Mekely besecheth your gracious lordship Humfrey Bawde and Johanne his wife that where one
Maude Olyff late perteyned and understond that the said Humfrey was in servyce with one Thomas
Hart Baker and residaunt with the same Thomas Baker in Smythfield of London. And also the same
Mawde Olyff havyng speciall acqueyntaunce of the forsaid Johanne wyf of your said besecher and
5   knowyng that the same Johanne was dwellyng in a howse a lone in the parissh of Seynt Gyles
withoute Cryppylgate labored sotilly to the seid Johanne seyng that ther was a man the which
ought to hir hertly luf and gladly wold be with her acqueynted to the which the same Johanne
answered seyng that she were loth to have any such acqueyntaunce by the which she in any wyse
myght be hurt of hur good name. And aftur the said Mawde Olyff of hir false lvyng and unclenly
10 disposicoun intendid to ayd the said man to have his fowll lust and will of the said Johanne, brow-
ght the same man into the howse of your said besecher Where as the said Johanne was dwellyng
and there the same Mawde Olyf caused the same man to ly down upon a benche unknow-
yng to the said Johanne for asmoche as the same Johanne was at that tyme wyrkyng within a
nother lytell howse and when the said Johanne had done her besenes she came into her utter
15 howse and there she founde the said man lying upon the benche. And the same man sodenly start
hym up and touke the said Johanne in his armys seyng that he wold have a doo with here or ellis
he wold dye for it. And the same Johanne strougguld sore with hym and by the help and grace of our
lady that blessed virgyn brake fro hym a clene woman not defylid. And the same Johane touke a
staf and there gaf to the seid man a dosen strypys and drove hym oute of her husbondes howse. And
20 after whan the same Johanne met next with the forsaid Maude Olyf she gaf to the same Maude a
knappe upon the cheik warnyng her that she fro that tyme forth never bryngg into the howse of
the same Johanne any man of such condicioun as the forsaid man was. And nowe it is so gracious
lord that the said Maude Olyff hath affermyd a playnt of trespas ayenst your said besecher and his
wyf and have declared and surmysed that the said Johanne wif of your besecher certen day yere and
25 parissh with a staf bet the same Maude Olyf to her damage xx. li. and howe be it that the said
Johanne your oratrice had soo greet occasion giffyn to her as is before declared yet the comen lawe
will not ayde hir to iustifie the betyng of the forsaid Maude. Wherfore withoute your gracious
ayde be to her shewed with the premysses she shalbe condempned and utterly undoon. Therefore
that it may please your good grace to graunte a *certiorari* to be direct to the Shireffes of London
30 commaundyng them to certefie the cause into the kynges chauncery there to be examined according to
conscience.

Source: TNA, C1/32/337 (contractions have been silently expanded where
needed).

NOTES

Kane with Williamson, 'Introduction'

1. The editors are grateful to the anonymous readers of the initial proposal for their insightful comments on developing the themes of this collection, and latterly to Dr Cordelia Beattie and Dr Simon Sandall for reading and commenting on an earlier version of this chapter.

2. S. H. Rigby, *English Society in the Later Middle Ages: Class, Status and Gender* (Basingstoke: Macmillan Press, 1995); M. K. McIntosh, *Controlling Misbehaviour in England, 1370–1600* (Cambridge: Cambridge University Press, 2002); J. M. Bennett, *Ale, Beer, and Brewsters in England: Women's Work in a Changing World, 1300 to 1600* (Oxford: Oxford University Press, 1996); J. M. Bennett, *Women in the Medieval English Countryside: Gender and Household in Brigstock before the Plague* (Oxford: Oxford University Press, 1987); see also several important articles: J. M. Bennett, 'Writing Fornication: Medieval Leyrwite and its Historians', *Transactions of the Royal Historical Society 6th series*, 13 (2003), pp. 131–62; J. M. Bennett, 'Compulsory Service in Late Medieval England', *Past and Present*, 209 (2010), pp. 7–51.

3. K. Wrightson, 'The Politics of the Parish in Early Modern England', in P. Griffiths, A. Fox and S. Hindle (eds), *The Experience of Authority in Early Modern England* (Basingstoke: Palgrave Macmillan, 1996), pp. 10–46, on p. 10.

4. J. C. Scott, *Weapons of the Weak: Everyday Forms of Peasant Resistance* (New Haven, CT: Yale University Press, 1985); A. Gramsci, *Selections from the Prison Notebooks* (New York: International Publishers, 1971). Their work has influenced, for example: Griffiths, Fox and Hindle (eds), *The Experience of Authority*; M. J. Braddick and J. Walter (eds), *Negotiating Power in Early Modern Society: Order, Hierarchy and Subordination in Britain and Ireland* (Cambridge: Cambridge University Press, 2001).

5. A. Shepard and G. Walker, 'Gender, Change and Periodisation', in Shepard and Walker (eds), *Gender and Change: Agency, Chronology and Periodisation* (Chichester: Wiley-Blackwell, 2009), pp. 1–12, on pp. 6–7.

6. Ibid., p. 5.

7. A. Montenach and D. Simonton, 'Introduction', in D. Simonton and A. Montenach (eds), *Female Agency in the Urban Economy: Gender in European Towns, 1640–1830* (New York and London: Routledge, 2013), p. 4.

8. W. Johnson, 'On Agency', *Journal of Social History*, 37:1 (2003), p. 117.

9. K. Canning, *Gender History in Practice: Historical Perspectives on Bodies, Class, and Citizenship* (Ithaca, NY, and London: Cornell University Press, 2006), p. 77.

10. For a groundbreaking and seminal piece on gender in history, see J. W. Scott, 'Gender: A Useful Category of Historical Analysis', *American Historical Review*, 91:5 (1986), pp. 1053–75; for an expansion and further discussion of these arguments, see also J. W. Scott, *Gender and the Politics of History* (New York: Columbia University Press, 1988).

11. J. M. Bennett, E. A. Clark, J. F O'Barr and B. A. Villen (eds), *Sisters and Workers in the Middle Ages* (Chicago, IL: University of Chicago Press, 1989), p. 6.

12. P. J. P. Goldberg, 'Marriage, Migration, Servanthood and Lifecycle in Yorkshire Towns of the Later Middle Ages: Some York Cause Paper Evidence', *Continuity and Change*, 1 (1986), pp. 141–69.

13. B. A. Hanawalt, *The Ties that Bound: Peasant Families in Medieval England* (Oxford: Oxford University Press, 1986); B. A. Hanawalt, *The Wealth of Wives: Women, Law, and Economy in Late Medieval London* (Oxford: Oxford University Press, 2007).

14. L. Gowing, *Domestic Dangers: Women, Words, and Sex in Early Modern London* (Oxford: Oxford University Press, 1998); L. Gowing, *Common Bodies: Women, Touch and Power in Seventeenth-Century England* (New Haven, CT, and London: Yale University Press, 2003); S. Kingsley Kent, *Gender and Power in Britain, 1640–1990* (London and New York: Routledge, 1999); G. Walker, 'Expanding the Boundaries of Female Honour in Early Modern England', *Transactions of the Royal Historical Society*, 6:6 (1996), pp. 235–45; G. Walker, *Crime, Gender and Social Order in Early Modern England* (Cambridge: Cambridge University Press, 2003); see also works including B. Capp, *When Gossips Meet: Women, Family and Neighbourhood in Early Modern England* (Oxford: Oxford University Press, 2003). R. Houlbrooke, 'Women's Social Life and Common Action in England from the Fifteenth Century to the Eve of the Civil War', *Continuity and Change*, 1:2 (1986), pp. 171–89.

15. P. Anagol, 'Agency, Periodisation and Change in the Gender and Women's History of Colonial India', *Gender & History*, 20:3 (2008), pp. 603–27.

16. J. M. Bennett, 'Confronting Continuity', *Journal of Women's History*, 9:3 (1997), pp. 73–94, on p. 74. See also the classic essay by J. Kelly-Gadol, 'Did Women have a Renaissance?', in R. Bridenthal and C. Koonz (eds), *Becoming Visible: Women in European History* (Boston, MA: Houghton Mifflin, 1997), pp. 137–64.

17. C. Barron, 'The "Golden Age of Women" in Late Medieval London', *Reading Medieval Studies*, 15 (1989), pp. 35–58; S. H. Rigby, 'Gendering the Black Death: Women in Later Medieval England', *Gender & History*, 12:3 (2000), pp. 745–54; Bennett, 'Compulsory Service in Late Medieval England'.

18. M. F. Stevens, 'London Women, the Courts and the "Golden Age": A Quantitative Analysis of Female Litigants in the Fourteenth and Fifteenth Centuries', *London Journal*, 37:2 (2012), pp. 67–88, on p. 70.

19. For an overview of the debate, see A. Vickery, 'Golden Age to Separate Spheres? A Review of the Categories and Chronology of English Women's History', *Historical Journal*, 36 (1993), pp. 383–414. See also A. L. Erickson, *Women and Property in Early Modern England* (New York and London: Routledge, 1993).

20. Shepard and Walker (eds), *Gender and Change*.

21. J. Kermode and G. Walker, 'Introduction', in Kermode and Walker (eds), *Women, Crime and the Courts in Early Modern England* (New York and London: Routledge, 1994), pp. 1–22.

22. L. Roper, *Oedipus and the Devil: Witchcraft, Religion and Sexuality in Early Modern Europe* (New York: Routledge, 1994).

23. J. H. Arnold, *Inquisition and Power: Catharism and the Confessing Subject in Medieval Languedoc* (Philadelphia, PA: University of Pennsylvania Press, 2001).

24. Walker, *Crime, Gender and Social Order*. For a medieval perspective on women and crime, see K. Jones, *Gender and Petty Crime in Late Medieval England: The Local Courts in Kent, 1460–1560* (Woodbridge: The Boydell Press, 2006).

25. Gowing, *Common Bodies*, pp. 12–13.

26. P. J. P. Goldberg, 'Masters and Men in Later Medieval England', in D. M. Hadley (ed.), *Masculinity in Medieval Europe* (New York and London: Longman, 1999), pp. 55–70. S. M. Butler, *The Language of Abuse: Marital Violence in Later Medieval England* (Leiden: Brill, 2007); D. G. Neal, *The Masculine Self in Late Medieval England* (Chicago, IL: University of Chicago Press, 2008).

27. F. E. Dolan, *Marriage and Violence: The Early Modern Legacy* (Philadelphia, PA: University of Pennsylvania Press, 2008).

28. M. Gaskill, 'Witchcraft, Emotion and the Imagination in the English Civil War', in J. Newton and J. Bath (eds), *Witchcraft and the Act of 1604* (Leiden: Brill, 2008), pp. 160–79; Walker, *Crime, Gender and Social Order*, pp. 24, 27, 60, 87.

29. Ibid.

30. N. J. Menuge (ed.), *Medieval Women and the Law* (Woodbridge: The Boydell Press, 2000).

31. Erickson, *Women and Property*; T. Stretton, *Women Waging Law in Elizabethan England* (Cambridge: Cambridge University Press, 1998); Menuge (ed.), *Medieval Women and the Law*; C. Beattie and M. F. Stevens (eds), *Married Women and the Law in Pre-modern Northwest Europe* (Woodbridge: The Boydell Press, 2013).

32. M. Howell, 'The Gender of Europe's Commercial Economy, 1200–1700', in A. Shepard and G. Walker (eds), Gender, Change and Periodisation, *Gender & History*, 20:3 (2008), pp. 83–108, on p. 89.

33. Ibid., p. 89.

34. C. Beattie and M. F. Stevens, 'Introduction', in Beattie and Stevens (eds), *Married Women and the Law*, pp. 7–8. Bronach Kane is very grateful to the editors of this collection for providing her with a copy of this volume prior to its publication.

35. F. Pollock and F. W. Maitland, *The History of English Law before the Time of Edward I*, 2 vols (Cambridge, 1911), pp. 405–6; for a recent discussion on Sir William Blackstone's *Commentaries on the Laws of England* (1765), see Beattie and Stevens, 'Introduction', pp. 2–3. Bronach Kane is grateful to Dr Cordelia Beattie for drawing her attention to this point.

36. J. Bailey, 'Favoured or Oppressed? Married Women, Property and "Coverture" in England, 1660–1800', *Continuity and Change*, 17:3 (2002), pp. 351–72, on pp. 351–2.

37. J. Bailey, *Unquiet Lives: Marriage and Marriage Breakdown in England, 1660–1800* (Cambridge: Cambridge University Press, 2003), p. 70.

38. Bailey, 'Favoured or Oppressed?', pp. 363–5; Erickson, *Women and Property*, p. 150.

39. Ibid.

40. A. Shepard, 'Manhood, Credit and Patriarchy in Early Modern England, c. 1580–1640', *Past & Present*, 167 (2000), pp. 75–106, on p. 92.

41. M. Müller, 'Peasant Women, Agency and Status in Mid-Thirteenth- to Later Fourteenth-Century England: Some Reconsiderations', in Beattie and Stevens (eds), *Married Women and the Law*, pp. 91–113, on p. 108.

42. C. Briggs, 'Empowered or Marginalized? Rural Women and Credit in Later Thirteenth- and Fourteenth-Century England', *Continuity and Change*, 19:1 (2004), pp. 13–43,

on p. 37. See also the comprehensive, cross-period study by W. C. Jordan, *Women and Credit in Pre-industrial and Developing Societies* (Philadelphia, PA: University of Pennsylvania Press, 1993).

43. Erickson, *Women and Property,* pp. 5–6.
44. E. Hawkes, "'She will ... Protect and Defend her Rights Boldly by Law and Reason...'": Women's Knowledge of Common Law and Equity Courts in Late-Medieval England', in Menuge (ed.), *Medieval Women and the Law,* pp. 145–61, on p. 150.
45. M. F. Stevens, 'London's Married Women, Debt Litigation and Coverture in the Court of Common Pleas', in Beattie and Stevens (eds), *Married Women and the Law,* pp. 115–31, on p. 125; see also Hawkes, "'She will ... Protect'", p. 147.
46. Erickson, *Women and Property,* pp. 32–3.
47. N. Z. Davis, *Fiction in the Archives: Pardon Tales and Their Tellers in Sixteenth-Century France* (Stanford, CA: Stanford University Press, 1987).
48. M. Goodich, *Voices from the Bench: The Narratives of Lesser Folk in Medieval Trials* (New York: Palgrave Macmillan, 2006).
49. J. Arnold, 'The Historian as Inquisitor: The Ethics of Interrogating Subaltern Voices', *Rethinking History,* 2:3 (1998), pp. 379–86, on p. 380.
50. Arnold, *Inquisition and Power.*
51. M. Gaskill, 'Witchcraft and Power in Early Modern England: The Case of Margaret More', in Kermode and Walker (eds), *Women, Crime and the Courts,* pp. 125–45, on p. 130.
52. Ibid., pp. 134–37.
53. Arnold, *Inquisition and Power,* p. 109.
54. Ibid.
55. Walker, *Crime, Gender and Social Order,* p. 8.
56. Arnold, *Inquisition and Power,* p. 12.
57. Ibid., p. 153; Stretton, *Women Waging Law,* pp. 25–7.
58. Ibid., p. 26.
59. J. Bedell, 'Memory and Proof of Age in England, 1272–1327', *Past and Present,* 162:1(1999), pp. 3–27; J. T. Rosenthal, *Telling Tales: Sources and Narration in Late Medieval England* (University Park, PA: Pennsylvania State University Press, 2003); A. Wood, 'The Place of Custom in Plebeian Political Culture: England, 1550–1800', *Social History,* 22:1 (1997), pp. 46–60.
60. M. Holford, "'Testimony (to Some Extent Fictitious)": Proofs of Ages in the First Half of the Fifteenth Century', *Historical Research,* 82:218 (2009), pp. 635–54. See also the recent edited collection, M. Hicks (ed.), *The Fifteenth-Century Inquisitions Post Mortem: A Companion* (Woodbridge: The Boydell Press, 2012). A number of works by B. R. Lee are useful in this context, see B. R. Lee, 'Men's Recollections of a Women's Rite: Medieval English Men's Recollections Regarding the Rite of Purification of Women After Childbirth', *Gender & History,* 14:2 (2002), pp. 224–41; B. R. Lee, 'A Company of Men and Women: Men's Recollections of Childbirth in Medieval England', *Journal of Family History,* 27:2 (2002), pp. 92–100.
61. Kermode and Walker, 'Introduction', pp. 4–5.
62. Hawkes, "'She will ... Protect'", pp. 157–60.
63. J. Bailey, 'Voices in Court: Lawyers' or Litigants'?', *Historical Research,* 74:186 (2001), pp. 392–408, on p. 408.
64. G. Williams, *Renewal and Reformation: Wales, c. 1415–1642* (Oxford: Oxford University Press, 1987, reprinted 2002), pp. 37–8. For an important volume of essays on

women in Wales in this period, see M. Roberts and S. Clarke (eds), *Women and Gender in Early Modern Wales* (Cardiff: University of Wales Press, 2000). See particularly M. Roberts, 'Introduction', and L. Beverley Smith, 'Towards a History of Women in Late Medieval Wales', in this collection.

65. J. M. Bennett, 'Public Power and Authority in the Medieval English Countryside', in M. C. Erler and M. Kowaleski (eds), *Women and Power in the Middle Ages* (Athens, GA: University of Georgia Press, 1998), pp. 18–36, on p. 23.

66. J. Loengard, '*Rationabilis dos*: Magna Carta and the Women's "Fair Share" in the Earlier Thirteenth Century', in S. S. Walker (ed.), *Wife and Widow in Medieval England* (Ann Arbor, MI: University of Michigan Press, 1993), pp. 59–80.

67. J. T. Rosenthal, 'Fifteenth-Century Widows and Widowhood: Bereavement, Reintegration and Life Choices', in Walker (ed.), *Wife and Widow*, pp. 33–58, on p. 48.

68. P. R. Schofield, 'The Late Medieval View of Frankpledge and the Tithing System: An Essex Case Study', in Z. Razi and R. M. Smith (eds), *Medieval Society and the Manor Court* (Oxford: Oxford University Press, 1996), pp. 408–49.

69. S. Bardsley, *Venomous Tongues: Speech and Gender in Late Medieval England* (Philadelphia, PA: University of Pennsylvania Press, 2006), p. 76; see also M. Müller, 'Social Control and the Hue and Cry in Two Fourteenth-Century Villages', *Journal of Medieval History*, 31 (2005), pp. 29–53.

70. D. Underdown, 'The Taming of the Scold: The Enforcement of Patriarchal Authority in Early Modern England', in A. Fletcher and J. Stevenson (eds), *Order and Disorder in Early Modern England* (Cambridge, 1985), pp. 116–36, on p. 119.

71. M. Ingram, '"Scolding Women Cucked or Washed": A Crisis in Gender Relations in Early Modern England?', in Kermode and Walker (eds), *Women, Crime and the Courts*, pp. 48–80, on p. 57.

72. L. Gowing, 'Language, Power and the Law: Women's Slander Litigation in Early Modern London', in Kermode and Walker (eds), *Women, Crime and the Courts*, pp. 26–47, on p. 43.

73. Ingram, '"Scolding Women"', p. 49.

74. Walker, 'Expanding the Boundaries', p. 236.

75. Ibid.

76. Wrightson, 'The Politics of the Parish', pp. 12–37, however p. 12 for his initial statement.

77. This is particularly the case for women's experiences of local custom, state governance and authority in manorial and parish contexts. See, however, N. Whyte, 'Custodians of Memory: Women and Custom in Rural England c. 1550–1700', *Cultural and Social History*, 8:2 (2011), pp. 153–73; T. Stretton, 'Women, Custom and Equity in the Court of Requests', in Kermode and Walker (eds), *Women, Crime and the Courts*, pp. 170–89.

78. For various aspects of orthodoxy and nonconformity, see P. Lake and M. C. Questier (eds), *Conformity and Orthodoxy in the English Church, c. 1560–1660* (Woodbridge: The Boydell Press, 2000).

79. See also F. Molekamp, *Women and the Bible in Early Modern England: Religious Reading and Writing* (Oxford: Oxford University Press, 2013), pp. 67–9.

80. S. Brown (ed.), *Women, Gender and Radical Religion in Early Modern Europe* (Leiden and Boston, MA: Brill, 2007).

81. C. Hughes Dayton, 'Rethinking Agency, Recovering Voices', *American Historical Review*, 109:3 (2004), pp. 827–43, on p. 836.

82. A. Flather, *Gender and Space in Early Modern England* (Woodbridge: The Boydell Press, 2007), pp. 5–6.

83. Vickery, 'Golden Age to Separate Spheres?'

84. Flather, *Gender and Space*; M. McKeon, *The Secret History of Domesticity: Public, Private, and the Division of Knowledge* (Baltimore, MD: The Johns Hopkins University Press, 2005); R. Kingston, 'Mind Over Matter? History and the Spatial Turn', *Cultural and Social History*, 7:1 (2010), pp. 111–21.

85. S. McSheffrey, *Marriage, Sex, and Civic Culture in Late Medieval London* (Philadelphia, PA: University of Pennsylvania Press, 2006); Flather, *Gender and Space*.

86. K. L. French, *The Good Women of the Parish: Gender and Religion After the Black Death* (Philadelphia, PA: University of Pennsylvania Press, 2008), p. 36.

87. Ibid., p. 48.

88. S. Hindle, 'A Sense of Place? Becoming and Belonging in the Rural Parish, 1550–1650', in A. Shepard and P. Withington (eds), *Communities in Early-Modern England* (Manchester: Manchester University Press, 2000), pp. 96–114, on p. 109.

89. Gowing, *Domestic Dangers*.

90. Goldberg, 'Masters and Men', pp. 56–70.

91. B. Capp, 'Separate Domains? Women and Authority in Early Modern England', in Griffiths, Fox and Hindle (eds), *The Experience of Authority*, pp. 117–45; K. Wrightson, *Earthly Necessities: Economic Lives in Early Modern Britain* (New Haven, CT: Yale University Press, 2000), p. 42; see also Flather, *Gender and Space*, p. 4.

92. Goldberg, 'Masters and Men', p. 58.

93. Walker, 'Expanding the Boundaries', p. 245.

94. Wood, 'The Place of Custom in Plebeian Political Culture'. See also Wrightson, 'Politics of the Parish', pp. 22–5.

95. Stretton, 'Women, Custom and Equity', pp. 170–89.

96. Ibid., p. 185.

97. Whyte, 'Custodians of Memory', pp. 153–73.

98. For a similar and more comprehensive justification, see Kermode and Walker, 'Introduction', p. 21.

99. M. C. Erler and M. Kowaleski, 'Introduction: A New Economy of Power Relations: Female Agency in the Middle Ages', in Erler and Kowaleski (eds), *Gendering the Master Narrative: Women and Power in the Middle Ages* (Ithaca, NY: Cornell University Press, 2003).

1 Beattie, 'Your Oratrice: Women's Petitions to the Late Medieval Court of Chancery'

1. National Archives, Kew, Surrey, Early Chancery Proceedings (hereafter TNA C 1), C 1/16/331; C 1/46/47; C 1/66/205. All quotations, here and elsewhere, have been modernized, although I have decided to keep Johanne in the original spelling as Joan, Joanne or Joanna are all possibilities. In the absence of other information, bills are dated by their address to a bishop or archbishop as Chancellor in combination with TNA's bundle number. Elizabeth Lamanva's bill can be dated more precisely as there is a matching writ, C 244/112/105, from October 1471. See P. M. Barnes, 'The Chancery Corpus Cum Causa File, 10–11 Edward IV', in R. F. Hunnisett and J. B. Post, *Medieval Legal Records, Edited in Memory of C. A. F. Meekings* (London, HMSO, 1978), pp. 429–76, on p. 464. I am grateful to Steve Rigby and John Arnold for comments on earlier versions of this essay.

2. On the numbers of women using the court, see T. S. Haskett, 'The Medieval English Court of Chancery', *Law and History Review*, 14 (1996), pp. 245–313, on pp. 282, 286 (21 per cent of petitioners in a sample of nearly seven thousand cases from a possible sixty-one thousand); E. Hawkes, '"She will ... Protect and Defend her Rights Boldly by Law and Reason ...": Women's Knowledge of Common Law and Equity Courts in Late-Medieval England', in N. J. Menuge (ed.), *Medieval Women and the Law* (Woodbridge: The Boydell Press, 2000), pp. 145–61, on pp. 148, 151. Compare Stevens, who argues that 'while women formed a larger proportion of petitioners to Chancery than they did litigants at Common Pleas (15 per cent as opposed to 5 per cent, respectively), the fifteenth-century Court of Common Pleas processed twenty to forty-five lawsuits for each one petition to Chancery': M. F. Stevens, 'London's Married Women, Debt Litigation and Coverture in the Court of Common Pleas', in C. Beattie and M. F. Stevens (eds), *Married Women and the Law in Premodern Northwest Europe* (Woodbridge: The Boydell Press, 2013), pp. 115–32, on p. 124; his figures for Chancery are from Hawkes for the proportion of women but from Haskett for the number of cases heard per year. However, a study of the surviving Chancery writs argues that the number of Chancery cases per year might have been much higher than that suggested by Haskett and others. For example, Tucker found over 900 writs for 1441–2, a period for which Pronay suggested an average of 136 bills: P. Tucker, 'The Early History of the Court of Chancery: A Comparative Study', *English Historical Review*, 115 (2000), pp. 791–811, on p. 799; N. Pronay, 'The Chancellor, the Chancery, and the Council at the End of the Fifteenth Century', in H. Hearder and H. R. Loyn (eds), *British Government and Administration: Studies Presented to S. B. Chrimes* (Cardiff: University of Wales Press, 1974), pp. 87–103, on p. 89.

3. Hawkes, "She will ... Protect", pp. 151–6, 160–1; M. K. McIntosh, *Working Women in English Society, 1300–1620* (Cambridge: Cambridge University Press, 2005), pp. 21, 23–4. Compare T. Stretton, *Women Waging Law in Elizabethan England* (Cambridge: Cambridge University Press, 1998), pp. 25–9.

4. For a discussion of the differences between conscience and equity, see Haskett, 'Medieval English Court', pp. 249–80; see also Tucker, 'Early History', p. 795. For a brief discussion of the background of Chancellors, 1396–1532, see Haskett, 'Medieval English Court', pp. 311–13.

5. For a discussion of how many complaints might have begun orally, see Tucker, 'Early History', pp. 793–4. 'Bill' is the proper term for a written document to Chancery but, as Dodd has argued, 'there is general consensus that the terms "bill" and "petition" refer to essentially the same phenomenon': G. Dodd, *Justice and Grace: Private Petitioning and the English Parliament in the Late Middle Ages* (Oxford: Oxford University Press, 2007), p. 1, n. 2.

6. T. S. Haskett, 'Country Lawyers?: The Composers of English Chancery Bills', in P. Birks (ed.), *The Life of the Law: Proceedings of the Tenth British Legal History Conference, Oxford, 1991* (London: Hambledon Press, 1993), pp. 9–23, esp. pp. 10, 14.

7. B. A. Hanawalt, *Growing Up in Medieval London: The Experience of Childhood in History* (New York: Oxford University Press, 1993), p. 15.

8. TNA, C 1/32/337 (*c.* 1480).

9. J. Bailey, 'Voices in Court: Lawyers' or Litigants'?', *Historical Research*, 74:186 (2001), pp. 392–408, on pp. 406–7. See also G. Walker, *Crime, Gender and Social Order in Early Modern England* (Cambridge: Cambridge University Press, 2003), pp. 1–9.

10. One of Bailey's examples is Lawrence Stone. See his *The Past and Present Revisited* (London: Routledge & Kegan Paul, 1987), p. 241, also pp. 81–95; *Road to Divorce: England 1530–1987* (Oxford: Oxford University Press, 1995), pp. 27–32; *Uncertain Unions and Broken Lives: Marriage and Divorce in England 1660–1857* (Oxford: Oxford University Press, 1995), pp. 5–8.

11. McIntosh, *Working Women*, pp. 20–8, quotation on p. 22. This work represents a change from her earlier view of Chancery bills as being good sources of people's own language: M. K. McIntosh, *Controlling Misbehaviour in England, 1370–1600* (Cambridge: Cambridge University Press, 1990), pp. 119–24.

12. For example, S. H. Mendelson, "'To Shift for a Cloak': Disorderly Women in the Church Courts", in V. Frith (ed.), *Women and History: Voices of Early Modern England* (Toronto: Coach House, 1995), pp. 3–17, on pp. 5–6; C. Bruschi, "'Magna diligentia est habenda per inquisitorem': Precautions before Reading Doat 21–26', in C. Bruschi and P. Biller (eds), *Texts and the Repression of Medieval Heresy*, York Studies in Medieval Theology, 4 (Woodbridge: York Medieval Press, 2003), pp. 81–110.

13. G. Walker, 'Rereading Rape and Sexual Violence in Early Modern England', *Gender and History*, 10:1 (1998), pp. 1–25, on p. 20, n. 4; see also M. Chaytor, 'Husband(ry): Narratives of Rape in the Seventeenth Century', *Gender & History*, 7 (1995), pp. 378–407, on p. 401, n. 1.

14. T. Kuehn, 'Reading Microhistory: The Example of Giovanni and Lusanna', *Journal of Modern History*, 61 (1989), pp. 512–34, on p. 533.

15. C. Cannon, 'The Rights of Medieval English Women: Crime and the Issue of Representation', in B. A. Hanawalt and D. Wallace (eds), *Medieval Crime and Social Control* (Minneapolis, MN: University of Minnesota Press, 1999), pp. 156–85, on p. 168.

16. N. Z. Davis, *Fiction in the Archives: Pardon Tales and their Tellers in Sixteenth-century France* (Cambridge: Polity Press, 1987), on pp. 18, 4.

17. Stretton, *Women Waging Law*, pp. 19, 179.

18. G. Walker, 'Just Stories: Telling Tales of Infant Death in Early Modern England', in M. Mikesell and A. Seeff (eds), *Culture and Change: Attending to Early Modern Women* (Newark, DE: University of Delaware Press, 2003), pp. 98–115, on p. 99.

19. See L. Gowing, *Domestic Dangers: Women, Words, and Sex in Early Modern London* (Oxford: Clarendon Press, 1996), pp. 234–5, 262.

20. Walker, 'Just Stories', p. 112. See also Walker, *Crime, Gender and Social Order*, pp. 7–8.

21. On language and composition see, for example *An Anthology of Chancery English*, ed. J. H. Fisher, M. Richardson and J. L. Fisher (Knoxville, TN: University of Tennessee Press, 1984), esp. pp. 20–5; Haskett, 'Country Lawyers?'; T. S. Haskett, 'The Presentation of Cases in Medieval Chancery Bills', in W. M. Gordon and T. D. Fergus (eds), *Legal History in the Making: Proceedings of the Ninth British Legal History Conference, Glasgow, 1989* (London: Hambledon Press, 1991), pp. 11–28. For a focus on petitioners, see M. Hettinger, 'Defining the Servant: Legal and Extra-Legal Terms of Employment in Fifteenth-Century England', in A. J. Frantzen and D. Moffat (eds), *The Work of Work: Servitude, Slavery, and Labor in Medieval England* (Glasgow: Cruithne Press, 1994), pp. 206–28; S. M. Butler, 'The Law as a Weapon in Marital Disputes: Evidence from the Late Medieval Court of Chancery, 1424–1529', *Journal of British Studies*, 43 (2004), pp. 291–316.

22. M. E. Avery, 'An Evaluation of the Effectiveness of the Court of Chancery under the Lancastrian Kings', *Law Quarterly Review*, 86 (1970), pp. 84–97, on p. 86; J. H. Baker, *An Introduction to English Legal History*, 3rd edn (London: Butterworths, 1990), p. 116.

23. Haskett, 'Country Lawyers?'; J. H. Fisher, 'Chancery and the Emergence of Standard Written English in the Fifteenth Century', *Speculum*, 52 (1977), pp. 870–99, on pp. 888–9.

24. G. Dodd, 'Writing Wrongs: The Drafting of Supplications to the Crown in Later Fourteenth-Century England', *Medium Aevum*, 80 (2011), pp. 217–46, on p. 224. See also *Anthology of Chancery English*, p. 21.

25. This view has been formed from a reading of the bills relating to women in TNA C 1, bundles 1–235 (pre 1500) and – based on which actions produced the most interesting bills – selected bills from bundles 236–356 (c. 1500–15), using the information given in the *List of Early Chancery Proceedings Preserved in the Public Record Office*, 10 vols, Lists and Indexes, 12, 16, 20, 29, 38, 48, 50–1, 54–5 (London: His Majesty's Stationery Office, 1901–38), vols 1–4. This amounts to around a thousand petitions.

26. Haskett, 'Presentation', p. 13.

27. Ibid., p. 25: 'materiam in hac supplicacione specificatam'.

28. Margaret Hargyll's bill, for example, states that 'she will depose afore your lordship' that she did not owe an alleged debt: TNA, C 1/64/1129 (1475–80 or 1483–5). Stretton makes a similar point in relation to the Elizabethan Court of Requests material: Stretton, *Women Waging Law*, pp. 210–11.

29. See Tucker, 'Early History', p. 798.

30. See Avery, 'Evaluation', pp. 90–2; W. J. Jones, *The Elizabethan Court of Chancery* (Oxford: Clarendon Press, 1967), pp. 11–15.

31. On cases being dismissed, see Haskett, 'Presentation', pp. 20–1. It has been estimated that a suit brought to Chancery cost between £50 and £400, although the poor might have received some legal assistance: Jones, *Elizabethan Court of Chancery*, pp. 309, 323–8. Compare Stretton, *Women Waging Law*, p. 82.

32. For a discussion of some common narrative frames, such as Servants' Tales and Old Widows' Tales, see C. Beattie, 'Meanings of Singleness: The Single Woman in Late Medieval England' (DPhil dissertation, University of York, 2001), pp. 155–205.

33. TNA, C 1/66/205.

34. TNA, C 1/64/1077 (1475–80 or 1483–5). Such subject positions are discussed further in Beattie, 'Meanings of Singleness', pp. 170–89.

35. Compare J. H. Arnold, *Inquisition and Power: Catharism and the Confessing Subject in Medieval Languedoc* (Philadelphia, PA: University of Pennsylvania Press, 2001), pp. 76–7, 199.

36. TNA, C 1/16/331. Avery suggests that this bill was presented to John Stafford as Chancellor in the 1430s but it is addressed to the Archbishop of Canterbury and Stafford only took up that post in 1443: Avery, 'Evaluation', p. 93.

37. Haskett sets out a more complex canon of form for Chancery bills, consisting of eleven sections, but the five-fold division will suffice for our purposes: Haskett, 'Presentation', pp. 12–13.

38. See Haskett, 'Medieval English Court', p. 312.

39. DL/C/B/043/MS09064/003 (*Acta quoad correctionem delinquentium*, 1475–7 and 1480–2), London Metropolitan Archives (hereafter DL/C/B/043/MS09064/003), fol. 30v; I owe the original reference to S. McSheffrey, *Marriage, Sex, and Civic Culture in Late Medieval London* (Philadelphia, PA: University of Pennsylvania Press, 2006), p. 250, n. 1.

40. TNA, C 1/32/337.

41. Compare Gowing, who found that female deponents, unlike male ones, used a variety of pronouns for the same places e.g. 'her [i.e. my] husband's house', 'her shop': Gowing, *Domestic Dangers*, p. 239.

42. As Gowing suggested for the narratives told in church court depositions, 'the two-way flow of influences between law and practice meant that legal personnel and witnesses might, very often, be working with the same plans, patterns, and conventions': Gowing, *Domestic Dangers*, p. 239.

43. Davis, *Fiction in the Archives*, pp. 89, 96.

44. Chaytor, 'Husband(ry)', pp. 382–5, quotation on p. 385.

45. Walker, 'Rereading Rape', pp. 14–15, quotation on p. 15. See also G. Walker, 'Expanding the Boundaries of Female Honour in Early Modern England', *Transactions of the Royal Historical Society*, 6:6 (1996), pp. 235–45; Walker, *Crime, Gender and Social Order*, pp. 52–3.

46. TNA, C 1/66/368 (1475–80 or 1483–5). There is also an example from London's Court of Aldermen, 1517, in which a young woman asks a waterman's wife to help her escape a life of prostitution 'for Our Lady's sake': R. M. Karras, *Common Women: Prostitution and Sexuality in Medieval England* (New York: Oxford University Press, 1996), p. 58.

47. On the widespread appeal and telling of miracles of the Virgin, see C. M. Meale, 'The Miracles of Our Lady: Context and Interpretation', in D. Pearsall (ed.), *Studies in the Vernon Manuscript* (Cambridge: D. S. Brewer, 1990), pp. 115–36, on pp. 115–17.

48. A. Wallensköld, *Le Conte de la femme chaste convoitée par son beau-frère*, Acta Societatis Scientiarum Fennicae, 34:1 (Helsinki: Société de Littérature Finnoise, 1907); *Florence de Rome: Chanson d'aventure du premier quart du XIIIe siècle*, ed. A. Wallensköld, Publications de la Société des anciens textes français, 2 vols (Paris: Librairie de Firmin-Didot, 1909), vol. 1, pp. 112–30. See also *Le Bone Florence of Rome*, ed. C. F. Heffernan (Manchester: Manchester University Press, 1976), pp. 3–17; C. F. Heffernan, *The Orient in Chaucer and Medieval Romance* (Cambridge: D. S. Brewer, 2003), pp. 111–15.

49. 'Chaste Empress', in S. Parkinson et al. (eds), 'The Oxford *Cantigas de Santa Maria* Database', at http://csm.mml.ox.ac.uk/index.php?p=poemdata_view&rec=5 [accessed 14 October 2009]; *Florence de Rome*, pp. 117–18; J. E. Connolly, 'Marian Intervention and Hagiographic Models in the Tale of the Chaste Wife: Text and Context', in A. M. Beresford (ed.), *'Quien hubiese tal ventura': Medieval Hispanic Studies in Honour of Alan Deyermond* (London: Department of Hispanic Studies, Queen Mary and Westfield College, 1997), pp. 35–44, esp. pp. 36–7. For fourteenth- and fifteenth-century Middle English examples, see *The Middle English Miracles of the Virgin*, ed. B. Boyd (San Marino, CA: Huntington Library, 1964), pp. 64–7; *An Alphabet of Tales*, ed. M. M. Banks, Early English Text Society, original series, 126–7 (London: K. Paul, Trench, Trübner, 1904–5), pp. 447–50.

50. See *Le Bone Florence of Rome*, pp. 113, 101; this is a fifteenth-century English version. For the circulation of the story in England, see F. Riddy, 'Temporary Virginity and the Everyday Body: *Le Bone Florence of Rome* and Bourgeois Self-making', in N. McDonald (ed.), *Pulp Fictions of Medieval England: Essays in Popular Romance* (Manchester: Manchester University Press, 2004), pp. 197–216, on p. 202.

51. Davis, *Fiction in the Archives*, pp. 98–103, quotation on p. 101. See also Walker, *Crime, Gender and Social Order*, pp. 96–8.

52. K. Jones, *Gender and Petty Crime in Late Medieval England: The Local Courts in Kent, 1460–156*, Gender in the Middle Ages, 2 (Woodbridge: The Boydell Press, 2006), pp. 70–5, 92–3, quotation on p. 93.

53. See, for example, *Select Cases on Defamation to 1600*, ed. R. H. Helmholz, Selden Society, 101 (London: Selden Society, 1985), pp. 4, 7, 9–10, 14–18, 22–5.

54. The man was perhaps John Travase, as the consistory court noted in 1480 that Humphrey Bawde and his wife had defamed Maud (here 'Matilda Olyve') by calling her *meretricem* (whore) and *pronubam* (bawd; go-between), especially with John Travase: DL/C/B/043/MS09064/003, fol. 30v.

55. DL/C/B/043/MS09064/003, fol. 9v. The *Middle English Dictionary* (hereafter *MED*), at http://quod.lib.umich.edu/m/med/ [accessed 14 October 2009], also records 'ado' with the meaning sexual intercourse and gives six examples, all from the fifteenth century: *MED*, ado (n.), 1. (b).

56. Compare Gowing, *Domestic Dangers*, p. 46: 'When ... testimonies concerned illicit sex, scribes, lawyers, or witnesses themselves shifted into a different register from everyday speech ... The legal presentation of sex involved an idiom common to all courts'.

57. See *MED*, hert(e)li(e) (adj.) 1. (a); *The English Poems of Charles of Orleans*, ed. R. Steele, Early English Text Society, original series, 215 (London: Oxford University Press, 1941), p. 225.

58. *MED*, hert(e)li(e) (adj.) 2. (a).

59. DL/C/B/043/MS09064/003. For more on London's commissary court, see McSheffrey, *Marriage, Sex, and Civic Culture*, pp. 155–6.

60. DL/C/B/043/MS09064/003, fol. 39v. See also ibid. fols 24 (Elena Morgon about William Swanton and his wife Johanna), 38v (Agnes Newell against Johanna Wrykkyls). Ibid., fol. 34 (Johanna Croysten and Maria White, her daughter, against Thomas Rodwyk) which even mixes languages with the phrase '*dicendo* that'.

61. Compare the fabliaux 'The Wright's Chaste Wife', which is preserved in a late fifteenth-century household manuscript, discussed in B. A. Hanawalt, '*Of Good and Ill Repute*': *Gender and Social Control in Medieval England* (New York: Oxford University Press, 1998), pp. 88–103.

2 Goldberg, 'Echoes, Whispers, Ventriloquisms: On Recovering Women's Voices from the Court of York in the Later Middle Ages'

1. For example, Robert Bartlett suggests that such testimony offers 'as good an idea as we are likely to get of the spoken words of the past': R. Bartlett, *The Hanged Man: A Story of Miracle, Memory, and Colonialism in the Middle Ages* (Princeton, NJ: Princeton University Press, 2004), p. xi.

2. J. H. Arnold, *Inquisition and Power: Catharism and the Confessing Subject in Medieval Languedoc* (Philadelphia, PA: University of Pennsylvania Press, 2001), p. 229.

3. P. J. P. Goldberg (ed. and trans.), *Women in England c. 1275–1525: Documentary Sources* (Manchester: Manchester University Press, 1995), p. 239.

4. For examples, see ibid., p. 145.

5. I have discussed this at length in P. J. P. Goldberg, 'Gender and Matrimonial Litigation in the Church Courts in the Later Middle Ages: The Evidence of the Court of York', *Gender and History*, 19:1 (2007), pp. 43–59. The only exception to the general legal equality permitted to women as deponents was where a mother, testifying for the validity of her daughter's marriage, could be shown to be striving unduly to promote an exceptionally advantageous union.

6. York, York Minster Library, M2(c)3. I have discussed this case in '"I Know What You Did Last Summer": Knowledge as Power among Parochial Clergy in Later Medieval England', in B. Bolton and C. Meek (eds), *Aspects of Power and Authority in the Middle Ages* (Turnhout: Brepols, 2007), pp. 185–96.
7. Sir Brian was the head of the armigerous family of de Rouclif of Rawcliffe and held property in Rawcliffe. Alice's family, despite the commonality of name, appears not to have been closely related, if at all, but probably held their land of Sir Brian as their feudal superior.
8. York, Borthwick Institute for Archives (hereafter BI), CP.E.89, translated in Goldberg (ed. and trans.), *Women in England*, pp. 58–80. The case is discussed at length in P. J. P. Goldberg, *Communal Discord, Child Abduction, and Rape in the Later Middle Ages* (New York: Palgrave Macmillan, 2008) and, somewhat inaccurately, in S. Niebrzydowski, 'From Bedroom to Courtroom: Home and the Memory of Childbirth in a Fourteenth-Century Marriage Dispute', *Home Cultures*, 6 (2009), pp. 123–34.
9. For discussions of the matrimonial litigation in the church courts, see R. H. Helmholz, *Marriage Litigation in Medieval England* (Cambridge: Cambridge University Press, 1974); C. Donahue, Jr, *Law, Marriage, and Society in the Later Middle Ages: Arguments about Marriage in Five Courts* (Cambridge: Cambridge University Press, 2007).
10. The relationship of a deponent to one or other of the litigants in terms of kinship or ties of service are routinely recorded in depositions precisely because the canon law recognized that such testimony might be partial.
11. This procedure and the personnel of the courts is discussed with admirable clarity in Helmholz, *Marriage Litigation*.
12. Canonical majority was understood to be twelve for girls and fourteen for boys. In fact, witnesses as young as this are not found since there was an understanding that younger witnesses would lack credibility.
13. P. J. P. Goldberg, *Women, Work, and Life Cycle in a Medieval Economy: Women in York and Yorkshire c. 1300–1520* (Oxford: Oxford University Press, 1992), table 5.3, p. 221.
14. Goldberg, 'Gender and Matrimonial Litigation', pp. 43–59, esp. p. 47.
15. Helmholz, *Marriage Litigation*, pp. 128–31.
16. For example, the insults Emma Lylle supposedly hurled at Agnes Popilton in 1422 as she walked across the churchyard after attending evensong in her parish church of Holy Trinity, King's Court in York, and recalled by witnesses appearing for Agnes were recorded not only in Latin, but also in the vernacular, namely 'ald munkhore and aldfrerehor' and 'ald rank tayntydthefe': Goldberg (ed. and trans.), *Women in England*, p. 230.
17. York, BI, CP.E.89; Goldberg (ed. and trans.), *Women in England*, p. 60.
18. Ibid., pp. 58–60, 62–5, 68–70, 73–5, 78.
19. B. Harvey, 'Work and *Festa Ferianda* in Medieval England', *Journal of Ecclesiastical History*, 23 (1972), pp. 289–308; R. Hutton, *The Rise and Fall of Merry England: The Ritual Year, 1400–1700* (Oxford: Oxford University Press, 1994).
20. Goldberg, *Communal Discord*, p. 37.
21. Goldberg (ed. and trans.), *Women in England*, pp. 65–6.
22. Helmholz, *Marriage Litigation*, pp. 13–20, 147–9.
23. I have written about his testimony at length in Goldberg, *Communal Discord*, pp. 38–41.
24. For this and what follows, see York, BI, CP.E.82; Goldberg (ed. and trans.), *Women in England*, pp. 156–7.
25. There is good scriptural precedent for this. The Biblical account of Susanna and the Elders (Susanna 1:1–63) tells how the Elders tried to blackmail Susanna into sleeping

with them, but on her refusal had her condemned to death for adultery with a young man they claimed to have caught her with. At the last moment, Daniel intervened urging that Susanna should not be condemned without the examination of her accusers. Daniel then interrogated the Elders separately, asking each the same question, namely what sort of tree had Susanna and her alleged lover lain beneath. Each named a different tree, the one large, the other small, and so were exposed as false witnesses and condemned by their own words.

26. Goldberg (ed. and trans.), *Women in England*, p. 59.
27. Ibid., p. 75.
28. Proof of Age, the procedure by which a jury of local men testified that the heir to a tenancy in chief, i.e. property held directly of the Crown, had achieved their majority for the purposes of inheritance, generated very large numbers of depositions, but a fairly narrow range of narrative strategies. Jurors might, for example, reference their presence at the baptism of the child, the recording of the birth in one of the books in the parish church, the births of their own children, personal accidents causing injury, or freak events such as gales that destroyed property. Scholars have been sceptical of the historicity of many of these depositions precisely because the same narrative strategies are so frequently repeated, but the broader point is that the proof of age procedure provided a cultural model for how past events might be evidenced. Compare J. T. Rosenthal, *Telling Tales: Sources and Narration in Late Medieval England* (University Park, PA: Pennsylvania State University Press, 2003), ch. 1, esp. p. 9.
29. Goldberg (ed. and trans.), *Women in England*, pp. 62–3.
30. I discuss this case in 'Brewing Trouble: The Devout Widow's Tale', in Goldberg, *Communal Discord*, pp. 129–45.
31. York, BI, CP.F.36 transcribed and translated in Helmholz, *Marriage Litigation*, p. 7.
32. York, BI, CP.E.221; Goldberg (ed. and trans.), *Women in England*, pp. 141–2.
33. Helmholz, *Marriage Litigation*, pp. 100–7, esp. p. 105. There was, however, another significant silence. Neither deponent explained how they came to witness the alleged attack at night. Nor were the witnesses kin or servants to the Nesfelds. Margery Speight would only have been 14 at the time. This raises questions as to whether either had actually been present, a concern that the court may well have shared. This need not imply that Thomas Nesfeld's cruelty was a fiction or that Margery Nesfeld's witnesses fabricated the attack, but rather the two young women ventriloquized actual, but unwitnessed domestic violence: Goldberg, 'Gender and Matrimonial Litigation', pp. 53–4.

3 Kane, 'Women, Memory and Agency in the Medieval English Church Courts'

1. I wish to thank the Leverhulme Trust for the award that supported much of this research. I am also very grateful to Dr Simon Sandall for his comments on an earlier version of this chapter. J. Gower, *Mirour de l'Omme*, trans. W. Burton Wilson, rev. N. Wilson Van Baak (East Lansing: Colleagues Press, 1992), ll. 17, 653–64.
2. In its anti-feminist rhetoric the *Mirour* resembles the *Vox Clamantis* rather than the *Confessio Amantis*, a text that approaches sexual politics on more equitable grounds. E. S. Bakalian, *Aspects of Love in John Gower's Confessio Amantis* (New York and London: Routledge, 2004), p. xvi.
3. Gower, *Mirour*, ll. 17, 656–62.

4. B. Kane, 'Custom, Memory and Knowledge in the Late Medieval English Church Courts', in R. C. E. Hayes and W. J. Sheils (eds), *Clergy, Church and Society in England and Wales, c. 1200–1800* (York: Borthwick Publications, 2013).

5. See M. Carruthers, *The Book of Memory: A Study of Memory in Medieval Culture* (Cambridge: Cambridge University Press, 1990); J. Coleman, *Ancient and Medieval Memories: Studies in the Reconstruction of the Past* (Cambridge: Cambridge University Press, 1992), pp. 150–2.

6. J. Enders, *The Medieval Theater of Cruelty: Rhetoric, Memory, Violence* (Ithaca, NY: Cornell University Press, 1999), pp. 3–8.

7. For a survey of *memoria* and the study of memory in the medieval period, see P. Geary, 'The Historical Material of Memory', in G. Ciapelli and P. Lee Rubin (eds), *Art, Memory and Family in Renaissance Europe* (Cambridge: Cambridge University Press, 2000), pp. 17–25.

8. E. van Houts, *Memory and Gender in Medieval Europe 900–1200* (Toronto: University of Toronto Press, 1999); E. van Houts (ed.), *Medieval Memories: Men, Women and the Past 700–1300* (London: Pearson Education Limited, 2001).

9. P. J. Geary, *Phantoms of Remembrance: Memory and Oblivion at the End of the First Millenium* (Princeton, NJ: Princeton University Press, 1994); Van Houts, *Memory and Gender*, pp. 65–8.

10. J. Everard, 'Sworn Testimony and Memory of the Past in Brittany, c. 1100–1250', in van Houts (ed.), *Medieval Memories*, pp. 72–91, on p. 80; P. Skinner, 'Gender and Memory in Medieval Italy', in van Houts (ed.), *Medieval Memories*, pp. 36–52, on p. 44.

11. J. Ward, *Women in England in the Middle Ages* (London: Hambledon Continuum, 2006), p. 24.

12. R. H. Helmholz, *Marriage Litigation in Medieval England* (Cambridge: Cambridge University Press, 1974); C. Donahue, Jr, *Law, Marriage, and Society in the Later Middle Ages: Arguments About Marriage in Five Courts* (Cambridge: Cambridge University Press, 2007); P. J. P. Goldberg, 'Gender and Matrimonial Litigation in the Church Courts in the Later Middle Ages', *Gender & History*, 19:1 (2007), pp. 43–59; F. Pedersen, 'Demography in the Archives: Social and Geographical Factors in Fourteenth-Century York Cause Paper Litigation', *Continuity and Change*, 10 (1995), pp. 405–36; S. McSheffrey, *Marriage, Sex, and Civic Culture in Late Medieval London* (Philadelphia, PA: University of Pennsylvania Press, 2006).

13. See, for example, P. R. Schofield, 'Peasants and the Manor Court: Gossip and Litigation in a Suffolk Village at the Close of the Thirteenth Century', *Past and Present*, 159 (1998), pp. 3–42.

14. P. R. Hyams, 'Deans and their Doings: The Norwich Inquiry of 1286', in S. Kuttner and K. Pennington (eds), *Proceedings of the Berkeley Congress of Medieval Canon Law, 1980* (Vatican City: Monumenta Iuris Canonici Series C: Subsidia, 1985), pp. 619–46, on p. 639.

15. J. A. Brundage, *Law, Sex, and Christian Society in Medieval Europe* (Chicago, IL, and London: The University of Chicago Press, 1987), pp. 319–23.

16. Ibid., p. 223.

17. Donahue, *Law, Marriage, and Society*, p. 8.

18. R. H. Helmholz, *The Oxford History of the Laws of England: Volume 1 The Canon Law and Ecclesiastical Jurisdiction from 597 to the 1640s* (Oxford: Oxford University Press, 2004), p. 229.

19. *Select Cases from the Ecclesiastical Courts of the Province of Canterbury, c. 1200–1301*, eds C. Donahue and N. Adams, Selden Society Publications 95 (London: London Selden Society, 1981), p. 6 (hereafter *Select Canterbury Cases*). The development of distinctive courts in the province and diocese of Canterbury was a gradual process that became more definitive towards the close of the thirteenth century. For an outline of the court systems from diocesan to provincial level, see *Select Canterbury Cases*, pp. 6–17. A useful survey of the court system in the province of Canterbury is B. Woodcock, *Medieval Ecclesiastical Courts in the Diocese of Canterbury* (London: Oxford University Press, 1952).

20. Helmholz, *Marriage Litigation*, pp. 7–11.

21. K. J. Lewis, 'Women, Testamentary Discourse and Life-Writing in Later Medieval England', in N. J. Menuge (ed.), *Medieval Women and the Law* (Woodbridge: The Boydell Press, 2000), pp. 57–75, on p. 58.

22. J. Butler, *The Psychic Life of Power: Theories in Subjection* (Stanford, CA: Stanford University Press, 1997), introduction.

23. C. Beattie, 'Married Women, Contracts and Coverture', in C. Beattie and M. F. Stevens (eds), *Married Women and the Law in Premodern Northwest Europe* (Woodbridge: The Boydell Press, 2013), pp. 133–54; M. Müller, 'Peasant Women, Agency and Status in Mid-Thirteenth- to Late Fourteenth-Century England: Some Reconsiderations', in Beattie and Stevens (eds), *Married Women and the Law*, pp. 91–113.

24. P. R. Schofield, *Peasant and Community in Medieval England, 1200–1500* (Basingstoke: Palgrave Macmillan, 2003), p. 182.

25. J. A. Brundage, 'Juridical Space: Female Witnesses in Canon Law', *Dumbarton Oaks Papers*, 52 (1998), pp. 147–56.

26. D. Ghosh, *Sex and the Family in Colonial India: The Making of Empire* (Cambridge: Cambridge University Press, 2006), p. 16.

27. B. A. Misztal, *Theories of Social Remembering* (Maidenhead and Philadelphia, PA: Open University Press, 2003), p. 134.

28. J. Fentress and C. Wickham, *Social Memory: New Perspectives on the Past* (Oxford: Blackwell, 1992), pp. 87–143; for an overview of the field, see J. K. Olick and J. Robbins, 'Social Memory Studies: From "Collective Memory" to the Historical Sociology of Mnemonic Practices', *Annual Review of Sociology*, 24 (1998), pp. 105–40.

29. Fentress and Wickham, *Social Memory*, p. 7.

30. C. G. A. Bryant and D. Jary, 'Introduction: Coming to Terms with Anthony Giddens', in Bryant and Jary (eds), *Giddens' Theory of Structuration: A Critical Appreciation* (New York and London, 1991), pp. 1–31, 7.

31. C. Hughes Dayton, 'Rethinking Agency, Recovering Voices', *American Historical Review*, 109:3 (2004), pp. 827–43, on p. 842.

32. M. Hirsch and V. Smith, 'Feminism and Cultural Memory: An Introduction', *Signs*, 28:1, Special Issue, Gender and Cultural Memory (2002), pp. 1–19, on p. 4.

33. K. Harvey and A. Shepard, 'What Have Historians Done with Masculinity? Reflections on Five Centuries of British History, circa 1500–1950', *Journal of British Studies*, 44:2 (2005), pp. 274–280, on p. 275.

34. W. Johnson, 'On Agency', *Journal of Social History*, 37:1 (2003), pp. 113–24, on p. 118.

35. D. G. Neal, *The Masculine Self in Late Medieval England* (Chicago, IL: University of Chicago Press, 2008), chs 1 and 2.

36. Canterbury Cathedral Archives (hereafter CCA), Ecclesiastical Suit Roll 11 (hereafter E.S. Roll).

37. For a study of femininity in the early modern ecclesiastical court material, see L. Gowing, *Common Bodies: Women, Touch and Power in Seventeenth-century England* (New Haven, CT, and London: Yale University Press, 2003), esp. ch. 3.

38. CCA, Sede Vacante Scrapbooks (hereafter SVSB), III, no. 33.

39. Geary, *Phantoms of Remembrance*, p. 17.

40. For a comprehensive study of rhetoric in medieval culture, see J. J. Murphy, *Rhetoric in the Middle Ages: A History of Rhetorical Theory from Saint Augustine to the Renaissance* (Berkeley, CA: University of California Press, 1974).

41. J. A. Brundage, 'The Teaching and Study of Canon Law in the Law Schools', in W. Hartmann and K. Pennington (eds), *The History of Medieval Canon Law in the Classical Period, 1140–1234: From Gratian to the Decretals of Pope Gregory IX* (Washington, DC: The Catholic University of America Press, 2008), p. 98–120, on p. 113.

42. For a useful summary of theories on memory in the twelfth and thirteenth centuries, see Coleman, *Ancient and Medieval Memories*, pp. 274–324.

43. Tancred, *Ordo iudiciarius*, in Pilli, *Tancredi, Gratiae, Libri de iudiciorum ordine* ed. F. C. Bergmann (Göttingen, 1842; reprinted Aalen, 1965), (hereafter Tancred, *Ordo*), 3.7, p. 228. C. Donahue, Jr notes that 'relatively little innovation occurs after Tancred's time', such that his *Ordo* is representative of Romano-canonic methods of proof through witnesses. C. Donahue, Jr, 'Proof by Witnesses in the Church Courts of Medieval England: An Imperfect Reception of the Learned Law', in M. S. Arnold, T. A. Green, S. A. Scully and S. D. White (eds), *On the Laws and Customs of England: Essays in Honor of Samuel E. Thorne* (Chapel Hill, NC: University of North Carolina Press, 1981), pp. 127–158, on p. 129.

44. Tancred, *Ordo*, 3.7, p. 228.

45. Ibid., 3.9, p. 238. The examiner should interrogate as follows: 'melius possit elicere veritatem, et de singulis circumstanciis prudenter inquirere, scilicet de personis, loco et tempore, visu, auditu, scientia et credulitate, fama et certitudine'.

46. Donahue, 'Proof by Witnesses', p. 131.

47. See, for example, the statement in the deposition of Lady Eleanor Bassett, CCA, E.S. Roll 57.

48. J. Fleming, 'The Friars and Medieval English Literature', in D. Wallace (ed.), *The Cambridge History of Medieval English Literature* (Cambridge: Cambridge University Press, 1999), pp. 349–75, on p. 356.

49. Quoted in J. Hughes, 'The Administration of Confession in the Diocese of York in the Fourteenth Century', in D. M. Smith (ed.), *Studies in Clergy and Ministry in Medieval England: Purvis Seminar Studies* (York: Borthwick Publications, 1991), pp. 87–163, on p. 107.

50. Butler, *The Psychic Life of Power*, pp. 18–19.

51. For a discussion of the subject in terms of power relations, see M. Foucault, 'The Subject and Power', in P. Rabinow and N. Rose (eds), *The Essential Foucault: Selections from Essential Works of Foucault, 1954–1984* (New York: New Press, 2003), pp. 126–44.

52. H. Solterer, *The Master and Minerva: Disputing Women in French Medieval Culture* (Berkeley, CA: University of California Press, 1995), p. 53.

53. J. Enders, 'Cutting off the Memory of Women', in C. Mason Sutherland and R. J. Sutcliffe (eds), *The Changing Tradition: Women in the History of Rhetoric* (Calgary: University of Calgary Press, 1999), pp. 47–55, on p. 49.

54. Van Houts, *Memory and Gender*, pp. 65–92.

55. Goldberg, 'Gender and Matrimonial Litigation', p. 50.

56. Borthwick Institute for Archives (hereafter BI), CP.E.89; BI, CP.F.89; CCA, E.S. Roll 10.
57. S. Justice, *Writing and Rebellion: England in 1381* (Berkeley, CA: University of California Press), p. 72; S. Federico, 'The Imaginary Society: Women in 1381', *Journal of British Studies*, 40:2 (2001), pp. 159–83, on p. 159. In the aftermath of the revolt in 1381, Justice notes that the chronicler, Henry Knighton, interpreted the rebels' letters as forms of speech rather than writing. Reflecting ideological associations with literacy and orality, distinctions were thus drawn between the letter of John Ball, a clerk, and the supposedly oral addresses from labouring 'insurgent authors'.
58. Justice, *Writing and Rebellion*, pp. 32–7.
59. BI, CP.E.174.
60. Ibid. 'quia ipsum testamentum sepius vidit et legi audivit'.
61. Brundage, 'Juridical Space', pp. 147–56.
62. Ibid., p. 148.
63. Tancred, *Ordo*, 3.12, p. 246.
64. BI, CP.F.104; for a discussion of this statement, see Goldberg, 'Gender and Matrimonial Litigation', p. 47.
65. Ibid., pp. 46–8.
66. P. Biller, 'Confession in the Middle Ages: Introduction', in P. Biller and A. J. Minnis (eds), *Handling Sin: Confession in the Middle Ages* (Woodbridge: York Medieval Press, 1998), pp. 3–33, on p. 13.
67. Ibid., p. 14.
68. M. Haren, 'Confession, Social Ethics and Social Discipline in the Memoriale Presbiterorum', in Biller and Minnis (eds), *Handling Sin*, pp. 109–22.
69. M. Haren, 'The Interrogatories for Officials, Lawyers and Secular Estates of the Memoriale presbiterorum', in Biller and Minnis (eds), *Handling Sin*, pp. 123–63, on p. 157.
70. Ibid., pp. 161–2.
71. *The Riverside Chaucer*, ed. L. D. Benson, 3rd edn (Oxford: Oxford University Press, 1988), vol. 3 (D) 1589. For a brief discussion of the summoner and his encounter with the old woman, see J. Scattergood, 'The "Lewed" and the "Lerede": A Reading of Satire on the Consistory Courts', in J. Scattergood (ed.), *The Lost Tradition: Essays on Middle English Alliterative Poetry* (Dublin: Four Courts Press, 2000), pp. 27–42, on p. 42.
72. *Riverside Chaucer*, vol. 3 (D) 1597.
73. CCA, E.S. Roll 11.
74. BI, CP.F.81. 'dicit que recolit de huiusmodi tempore ex eo que sepius reduxit memorie sue dictum contractum ne forte in futurum dictus Johannes vellet esse falsus huiusmodi contractum negando'.
75. Helmholz, *Marriage Litigation*, p. 26.
76. Ibid., p. 25.
77. P. J. P. Goldberg, *Women, Work, and Life Cycle in a Medieval Economy: Women in York and Yorkshire, c.1300–1520* (Oxford: Oxford University Press, 1992), p. 278.
78. Ibid., p. 275.
79. Gratian, *Decretum Magistri Gratiani, in Corpus Iuris Canonici*, ed. E. Friedberg, 2 vols (1879–81; reprint, Graz: Akademische Druck- und Verlagsanstalt, 1955), C. 27 q. 2 c. 29.
80. For an analysis of cases relating to spousal impotence, see B. Kane, 'Impotence and Virginity in the Late Medieval Ecclesiastical Court of York', *Borthwick Papers*, 114 (2008); see also B. Kane, 'Reading Emotion and Gender in the Later Medieval English Church Courts', *Frühneuzeit-Info*, Special Issue, 'The Use of Court Records and Petitions as Historical Sources', 23:1–2 (2012), pp. 53–63, on pp. 58–60.

81. M. Korpiola, 'Introduction', in M. Korpiola (ed.), *Regional Variations in Matrimonial Law and Custom in Europe, 1150–1600* (Leiden: Brill, 2011), pp. 1–20, on p. 14.

82. Kane, 'Impotence and Virginity'; ; P. J. P. Goldberg, 'John Skathelok's Dick: Voyeurism and "Pornography" in Late Medieval England', in N. McDonald (ed.), *Medieval Obscenities* (York: Boydell and Brewer, York Medieval Press, 2006), pp. 105–23; see also J. Murray, 'On the Origins and Role of "Wise Women" in Causes for Annulment on the Grounds of Male Impotence', *Journal of Medieval History*, 16 (1990), pp. 235–49.

83. BI, CP.F.175.

84. Ibid. 'posset venire domum faceret dictam uxorem suam sacerdoti confiteri ac penetentiam recipere pro periurio quod in hac parte incurrebat'.

85. CCA, E.S. Roll 10.

86. Brundage, *Law, Sex, and Christian Society*, p. 357; for a summary of litigation in cases of nonage, see Helmholz, *Marriage Litigation*, p. 98–9.

87. J. Bedell, 'Memory and Proof of Age in England 1272–1327', *Past and Present*, 162:1 (1999), pp. 3–27; J. T. Rosenthal, *Telling Tales: Sources and Narration in Late Medieval England* (University Park, PA: Pennsylvania State University Press, 2003), ch. 1; for a study of memory in proof of age statements, see B. R. Lee, 'Men's Recollections of a Women's Rite: Medieval English Men's Recollections Regarding the Rite of the Purification of Women after Childbirth', *Gender & History*, 14 (2002), pp. 224–41.

88. C. Given-Wilson, *Chronicles: The Writing of History in the Medieval England* (London: Hambledon Continuum, 2004), p. 79.

89. For a summary of the process involved in inquisitions *post mortem*, see M. Hicks, 'Introduction', in M. Hicks (ed.), *The Fifteenth-Century Inquisitions Post Mortem: A Companion* (Woodbridge: The Boydell Press, 2012), pp. 1–24, on pp. 1–7.

90. Donahue, 'Proof by Witnesses', pp. 136–7.

91. M. Holford, '"Thrifty Men of the Country"? The Jurors and their Role', in Hicks (ed.), *The Fifteenth-Century Inquisitions Post Mortem*, pp. 201–21, on pp. 213–14.

92. CCA, E.S. Roll 10. 'iurata et examinata idem dicit in omnibus cum preiuratis causam sue sciencie assignata quod deflorata fuit in carniprimo'.

93. K. M. Phillips, 'Four Virgins' Tales: Sex and Power in Medieval Law', in A. Bernau, R. Evans and S. Salih (eds), *Medieval Virginities* (Cardiff: University of Wales Press, 2003), pp. 80–101, on pp. 86–9.

94. J. M. Bennett, 'Writing Fornication: Medieval Leyrwite and its Historians', *Transactions of the Royal Historical Society*, 13 (2003), pp. 131–62, on p. 142. Bennett notes the use of the term 'quia deflorata est' in this context.

95. J. M. Bennett, 'Compulsory Service in Late Medieval England', *Past and Present*, 209 (2010), pp. 7–51, on p. 39.

96. Brundage, *Law, Sex, and Christian Society*, p. 519.

97. Phillips, 'Four Virgins' Tales', p. 87.

98. Boncompagno da Signa, 'On Memory', in M. Carruthers and J. M. Ziolkowski (eds), *The Medieval Craft of Memory* (Philadelphia, PA: University of Pennsylvania Press, 2002), pp. 103–17, on p. 115.

99. R. H. Helmholz, 'Bastardy Litigation in Medieval England', *American Journal of Legal History*, 13 (1969), pp. 360–83, on p. 361.

100. *Select Canterbury Cases*, pp. 1–3, pp. 30–1, pp. 612–27.

101. CCA, E.S. Roll 57, 233, 265, 88.

102. *Select Canterbury Cases*, pp. 535–67.

103. Brundage, *Law, Sex, and Christian Society*, p. 215.

104. *The Complete Peerage of England, Scotland, Ireland, Great Britain and the United Kingdom, Extant, Extinct, Or Dormant*, ed. G. E. Cockayne (London: G. Bell and Sons, 1889), vol. 2, p. 9. For a discussion of lands held in serjeanty, see J. Hudson, *The Oxford History of the Laws of England, volume II, 871–1216* (Oxford: Oxford University Press, 2012), pp. 339–40.

105. R. Dace, 'Lesser Barons and Greater Knights: The Middling Group within the English Nobility, *c.* 1086–1265', in S. Morillo (ed.), *Haskins Society Journal: Studies in Medieval History*, 10 (2002), pp. 57–77, on p. 58.

106. CCA, E.S. Roll 57. 'Requisita qualiter hoc recolit de tanto temporis dicit quod per hoc quod dictus Johannes fuit assecutus dictam ecclesiam ante bellum de Evesham et tantum tempus est elapsum post illud bellum'.

107. CCA, E.S. Roll 88. 'iste iuratus dicit quod officialis Linc' scripsit Elyanore Bassett quod ipsa faceret huc venire testes qui melius deponere scirent de facto isto et misit huc istum iuratum et alios contestes suos'.

108. E. Hawkes '"She will ... Protect and Defend her Rights Boldly by Law and Reason ...": Women's Knowledge of Common Law and Equity Courts in Late-Medieval England', in N. J. Menuge (ed.), *Medieval Women and the Law* (Woodbridge: The Boydell Press, 2000), pp. 157–61.

109. S. Bardsley, *Venomous Tongues: Speech and Gender in Late Medieval England* (Philadelphia, PA: University of Pennsylvania Press, 2006), p. 76.

110. Ibid.; see also M. Müller, 'Social Control and the Hue and Cry in Two Fourteenth-Century Villages', *Journal of Medieval History*, 31 (2005), pp. 29–53.

111. Neal, *The Masculine Self*, p. 82.

112. Ibid., chs 1 and 2.

113. CCA, E.S. Roll 62, 56; SVSB III no. 418.

114. BI, CP.F.205.

115. Ibid.

116. K. L. French, *The Good Women of the Parish: Gender and Religion after the Black Death* (Philadelphia, PA: University of Pennsylvania Press, 2008), pp. 48–9.

117. P. Górecki, 'Communities of Legal Memory in Medieval Poland, *c.* 1200–1240', *Journal of Medieval History*, 24:2 (1998), pp. 127–54, on p. 136.

118. S. McSheffrey, 'Jurors, Respectable Masculinity, and Christian Morality: A Comment on Marjorie McIntosh's *Controlling Misbehaviour*', *Journal of British Studies*, 37:3 Controlling (Mis)behavior: Medieval and Early Modern Perspectives (1998), pp. 269–78, on p. 269.

119. L. Gowing, 'Language, Power and the Law: Women's Slander Litigation in Early Modern London', in J. Kermode and G. Walker (eds), *Women, Crime and the Courts in Early Modern England* (London: Routledge, 1994), pp. 26–47, on pp. 30–1.

120. French, *The Good Women of the Parish*, pp. 118–56.

121. C. Wickham, '*Fama* and the Law in Twelfth-Century Tuscany', in T. Fenster and D. Lord Smail (eds), *Fama: The Politics of Talk and Reputation in Medieval Europe* (Ithaca, NY, and London: Cornell University Press, 2003), pp. 15–26, on pp. 16–17.

122. BI, C.P.F.307.

123. CCA, E.S. Roll 77.

124. Ibid. 'de antiqua et approbata consuetudine'.

125. R. H. Helmholz, 'Mortuaries and the Law of Custom', in Helmholz, *The Ius Commune in England: Four Studies* (Oxford: Oxford University Press, 2001), pp. 135–86; for the relation between custom and memory in the later medieval parish, see Kane, 'Custom, Memory and Knowledge'.

126. CCA, E.S. Roll 77. 'pro timore domine sue de Foxcote que huiusmodi solutioni resistit solvere non audebat'.
127. BI, C.P.F.221.
128. J. Murray, 'Gendered Souls in Sexed Bodies: The Male Construction of Female Sexuality in Some Medieval Confessors' Manuals', in Biller and Minnis (eds), *Handling Sin*, pp. 79–93, on p. 81.
129. Ibid., p. 91.

4 Horrox, "'Utterly and Untruly He Hath Deceived Me": Women's Inheritance in Late Medieval England'

1.   E. Powell, 'Law and Justice', in R. Horrox (ed.), *Fifteenth-Century Attitudes: Perceptions of Society in Late-Medieval England* (Cambridge: Cambridge University Press, 1994), pp. 29–41 offers a valuable survey of the issues.
2.   B. McRee, 'Religious Gilds and Regulation of Behavior in Late Medieval Towns', in J. Rosenthal and C. Richmond (eds), *People, Politics and Community in the Later Middle Ages* (Alan Sutton: Gloucester, 1987), pp. 108–22, 113.
3.   The phrase quoted recurs in Margaret of Anjou's letters on behalf of her servants and was clearly a common form: C. Monro (ed.), *Letters of Queen Margaret of Anjou and Bishop Beckington and others, written in the reigns of Henry V and Henry VI*, Camden Society 86 (1863), pp. 89–165.
4.   F. Blomefield (continued by C. Parkin), *An Essay towards a Topographical History of the County of Norfolk*, 5 vols (Lynn and London: published by the author, 1739–75), vol. 5, pp. 872–4; N. Pevsner, *The Buildings of England: North-East Norfolk and Norwich* (London: Penguin Books, 1962), pp. 176–8.
5.   H. Castor, *The King, the Crown and the Duchy of Lancaster* (Oxford: Oxford University Press, 2000), p. 173. Colin Richmond agrees: *The Paston Family in the Fifteenth Century: The First Phase* (Cambridge: Cambridge University Press, 1990), p. 248, but (n. 199) warns against the over-simplification of political connections.
6.   Because of the tendency of the de la Poles to use the same names in successive generations, Katherine has sometimes been misidentified as William's niece: the daughter of his younger brother Thomas, e.g. by J. C. Wedgwood, *History of Parliament: Biographies of the Members of the Commons House, 1439–1509* (London: HMSO, 1936), p. 804. Katherine's father was Thomas de la Pole of Grafton (Northants), the younger son of the first, rather than the second, Earl of Suffolk: *Victoria County History of Northamptonshire* (Woodbridge: VCH and The Boydell Press, 2002), vol. 5, p. 149.
7.   *Calendar of Inquisitions Post Mortem*, Henry VII (London: HMSO, 1898), vol. 1, nos 518, 1096–7; H. E. Chetwynd-Stapylton, *The Stapeltons of Yorkshire* (London: Longmans, Green, 1897), pp. 108–9. In her widowhood Katherine and her second husband evidently also retained possession of the Yorkshire lands (for which no inquisition *post mortem* survives), see n. 16 below.
8.   Wedgwood, *Biographies*, pp. 149–50 identifies Elizabeth's husband as William Calthorpe (1410–94). This is not impossible, but Calthorpe was not knighted until 1464 and the indenture incorporating the marriage settlement mentioned in Miles's will was made between Miles and *Sir* William Calthorpe, which suggests the existence of two namesakes, father and son: The National Archives (hereafter TNA), Prob 11/5 fol. 126 and compare the 'yong' Calthorp of N. Davis (ed.), *Paston Letters and Papers of the*

Fifteenth Century, 2 vols (Oxford: Clarendon Press, 1971–6), vol. 2, pp. 140, 167 [references to the 1450s] and William Calthorp 'junior' in R. Somerville, *Duchy of Lancaster* I (London: Chancellor and Council of the Duchy of Lancaster, 1953), p. 598 [1464].

9. Blomefield, *An Essay*, vol. 5, p. 870.

10. TNA, Prob 11/5 fol. 126.

11. *Calendarium Inquisitionum post mortem sive Escaetarum*, 4 vols (Record Commissioners: London, 1806–28), vol. 4, pp. 333–4.

12. Blomefield, *An Essay*, vol. 5, p. 871. Wedgwood, *Biographies*, p. 419, claims that Edith was still alive in 1467 but the context is a reference to an earlier grant made to the couple: C. Given-Wilson et al. (eds), *Parliament Rolls of Medieval England*, 16 vols (The Boydell Press and The National Archives: Woodbridge & London, 2005), vol. 13, p. 284.

13. The writ of *diem clausit extremum* was dated 22 June 1482: *Calendar of Fine Rolls, 1471–85* (London: HMSO, 1961), no. 664. This corrects the pedigree in J. C. Wedgwood, 'Harcourt of Ellenhall', *Collections for a History of Staffordshire, William Salt Archaeological Society* (London: Harrison, 1914), pedigree facing p. 187, which gives Christopher's death as 1474. The writ authorizes inquisitions in Oxfordshire, Berkshire and Leicestershire but none apparently survives.

14. TNA, PRO 11/7 fol. 206; *Cal.Inq.p.m.*, Henry VII, I no. 201. The pedigree in Wedgwood, 'Harcourt of Ellenhall' suggests that Miles had been born in 1468. It also names a fourth son, Edmund, who does not feature in any of the family wills and seems, to judge by the dates assigned to him, to have strayed in from another generation altogether.

15. There were three consecutive generations of John Huddlestons and most published pedigrees muddle them to a greater or lesser extent. In what follows Jane's father-in-law (d. 1492), her husband (d. 1512) and her son are identified as John I, II and III respectively.

16. G. Wrottesley, 'Pedigrees from the Plea Rolls', *Genealogist*, new series 19 (1903), pp. 158–63, on p. 161.

17. H. B. McCall, *The Early History of Bedale* (London: Elliot Stock, 1907), pp. 48, 55.

18. L. C. Attreed (ed.), *York House Books 1461–1490*, 2 vols (Stroud: Alan Sutton Publishing for Richard III and Yorkist History Trust, 1991), vol. 2, p. 707.

19. British Library, Cotton Julius BXII fols 122–3.

20. L. T. Smith, *The Itinerary of John Leland*, 5 vols (London: Centaur Press reprint, 1964), vol. 2, p. 56.

21. *Calendar of Patent Rolls, 1476–85* (London: HMSO, 1901), p. 93. John was described as a king's esquire.

22. W. St Clair Baddeley, *A Cotteswold Shrine: Being a Contribution to the History of Hailes* (Gloucester & London: J. Bellows, 1908), p. 102. Under Richard III, Christopher was promised the next vacancy in King's Hall, Cambridge: R. Horrox and P. W. Hammond (eds), *British Library Harleian Manuscript, 433*, 4 vols (Upminster: Richard III Society, 1979–83), vol. 1, p. 142.

23. For what follows, see Wedgwood, *Biographies*, pp. 477–8.

24. TNA, Prob 11/17 fol. 164.

25. At his father's death in 1512, John III was said to be aged 24 – i.e. had been born in 1488 – but ages given in inquisitions *post mortem* are notoriously unreliable.

26. W. Hutchinson, *The History of the County of Cumberland*, 2 vols (originally published 1794–5; reprinted East Ardsley: EP Publishing, 1974), vol. 1, p. 528. This gives John III two further wives: Joan Seymour and Joyce. The latter, only tentatively identified by Hutchinson, was the daughter of Margery Harris of Martley (Worcs): Shakespeare

Centre Library and Archives, Stratford upon Avon, ER5/1355. Jane was evidently dead, and John remarried, by 1518, when his mother's will refers to her as her son's *first* wife.

27. TNA, Prob 11/17 fol. 164. The deathbed will is undated, but probate was granted on 30 June 1512.

28. The 'first entail' is presumably not that of 1355, which would have disinherited Jane of all but Bainton, but the settlement made before the marriage of Miles and Katherine.

29. Her will suggests that by this date only Simon was alive. Richard, the second son, made his will in January 1513: TNA, Prob 11/18 fol. 15v. Neither he nor Jane mention Miles, Richard Harcourt's eldest son.

30. All the quotations from Jane's will are taken from TNA, Prob 11/19 fols 140v–2v.

31. Royal letters under the great seal were sent to individuals and sealed folded, so that the seal needed to be broken to open them. These were distinct from letters patent, used for public grants and commands, where the seal was suspended from the open document. It was common practice, especially in London, to have private material enrolled on the dorse as a permanent (and quasi-official) record: *Guide to the Contents of the Public Record Office I: Legal Records, etc* (London: HMSO, 1963), p. 16.

32. Both men were active in the execution of John II's will. They secured probate and were subsequently sued by one of John II's servants, Thomas Fryers, for non-payment of wages: TNA, C1/135/18. Urswick, as executor, also commissioned two large illuminated books from Pieter Meghan to be given to Hailes Abbey: a psalter (1514) and St John Chrysostom on St Matthew (1517): *ODNB*. The commission is not explicitly mentioned in Huddleston's will, which simply asks his executors to expend the residue of the estate for the good of his and Jane's souls.

33. *ODNB*.

34. There is an echo here of Margery Kempe having her *Book* read back to her by its scribe: 'And therfor sche dede no thing wryten but that sche knew rygth wel for very trewth': *The Book of Margery Kempe*, eds S. B. Meech and H.E. Allen, Early English Text Society, original series, 212 (1940), p. 5.

35. Her will speaks of finishing and making the aisles as well as leading and buttressing them, but it is unlikely to have been a complete rebuild. Roof bosses with the Huddleston and Stapleton arms survive in the on-site museum at Hailes.

36. It is not clear who the 'temporal judge' was before whom Jane made this declaration or when she had made it.

37. Although she was anxious for the land to revert to her Harcourt heirs, which by this date meant Simon, her third and only surviving son of the marriage, Jane makes no mention of her Harcourt grandchildren in her will, or of any of her Stapleton or Huddleston kin. John II's will had mentioned a daughter, Alice, the wife of Thomas Beyll, who was bequeathed £20.

38. W. S. Holdsworth, *A History of English Law* (London: Methuen & Co, 1923, rev. 3rd edn), vol. 3, p. 22.

39. These were held under male entail, and when Sir Robert Harcourt died leaving only daughters sometime before 1509, they had passed to Richard Harcourt, Jane's second son by Christopher. On Richard's death in 1513, they had come to Simon.

40. *Feet of Fines of the Tudor Period* IV, Yorkshire Archaeological Society record series, 8 (1890 for 1889), p. 50.

41. Michael Goodich in his introduction to *Voices from the Bench: The Narratives of Lesser Folk in Medieval Trials* (New York and Basingstoke: Palgrave, 2006), describes legal personnel as 'hidden puppeteers', p. 3.

5 Youngs, '"She Hym Fresshely Folowed and Pursued": Women and Star Chamber in Early Tudor Wales'

1. See, for example, E. Hawkes, '"She will ... Protect and Defend her Rights Boldly by Law and Reason ..."': Women's Knowledge of Common Law and Equity Courts in Late-Medieval England', in N. J. Menuge (ed.), *Medieval Women and the Law* (Woodbridge: The Boydell Press, 2000), pp. 145–61; M. F. Stevens, 'London's Married Women, Debt Litigation and Coverture in the Court of Common Pleas', in C. Beattie and M. F. Stevens (eds), *Married Women and the Law in Pre-modern Northwest Europe* (Woodbridge: The Boydell Press, 2013), pp. 115–32.

2. T. Stretton, *Women Waging Law in Elizabethan England* (Cambridge: Cambridge University Press, 1998), p. 40.

3. G. R. Elton, *Star Chamber Stories* (London: Methuen, 1958), p. 9.

4. R. A. Griffiths, 'The English Realm and Dominions and the King's Subjects in the Later Middle Ages', in J. G. Rowe (ed.), *Aspects of Late Medieval Government: Essays presented to J. R. Lander* (Toronto: Toronto University Press, 1986), p. 99.

5. G. Walker, '"A Strange Kind of Stealing": Abduction in Early Modern Wales', in S. Clarke and M. Roberts (eds), *Women and Gender in Early Modern Wales* (Cardiff: University of Wales Press, 2000), pp. 50–74. See too Nicola Whyte's essay in this volume, pp. 141–55.

6. These are housed in the National Archives as STAC 2.

7. For a list of categories, see J. A. Guy, *The Cardinal's Court: The Impact of Thomas Wolsey's Star Chamber* (Hassocks: Harvester Press, 1977), pp. 52–3.

8. J. A. Guy, *The Court of Star Chamber and its Records to the Reign of Elizabeth I* (London: HMSO, 1985), pp. 26, 52.

9. Guy, *The Cardinal's Court*, p. 79.

10. Guy, *The Court of Star Chamber*, p. 29.

11. Guy, *The Cardinal's Court*, p. 109. M. K. Lloyd, 'The Privy Council, Star Chamber and Wales, 1540–1572' (PhD dissertation, Swansea University, 1987), p. 91.

12. Guy, *The Cardinal's Court*, p. 30.

13. Guy, *The Court of Star Chamber*, p. 26; Lloyd, 'The Privy Council, Star Chamber and Wales', p. 93.

14. Lloyd, 'The Privy Council, Star Chamber and Wales', p. 6.

15. P. Williams, *The Council in the Marches of Wales under Elizabeth I* (Cardiff: University of Wales Press, 1958), pp. 11–15.

16. Ifan ab Owen Edwards, *A Catalogue of Star Chamber Proceedings Relating to Wales* (Cardiff: University of Wales Press, 1929), pp. 1–13; Lloyd, 'The Privy Council, Star Chamber and Wales', p. 400.

17. Guy, *The Court of Star Chamber*, p. 20; Guy, *The Cardinal's Court*, p. 110.

18. Women took part in 10 per cent of Star Chamber cases under Elizabeth, dropping to 8.5 per cent under James I: Stretton, *Women Waging Law*, p. 40, fn. 80; Hawkes's study of Lincolnshire and Yorkshire cases going to King's Bench and Common Pleas reveal that only 5 per cent of litigants in her sample years were women, although a higher proportion went to Chancery: "She will ... Protect", pp. 148–50.

19. This differs from Flintshire and Denbighshire where most litigation was over land: Lloyd, 'The Privy Council, Star Chamber and Wales', p. 405.

20. Ifan ab Owen Edwards, *A Catalogue of Star Chamber Proceedings*, pp. iii–iv.

21. For example G. Williams, *Recovery, Reorientation and Reformation: Wales c. 1415–1642* (Oxford: Clarendon Press, 1987).
22. T. B. Pugh (ed.), *Glamorgan County History, vol. III* (Cardiff: University of Wales Press, 1971), p. 268.
23. Williams, *Recovery*, p. 45.
24. Pugh, *Glamorgan County History, vol. III*, p. 266.
25. Ibid., p. 279.
26. Williams, *Recovery*, p. 46; W. R. B. Robinson, 'Sir George Herbert of Swansea (d. 1570), *Bulletin of the Board of Celtic Studies*, 27 (1977), p. 304.
27. For example, petition of Jenet verch Thomas of Gelligaer (Glamorgan): The National Archives (hereafter TNA), C1/1094/77.
28. J. S. Brewer, J. Gairdner and R. H. Brodie (eds), *Letters and Papers, Foreign and Domestic, of the Reign of Henry VIII*, 22 vols (London, 1862–1932), xiii (2), no. 732 (hereafter *LP*).
29. W. R. B. Robinson, 'The Officers and Household of Henry, Earl of Worcester 1529–49', *Welsh History Review*, 8 (1976–7), p. 34.
30. Williams, *Recovery*, p. 257.
31. *LP*, v, 991.
32. *LP*, vi, 210, 946.
33. *LP*, vi, 1381 (3); 1487 (2); Guy, *The Cardinal's Court*, p. 137; Williams, *The Council in the Marches of Wales*, p. 15.
34. TNA, STAC 2/22/206.
35. TNA, STAC 2/29/146; STAC 2/30/70.
36. TNA, STAC 2/8/8; STAC 2/34/8.
37. D. Rhys Phillips, *The History of the Vale of Neath* (Swansea: published by the author, 1925), p. 662; S. Bardsley, *Venomous Tongues: Speech and Gender in Late Medieval England* (Philadelphia, PA: University of Pennsylvania Press: 2006).
38. TNA, STAC 2/19/224.
39. B. A. Hanawalt, *'Of Good and Ill Repute': Gender and Social Control in Medieval England* (Oxford: Oxford University Press, 1998), p. 124.
40. Guy, *The Court of Star Chamber*, p. 19. It should be noted that four other unrelated cases share the same reference.
41. Stretton, *Women Waging Law*, p. 179; Walker, '"A Strange Kind of Stealing"', p. 69; Guy, *The Court of Star Chamber*, p. 26.
42. Hopkyn was Denise's first husband and genealogies show a long relationship with nine children generated from the union: G. T. Clark, *Limbus Patrum Morganiae et Glamorganiae* (London, 1886), pp. 525–6; P. C. Bartrum (ed.), *Welsh Genealogies, AD 1400–1500*, 18 vols (Aberystwyth: National Library of Wales, 1983), vol. 4, p. 609; vol. 5, p. 859.
43. TNA, STAC 2/26/105.
44. Clark, *Limbus Patrum*, pp. 206–7; Bartrum, *Welsh Genealogies*, vol. 2, p. 250.
45. W. R. B. Robinson, 'The First Subsidy Assessment of the Hundreds of Swansea and Llangyfelach, 1543', *Welsh History Review*, 2:2 (1964), pp. 125–145, on pp. 142–3.
46. West Glamorgan Archives, D/D Yc 295, 296.
47. G. T. Clark, *Cartae et alia munimenta quae ad dominim de Glamorgancia pertinent*, 6 vols (Cardiff: William Lewis, 1910), vol. 2, pp. 1864–5.
48. W. R. B. Robinson, 'The County Court of the Englishry of Gower 1498–1500: A Preliminary Study', *National Library of Wales Journal*, 29 (1996), pp. 357–89, on p. 363.

49. W. R. B. Robinson, 'The Lands of Henry, Earl of Worcester in the 1530s', Part 1: Gower, Glamorgan and Breconshire', *Bulletin of the Board of Celtic Studies*, 25:2 (1973), pp. 204, 214–15.

50. TNA, STAC 2/24/365; STAC 3/9/54.

51. William Devereux, Lord Ferrers, had been appointed justice of South Wales in 1525, Chamberlain of South Wales in 1526, and the same year made steward of Princess Mary's household and a member of her council in Wales: Williams, *Recovery*, p. 253.

52. Pardon for 'David ap Griffith of the lordship of Gower, yeoman: *LP*, iv (2), no. 4594 (1).

53. TNA, STAC 2/21/114.

54. TNA, STAC 2/9/46–59.

55. TNA, STAC 2/32/23.

56. TNA, STAC 2/9/58. In January 1540, Rowland Lee showed his awareness of Jane's allegations in a letter written to Cromwell, and in February depositions were taken at Gloucester in relation to this case: *LP*, xv, no. 129.

57. This appeared to be the main purpose of Star Chamber for the Jacobean litigant: T. G. Barnes, 'Star Chamber Litigants and their Counsel, 1596–1641', in J. H. Baker (ed.), *Legal Records and the Historian* (London; Royal Historical Society, 1978), pp. 12–15.

58. Jane Carne's bill made this explicit when it proclaimed her husband's murder was the 'utter undoing' of the plaintiff: TNA, STAC 2/9/46–59.

59. This is also catalogued as TNA, STAC 2/26/105. Bartrum, *Welsh Genealogies*, vol. 4, p. 605.

60. E. W. Ives, '"Agaynst Taking Awaye of Women": The Inception and Operation of the Abduction Act of 1487', in E. W. Ives, R. J. Knecht and J. J. Scarisbrick (eds), *Wealth and Power in Tudor England* (London: Athlone, 1978), pp. 21–44; K. M. Phillips, 'Written on the Body: Reading Rape from the Twelfth to the Fifteenth Centuries', in Menuge (ed.), *Medieval Women and the Law*, pp. 125–44, on p. 137. Walker, '"A Strange Kind of Stealing"', p. 63.

61. M. E. Owen, 'Shame and Reparation: Woman's Place in the Kin', in M. E. Owen and D. Jenkins (eds), *The Welsh Law of Women* (Cardiff: University of Wales Press, 1980), p. 48.

62. G. Walker, 'Rereading Rape and Sexual Violence in Early Modern England' *Gender and History*, 10:1 (1998), pp. 1–25.

63. Similar language was used in the abduction of Joan verch Howell at Llanwern Church (Monmouthshire): TNA, STAC 2, 20/223.

64. I. Soulsby, *The Towns of Medieval Wales* (Chichester: Phillimore, 1983), p. 191.

65. T. Hopkins, *Neath: the Town and its People* (Swansea: West Glamorgan Archives, 2010), pp. 5–6, 27–8.

66. J. G. Bellamy, *The Criminal Trial in Later Medieval England* (Stroud: Sutton, 1998), p. 173.

67. Walker, '"A Strange Kind of Stealing"', p. 66.

68. West Glamorgan Archives, D/D Yc 354.

69. W. P. Griffith, 'Tudor Prelude', in E. Jones (ed.), *The Welsh in London, 1500–2000* (Cardiff: University of Wales Press, 2001), pp. 9–11, 23.

70. TNA, C1/705/23.

71. J. Noorthouck, *A New History of London including Westminster and Southwark* (London: 1773), book 2, pp. 558–60.

72. An analysis of the case can be found in Ives, '"Agaynst Taking Awaye of Women"', pp. 31–43.

73. E. Hawkes, "'She was Ravished against Her Will What So Ever She Say": Female Consent in Rape and Ravishment in Late-Medieval England', *Limina*, 1 (1995), pp. 47–54, on p. 52.

74. Stretton, *Women Waging Law*, pp. 180, 212; C. Dunn, *Stolen Women in Medieval England: Rape, Abduction and Adultery, 1100–1500* (Cambridge: Cambridge University Press, 2013), p. 95.

75. Dunn, *Stolen Women*, pp. 55–6.

76. Bellamy, *The Criminal Trial*, p. 173.

77. Dunn, *Stolen Women*, pp. 83–5; Ives, "'Agaynst Taking Awaye of Women'", p. 22. Bellamy, *The Criminal Trial*, p. 175.

78. Later known as Longford Court. Phillips, *The History of the Vale of Neath*, pp. 66, 404–5.

79. L. Johnson, 'Married Women, Crime and the Courts in Late Medieval Wales', in Beattie and Stevens (eds), *Married Women and the Law*, pp. 74–7.

80. TNA, SC6/HenVIII/5156. I am grateful to Dr Rhianydd Biebrach for this reference.

81. Bartrum, *Welsh Genealogies*, vol. 4, p. 605.

82. West Glamorgan Archives, D/D Yc 371, 372.

83. Bartrum, *Welsh Genealogies*, vol. 2, p. 250.

84. B. J. Harris, *English Aristocratic Women, 1450–1550* (Oxford: Oxford University Press, 2002), p. 162.

6 Rodziewicz, 'Women and the Hue and Cry in Late Fourteenth-Century Great Yarmouth'

1. S. H. Rigby, *English Society in the Later Middle Ages: Class, Status and Gender* (Basingstoke: Macmillian Press, 1995), pp. 243–52.

2. D. Neal, 'Suits Make the Man: Masculinity in Two English Law Courts, c. 1500', *Canadian Journal of History*, 37:1 (2002), pp. 1–22, on p. 6.

3. Ibid., p. 15.

4. E. Hawkes, "'[S]he will … Protect and Defend her Rights Boldly by Law and Reason…'": Women's Knowledge of Common Law and Equity Courts in Late-Medieval England', in N. J. Menuge (ed.), *Medieval Women and the Law* (Woodbridge: The Boydell Press, 2003), pp. 145–162, on p. 146; B. A. Hanawalt, *'Of Good and Ill Repute': Gender and Social Control in Medieval England* (Oxford: Oxford University Press, 1998), p. 7.

5. J. M. Bennett, *Women in the Medieval English Countryside: Gender and Household in Brigstock before the Plague* (Oxford: Oxford University Press, 1987), pp. 172–6.

6. Only three Great Yarmouth court rolls have not survived from this period, for the years 1368–9, 1372–3 and 1375–6.

7. Two of these raisings were by the same woman in the course of an attack by two other women. Norfolk Record Office (hereafter NRO), Y/C4/88, m. 8v.

8. M. Müller, 'Social Control and the Hue and Cry in Two Fourteenth-Century Villages', *Journal of Medieval History*, 31 (2005), pp. 29–53, on pp. 38–9.

9. F. Pollock and F. W. Maitland, *The History of English Law before the Time of Edward I*, 2nd edn, 2 vols (Cambridge, 1898), vol. 2, pp. 578–9.

10. Ibid.; R. F. Hunnisett, *The Medieval Coroner* (Cambridge: Cambridge University Press, 1961), p. 10.

11. Müller, 'Social Control and the Hue and Cry ; M. P. Hogan, 'Medieval Villainy: A Study in the Meaning and Control of Crime in an English Village', *Studies in Medieval and Renaissance History*, new series 2 (1979), pp. 121–215.

12. For example, VI Athelstan 3; *The Laws of the Earliest English Kings*, ed. and trans by F. L. Attenborough (Cambridge: Cambridge University Press, 1963), p. 159.

13. F. W. Maitland, *Selected Historical Essays of F. W. Maitland: Chosen and Introduced by H. M. Cam* (Cambridge: Beacon Press, 1957), p. 43.

14. D. A. Crowley, 'The Later History of the Frankpledge', *Bulletin of the Institute of Historical Research* (PhD dissertation, University of Sheffield, 1971), pp. 290–1.

15. A. Saul, 'Great Yarmouth in the Fourteenth Century: A Study in Trade, Politics and Society' (PhD dissertation, University of Oxford, 1975), pp. 8–9.

16. D. A. Crowley, *Frankpledge and Leet Jurisdiction in Later Medieval Essex* (PhD dissertation, University of Sheffield, 1971); Crowley, 'History of the Frankpledge', pp. 1–15; P. R. Schofield, 'The Late Medieval View of Frankpledge and the Tithing System: An Essex Case Study', in Z. Razi and R. M. Smith (eds), *Medieval Society and the Manor Court* (Oxford: Oxford University Press, 1996), pp. 408–49.

17. W. A. Morris, *The Frankpledge System* (New York: Longmans, Green, and Co., 1910).

18. E. Rutledge, 'Immigration and Population Growth in Early Fourteenth-Century Norwich: Evidence from the Tithing Roll', *Urban History Yearbook* (1988), pp. 15–30; P. Dunn, 'Norwich after the Black Death: Society and Economy in Late Fourteenth-Century Norwich' (PhD dissertation, University of East Anglia, 2003).

19. L. R. Poos, *A Rural Society after the Black Death: Essex 1350–1525* (Cambridge: Cambridge University Press, 1991), pp. 91–110, 160–1.

20. S. Olson, *A Chronicle of All that Happens: Voices from the Village Court in Medieval England* (Toronto: Pontifical Institute of Mediaeval Studies, 1996); E. B. DeWindt, *Land and People in Holywell-cum-Needingworth: Structures of Tenure and Patterns of Social Organisation in an East Midlands Village, 1252–1457* (Toronto, 1972); A. R. DeWindt, 'Local Government in a Small Town: A Medieval Leet Jury and its Constituents', *Albion*, 23 (1991), pp. 627–54.

21. M. Mulholland, 'The Jury in English Manorial Courts', in J. W. Cairns and G. McLeod (eds), *The Dearest Birth Right of the People of England: The Jury in the History of the Common Law* (Oxford: Hart, 2002), pp. 63–74; M. Mulholland, 'Trials in Manorial Courts in Late Medieval England', in M. Mulholland and B. Pullan (eds), *Judicial Tribunals in England and Europe 1200–1700*, The Trial in History Series, vol. 1 (Manchester: Manchester University Press, 2003), pp. 81–101; DeWindt, 'Local Government', pp. 627–54; M. K. McIntosh, 'Finding Language for Misconduct: Jurors in Fifteenth-Century Local Courts', in B. A. Hanawalt and D. Wallace (eds), *Bodies and Disciplines: Intersections of Literature and History in Fifteenth-Century England*, Medieval Cultures Series, 9 (Minneapolis, MN: Minnesota University Press, 1996), pp. 87–122.

22. J. G. Bellamy, *Crime and Public Order in England in the Later Middle Ages* (London: Routledge and Kegan Paul, 1973); J. G. Bellamy, *The Criminal Trial in Later Medieval England: Felony before the Courts from Edward I to the Sixteenth Century* (Stroud: Sutton, 1998).

23. S. Roberts, *Order and Dispute: An Introduction to Legal Anthropology* (Harmondsworth: Penguin, 1979), pp. 40–1.

24. S. Bardsley, *Venomous Tongues: Speech and Gender in Late Medieval England* (Philadelphia, PA: University of Pennsylvania Press, 2006); S. McSheffrey, 'Men and Masculinity in Late Medieval London Civic Culture: Governance, Patriarchy and Reputation', in J.

Murray (ed.), *Conflicted Identities and Multiple Masculinities: Men in the Medieval West* (New York: Garland, 1999), pp. 243–78.

25. For more on this topic, see T. Fenster and D. Lord Smail (eds), *Fama: The Politics of Talk and Reputation in Medieval England* (Ithaca, NY: Cornell University Press, 2003) and B. A. Hanawalt, '"Of Good and Ill Repute": The Limits of Community Tolerance', in B. A. Hanawalt (ed.), *'Of Good and Ill Repute': Gender and Social Control in Medieval England* (Oxford: Oxford University Press, 1998), pp. 1–17.

26. Hawkes, "She will ... Protect", p. 146.

27. H. de Bracton, *Bracton on the Laws and Customs of England*, ed. and trans. S. E. Thorne, 4 vols (Cambridge, MA: Belknap Press in association with Selden Society, 1968), vol. 2, p. 31.

28. Olson, *Chronicle*, pp. 60–4; D. Postles, 'Personal Pledging in Manorial Courts in the Later Middle Ages', *Bulletin of the John Rylands University Library of Manchester*, 75 (1993), pp. 419–35, on p. 427.

29. Bennett, *Women in the Medieval English Countryside*, p. 154.

30. NRO, Y/C4/85, m. 15r; NRO, Y/C4/86, m. 14r.

31. J. Rodziewicz, 'Order and Society: Great Yarmouth 1366–1381' (PhD dissertation, University of East Anglia, 2009), pp. 264–82.

32. Olson, *Chronicle*, p. 58.

33. *Statutes of the Realm Printed by Command of His Majesty King George the Third in Pursuance of an Address of the House of Commons of Great Britain, from Original Records and Authentic Manuscripts*, ed. A. Luders and others, 11 vols (London: Record Commission, 1810), vol. 1, p. 41.

34. For more on this claim, see Rodziewicz, 'Order and Society', pp. 178–90; Müller, 'Social Control and the Hue and Cry'; Bardsley, *Venomous Tongues*, pp. 70–7; Olson, *Chronicle*, pp. 92–100.

35. *Bracton on the Laws and Customs of England*, vol. 2, p. 350; Morris, *Frankpledge System*, pp. 91, 96–7.

36. Crowley, 'History of the Frankpledge', pp. 289–91. L. R. Poos has argued that, although the tithing was in decline in some places, in 'other communities the institution remained a vital organ of local administration': Poos, *Rural Society*, p. 92.

37. *Bracton on the Laws and Customs of England*, vol. 2, p. 350; Morris, *Frankpledge System*, pp. 91, 96–7.

38. P. Brand, 'The Travails of Travel: The Difficulties of Getting to Court in Later Medieval England', in P. Horden (ed.), *Freedom of Movement in the Middle Ages: Proceedings of the 2003 Harlaxton Symposium*, Harlaxton Medieval Studies, 15 (Donington: Shaun Tyas, 2007), pp. 226, 228.

39. John was eventually fined 'for the aforesaid trespass': D. W. Sutherland, *Eyre of Northamptonshire*, Selden Society, 97 (Seldon Society, 1981), p. 152.

40. NRO, Y/C4/91, m. 10v.

41. NRO, Y/C4/88, m. 8r.

42. For the punishment of the provoker of an assault rather than the attacker, see K. Jones, *Gender and Petty Crime in Late Medieval England: The Local Courts in Kent, 1460–1560*, Gender in the Middle Ages, 2 (Woodbridge: The Boydell Press, 2006), p. 67.

43. NRO, Y/C4/89, m. 2v.

44. NRO, Y/ C4/91, m. 10r.

45. NRO, Y/C4/92, m. 14v.

46. There was also one instance where the gender of the raiser is unknown, identified only as the servant of Agatha Legat.

47. B. A. Hanawalt, 'Violent Death in Fourteenth- and Fifteenth-Century England', *Comparative Studies in Social History*, 18 (1976), 297–320, on p. 307.

48. Ibid., p. 310, 319; A. J. Finch, 'The Nature of Violence in the Middle Ages: An Alternative Perspective', *Historical Research*, 70 (1997), pp. 249–68, on pp. 257, 267.

49. NRO, Y/C4/88, m. 8v.

50. NRO, Y/C4/88, m. 8v; NRO, Y/C4/91, m. 10v.

51. Bardsley, *Venomous Tongues*, pp. 76–7.

52. NRO, Y/C4/85, m. 2r.

53. Bardsley, *Venomous Tongues*, pp. 70–7.

54. NRO, Y/C4/88, m. 8v.

55. NRO, Y/C4/92, m. 14v.

56. Müller, 'Social Control and the Hue and Cry', p. 39.

57. For example, NRO, Y/C4/91, m. 10r; NRO, Y/C4/82, m. 16v.

58. Müller, 'Social Control and the Hue and Cry', p. 39; Karen Jones and others have emphasized that violence was central to the medieval masculine ideal: Jones, *Gender and Petty Crime*, pp. 63–9. Jones also discusses the available literature on this subject. R. M. Karras, *From Boys to Men: Formations of Masculinity in Late Medieval Europe* (Philadelphia, PA: University of Pennsylvania Press, 2003), pp. 11–17.

59. Müller, 'Social Control and the Hue and Cry', pp. 45, 47.

60. Müller, 'Social Control and the Hue and Cry', pp. 44, 47; Bardsley, *Venomous Tongues*, pp. 73–4.

61. S. Chojnacki, 'The Power of Love: Wives and Husbands in Late Medieval Venice', in M. C. Erler and M. Kowaleski (eds), *Women and Power in the Middle Ages* (Athens, GA: University of Georgia Press, 1998), pp. 126–48.

62. E. Adamson Hoebel, *The Law of Primitive Man: A Study in Comparative Legal Dynamics* (Cambridge, MA: Harvard University Press, 1954), p. 286.

63. Müller, 'Social Control and the Hue and Cry', pp. 41–2; Rigby, *English Society in the Later Middle Ages*, pp. 243–52; P. Maddern, *Violence and Social Order: East Anglia 1422–1442* (Oxford: Clarendon Press, 1992), pp. 98–9, 232–3.

64. Hoebel, *Primitive Man*, pp. 275–6, 287; Roberts, *Order and Dispute*, p. 13.

65. J. M. Bennett, 'Public Power and Authority in the Medieval English Countryside', in Erler and Kowaleski (eds), *Women and Power*, pp. 18–36; B. A. Hanawalt, 'Lady Honor Lisle's Networks of Influence', in Erler and Kowalski (eds), *Women and Power*, pp. 188–212; J. A. McNamara and S. F. Wemple, 'The Power of Women through Family in Medieval Europe, 500–1100', in Erler and Kowalski (eds), *Women and Power*, pp. 83–101; J. A. McNamara, 'Women and Power through the Family Revisited', in M. C. Erler and M. Kowaleski (eds), *Gendering the Master Narrative: Women and Power in the Middle Ages* (London: Cornell University Press, 2003), pp. 17–30.

66. F. Rexroth, *Deviance and Power in Late Medieval London* (Cambridge: Cambridge University Press, 2007), p. 220; H. Garfinkel, 'Conditions of Successful Degradation Ceremonies', *American Journal of Sociology*, 61 (1956), pp. 420–4.

67. Rodziewicz, 'Order and Society', pp. 122–3.

68. B. C. Kane, 'Memory and Gender in the Late Medieval Church Courts of York' (PhD dissertation, University of York, 2008).

7 Flather, 'Gender and the Control of Sacred Space in Early Modern England'

1. I am grateful to John Walter, Alison Rowlands and Tom Freeman for their helpful comments on earlier drafts of this essay.
2. M. Aston, *England's Iconoclasts Vol. 1: Laws against Images* (Oxford: Clarendon Press, 1988); M. Aston, *Faith and Fire, Popular and Unpopular Religion in England, 1350–1600* (London: The Hambledon Press, 1993); M. Aston, *The King's Bedpost: Reformation and Iconography in a Tudor Group Portrait* (Cambridge: Cambridge University Press, 1993); M. Aston, 'Puritans and Iconoclasm 1560–1660', in C. Durston and J. Eales (eds), *The Culture of English Puritanism, 1560–1700* (Basingstoke: Palgrave, 1996); D. Cressy, 'The Battle of the Altars: Turning the Tables and Breaking the Rails', in D. Cressy, *Travesties and Transgressions in Tudor and Stuart England* (Oxford: Oxford University Press, 2000); P. Collinson, *From Iconoclasm to Iconophobia, The Cultural Impact of the Second Reformation* (Reading: University of Reading, 1986); J. Eales, 'Iconoclasm, Iconography and the Altar in the English Civil War', in D. Wood and W. Sheils (eds), *The Church and the Arts: Studies in Church History*, 28 (Oxford: Blackwell, 1992); J. Spraggon, *Puritan Iconoclasm during the English Civil War* (Woodbridge: Boydell and Brewer, 2003); J. Walter, '"Abolishing Superstition with Sedition?" The Politics of Popular Iconoclasm in England 1640–1642', *Past and Present*, 183 (2004), pp. 79–123; J. Walter, 'Popular Iconoclasm and the Politics of the Parish in Eastern England, 1640–1642', *Historical Journal*, 47 (2004), pp. 261–90; J. Walter, 'Confessional Politics in Pre-Civil War Essex: Prayer Books, Profanations, and Petitions', *Historical Journal*, 44 (2001). pp. 677–701; J. Walter, '"Affronts & Insolencies": The Voices of Radwinter and Popular Opposition to Laudianism', *English Historical Review*, 122 (2007), pp. 35–60.
3. D. Cressy, *Birth, Marriage and Death: Ritual, Religion and the Lifecycle in Tudor and Stuart England* (Oxford: Oxford University Press, 1997), p. 11.
4. P. Collinson, *The Elizabethan Puritan Movement* (London: Jonathan Cape, 1967), p. 93; C. Peters, *Patterns of Piety: Women, Gender and Religion in Late Medieval and Reformation England* (Cambridge: Cambridge University Press, 2003), pp. 154–5.
5. Walter, 'Abolishing Superstition', pp. 80–1.
6. E. Carlson, 'The Origins, Function, and Status of Churchwardens', in M. Spufford (ed.), *The World of Rural Dissenters, 1520–1725* (Cambridge: Cambridge University Press, 1995), p. 192.
7. The Parochial Inquisition of 1650 lists 22 female patrons out of 370 Essex parishes, all widows: H. Smith, *The Ecclesiastical History of Essex under the Long Parliament and Commonwealth* (Colchester: Benham, 1933), pp. 233–320.
8. M. Sommerville, *Sex and Subjection* (London: Arnold, 1995), p. 50.
9. S. Mendelson and P. Crawford, *Women in Early Modern England 1550–1720* (Oxford: Clarendon Press, 1998), p. 229.
10. R. B. Shoemaker, *Gender in English Society 1650–1850: The Emergence of Separate Spheres?* (London: Longman, 1998), p. 210; P. Collinson, *Birthpangs of Protestant England* (Basingstoke: Macmillan, 1988), pp. 74–7.
11. A. Flather, *Gender and Space in Early Modern England* (Woodbridge: The Boydell Press, 2007), pp. 135–73.

12. F. G. Emmison, *Essex Wills (England): Archdeaconry of Essex, Archdeaconry of Colchester, Archdeaconry of Middlesex (Essex Division), preserved in the Essex Record Office, Vol. 4, 1577–1584*, p. 55; *Vol. 6, 1591–1597*, p. 62.

13. Cressy, *Birth, Marriage and Death*, pp. 428–9, 436.

14. P. Crawford, *Women and Religion in England, 1500–1720* (London: Routledge, 1993), p. 56; M. Hayward, 'Reflections on Gender and Status Distinctions: An Analysis of the Liturgical Textiles Recorded in Mid-Sixteenth Century London', *Gender & History*, 14:3 (2002), pp. 403–25, on p. 420.

15. Essex Record Office (hereafter ERO), T/P 99/3.

16. ERO, D/P 44/5.

17. W. Cliftlands, 'The "Well-Affected" and the "Country": Politics and Religion in English Provincial Society, *c.* 1640–1645' (PhD dissertation, University of Essex, 1987), p. 148.

18. ERO, Q/SR 314/92; 318/29; Q/SBa 2/43, 47; Cliftlands, "Well-Affected", p. 153.

19. Cressy, *Birth, Marriage and Death*, pp. 208–10.

20. For examples, see ERO, D/AEA 40 fol. 122; ERO, D/AEA 43 fol. 10; ERO, D/ACA 47 fol. 98v.

21. W. Hale, *A Series of Precedents and Proceedings in Criminal Causes Extending from the Year 1475 to 1640* (London: Francis and John Rivington, 1847), p. 237. See also ERO, D/ACA 21 fols 55v, 56; ERO, D/ACA 21 fol. 90v.

22. ERO, D/ACA 39 fols 27, 34, 45. Thanks to Robert Dean Smith for biographical details.

23. Cressy, *Birth, Marriage and Death*, p. 11.

24. Ibid., pp. 218–24.

25. ERO, D/AEA 42 fol. 35.

26. ERO, D/ACA 54 fol. 113. See also ERO, D/ACA 51 fol. 228; ERO, D/ACA 51 fol. 237v.

27. ERO, D/AEA 41 fol. 181v.

28. Walter, 'Prayer Book', p. 683. On the sign of the cross, see Cressy, *Birth, Marriage and Death*, pp. 124–48.

29. For examples at Radwinter and Halstead, see Smith, *Ecclesiastical History*, pp. 87–8, 182.

30. Cressy, *Birth, Marriage and Death*, p. 133.

31. ERO, D/ABA 8 fol. 2.

32. Cited in Smith, *Ecclesiastical History*, p. 183.

33. Cressy, *Birth, Marriage and Death*, p. 133.

34. Ibid., p. 410.

35. ERO, D/ABA 8 fol. 17.

36. Cressy, *Birth, Marriage and Death*, p. 405.

37. Collinson, *Elizabethan Puritan Movement*, pp. 71, 94–5; N. Jones, *The Birth of the Elizabethan Age* (Oxford: Blackwell, 1995), pp. 53–65; R. Crowley, *A Briefe Discourse against the Outwarde Apparell and Ministring Garmentes of the Popishe Church* (Emden, 1566). On the vestments controversy, see P. Collinson, *The Religion of Protestants: The Church in English Society 1559–1625* (Oxford: Clarendon Press, 1982); M. M. Knappen, *Tudor Puritanism: A Chapter in the History of Idealism* (Chicago, IL: University of Chicago Press, 1939). For clergy dress, see G. Murdock, 'Dressed to Repress?: Protestant Clergy Dress and the Regulation of Morality in Early Modern Europe', *Fashion Theory: The Journal of Dress, Body and Culture*, 4 (2000), pp. 179–99.

38. W. Hunt, *The Puritan Moment, The Coming of Revolution in an English County* (Cambridge, MA, and London: Harvard University Press, 1983), pp. 87–112; Walter, 'Confessional Politics'; Walter, "Abolishing Superstition", pp. 79–123.

39. 'The Roots and Branches Petition, 1640', in D. Cressy and L. A. Ferrell (eds), *Religion and Society in Early Modern England: a Sourcebook* (London: Routledge, 1996), pp. 174–5.

40. Collinson, *Elizabethan Puritan Movement*, p. 93; Young radical soldiers in the Parliamentary army made a mockery of the surplice during the 1640s, but women also seized the initiative at local parish level. Walter, "Abolishing Superstition", p. 90.

41. 'Historical Memoranda of John Stowe: General, 1564–7', in J. Gairdner (ed.), *Three Fifteenth-Century Chronicles: With Historical Memoranda by John Stowe* Camden Society new series 28 (1880), p. 140.

42. Collinson, *Elizabethan Puritan Movement*, p. 94.

43. Anon., *An Order from the High Conrt [sic] of Parliament, which was Read on Sunday Last, in Every Church, being the 19. day of December, 1641* (London, 1641).

44. 'Historical Memoranda of John Stowe', p. 140; W. Nicholson (ed), *The Remains of Edmund Grindal, D.D.* (Cambridge: Cambridge University Press, 1843), p. 288.

45. Cited in Smith, *Ecclesiastical History*, p. 182.

46. On clothing, damage and status, see A. Shepard, *Meanings of Manhood in Early Modern England* (Oxford: Oxford University Press, 2003), p. 145.

47. ERO, Q/SR 312/58, 60, 61, 112, 136; *Journal of the House of Lords Vol 4: 1629–42* (1802), pp. 107–8.

48. Royal Manuscripts Commission Buccleuch Estate Archive, *Buccleuch* MSS, iii, 395.

49. ERO, D/ACA 69 fol. 307.

50. N. Z. Davis, 'The Rites of Violence', in N. Z. Davis, *Society and Culture in Early Modern France* (Stanford, CA: Stanford University Press, 1965), p. 159.

51. ERO, D/ACA 68 fol.19.

52. P. Crawford, 'Attitudes to Menstruation in Seventeenth Century England', *Past and Present*, 91 (1981), pp. 57–65, 60–1; Walter, 'Confessional Politics', pp. 680–1; Walter, "Abolishing Superstition", pp. 90–1.

53. ERO, D/ACA 41 fol. 43v.

54. N. Z. Davis, 'Women on Top', in N. Z. Davis (ed.), *Society and Culture in Early Modern France* (Stanford, CA: Stanford University Press, 1975), pp. 124–51.

55. ERO, Q/SR 311/14. Men performed all other attacks on altar rails, Cliftlands, "Well-Affected", pp. 150–1.

56. Cressy, *Birth, Marriage and Death*, p. 20.

57. For Brian Walton, see A. G. Matthews, *Walker Revised. Being a Revision of John Walker's Sufferings of the Clergy during the Grand Rebellion 1642–1660* (Oxford: Clarendon Press, 1948), p. 61.

58. Cliftlands, "Well-Affected", p. 151.

59. ERO, D/AEA 41 fol. 129v.

60. For hat honour, see A. Davies, *The Quakers in English Society 1655–1725* (Oxford: Oxford University Press, 2000), pp. 133–5; J. Walter, 'Gesturing at Authority: Deciphering the Gestural Code of Early Modern England', in M. Braddick (ed), *The Politics of Gesture: Historical Perspectives,* vol. 203, Supplement 4 (Past and Present, 2009), pp. 96–127.

61. ERO, D/AEA 39 fol. 210.

62. ERO, D/ABA 6 fol. 57v.

63. Collinson, *Elizabethan Puritan Movement*, p. 92.

64. ERO, D/AEA 40 fol. 84.

65. ERO, D/AEA 39 fol. 74v.

66. ERO, D/ACA 52 fol. 250v.

67. Cliftlands, "Well-Affected", p. 205; ERO, Q/SR 332/70; British Library (hereafter BL) Add MSS 5829, fols 9, 10, 21.

68. Cliftlands, "Well-Affected", p. 205. For stoning and female violent protest, see J. Walter, 'Faces in the Crowd: Gender and Age in the Early Modern English Crowd', in H. Berry and E. Foyster (eds), *The Family in Early Modern England* (Cambridge: Cambridge University Press, 2007), p. 118.

69. L. Gowing, *Domestic Dangers: Women, Words, and Sex in Early Modern London* (Oxford: Oxford University Press, 1996), pp. 111–38; B. Capp, *When Gossips Meet: Women, Family and Neighbourhood in Early Modern England* (Oxford: Oxford University Press, 2003), pp. 268–87.

70. I. M. Green, 'The Persecution of "Scandalous" and Malignant Parish Clergy during the English Civil War', *English Historical Review*, 94 (1979), pp. 507–31.

71. C. Holmes (ed.), *Suffolk Committees for Scandalous Ministers 1644–1646*, Suffolk Records Society 13 (1970), pp. 9–14.

72. Cliftlands, "Well-Affected", pp. 195–257.

73. BL Add. MSS 5829.

74. BL Add. MSS 5829, fol. 37. On Wall, see Cliftlands, "Well-Affected", p. 220.

75. BL Add. MSS 5829, fols 32–3; PRO SP16/31; Cliftlands, "Well-Affected", p. 220.

76. BL Add. MSS 5829, fol. 10.

77. BL Add. MSS 5829, fol. 45.

78. BL Add. MSS 5829, fol. 47.

79. BL Add. MSS 5829, fol. 15. ERO, T/A 42 fol. 146. Henry Smith rated at £1.2s.; Widow Osborne rated at 2s.4d.

80. BL Add. MSS 5829, fol. 16; ERO, D/ABA 8, fol.142; Cliftlands, "Well-Affected", p. 220.

81. BL Add. MSS 5829, fol. 23.

82. ERO, Q/SBa 2/57.

83. ERO, Q/SR 171/60d, John Neville, 'church-warden'; F. G. Emmison, *Wills at Chelmsford*, vol. 8 (Chelmsford: Essex Records Office, 1958), p. 210.

84. ERO, Q/SBa 2/57; ERO, Q/SR 310/72, Thomas Beare, 'husbandman'.

85. P. Morant, *The History and Antiquities of the County of Essex, Vol. 1* (London: T. Osborne, 1768), p. 281; ERO, Q/SBa 2/57.

86. Smith, *Ecclesiastical History*, p. 296.

87. L. Gowing, 'Ordering the Body: Illegitimacy and Female Authority in Seventeenth-Century England', in M. J. Braddick and J. Walter (eds), *Negotiating Power in Early Modern Society: Order, Hierarchy and Subordination in Britain and Ireland* (Cambridge: Cambridge University Press, 2001), pp. 43–62.

88. L. Gowing, *Common Bodies: Women, Touch and Power in Seventeenth Century England* (New Haven, CT: Yale University Press, 2003), pp. 47–8.

89. Cressy, *Birth, Marriage and Death*, pp. 117–24.

90. J. White, *The First Century of Scandalous, Malignant Priests Made and Admitted into, by the Prelates in whose Hands the Ordination of Ministers and Government of the Church hath been. Or, A Narration of the Causes for which the Parliament hath ordered the Sequestration of the Beneficies of Severall Ministers Complained of before them for Vitiousness of Life, Errors of Doctrine, contrary to the Articles of our Religion, and for Practising and Pressing Superstitious Innovations against Law for Malignancy Against Parliament* (London: Printed by George Miller, [1643]), pp. 50–2.

91. M. Byford, 'The Birth of a Protestant Town: The Process of Reformation in Tudor Colchester, 1530–80', in P. Collinson and J. Craig (eds), *The Reformation in English Towns, 1500–1640* (London: Palgrave Macmillan, 1998), p. 41.
92. Hale, *A Series of Precedents*, pp. 248–9.
93. Cliftlands, "Well-Affected", pp. 150–6.
94. ERO, Q/SR 312/58, 60, 61, 112, 136.
95. ERO, Ass. 35/88/6/48; Cliftlands, "Well-Affected", p. 154, n. 322.
96. H. Grieve, *Sleepers in the Shadows: Chelmsford, A Town, Its People And Its Past. vol. 2, From Market Town to Chartered Borough, 1608–1688* (Chelmsford: Essex Record Office, 1994), pp. 23, 47, 52.

8 Capp, 'The Travails of Agnes Beaumont'

1. *ODNB.*
2. The first modern edition, with modernized spelling, is *The Narrative of the Persecutions of Agnes Beaumont*, ed. V. J. Camden (East Lansing, MI: Colleagues Press, 1992), hereafter *The Narrative of the Persecutions*. The most accessible text is now in *John Bunyan: Grace Abounding with Other Spiritual Autobiographies*, eds J. Stachniewski and A. Pacheco (Oxford: Oxford University Press, 1998), hereafter *John Bunyan*. Citations to Agnes's *Narrative* in the text and notes are to this edition unless otherwise stated. The original manuscript, possibly penned by Agnes, is Egerton MS 2414, London, British Library; Egerton MS 2128 is a fair copy, written after her death.
3. *The Narrative of the Persecutions*, p. 22n.
4. H. G. Tibbutt (ed.), *The Minutes of the First Independent Church (now Bunyan Meeting) at Bedford 1656–1766*, Bedfordshire Historical Record Society, 55 (1976), pp. 75, 215. The Gamlingay Dissenters requested affiliation with the Bedford church in December 1669. Their teacher was Luke Ashwood (or Astwood), oatmeal-maker, and meetings were held at his house. He was licensed in 1672: Tibbutt, *Minutes*, p. 42; G. Lyon Turner (ed.), *Original Records of Early Nonconformity* 3 vols (London: T. Fisher Unwin, 1911–14), vol. 2, p. 869. Several members came from Edworth, where meetings were sometimes held at George Pridden's house, with Edward Dent as teacher: Tibbutt, *Minutes*, pp. 76, 86; Lyon Turner, *Original Records*, vol. 2, p. 858. Sister Pridden was Agnes's friend and *confidante*: *The Narrative of the Persecutions*, p. 195; Tibbutt, *Minutes*, p. 73.
5. *The Narrative of the Persecutions*, p. 209.
6. Anthony Lane was minister of Langford, Beds., 1670–5, and was buried at Bedford in 1676: J. Venn and J. A. Venn, *Alumni Cantabrigienses*, 4 vols (Cambridge: Cambridge University Press, 1924), vol. 3, p. 40.
7. Bunyan was smeared as a sexual libertine, witch, highwayman and Jesuit: *John Bunyan*, pp. 84–5.
8. Identified as Mr Halfehead of Potton, physician and surgeon (*The Narrative of the Persecutions*, p. 216). A kinswoman, Sister Halfhead, joined the affiliated congregation at Cotten End in 1677: Tibbutt, *Minutes*, p. 81.
9. She refers to the town throughout as Biglesworth.
10. *The Narrative of the Persecutions*, pp. 29–30.
11. The Edworth churchwardens had presented John Beaumont in 1669 for refusing to take the sacrament (*The Narrative of the Persecutions*, p. 22). It was not unusual in some areas for nonconformists to hold parish office: J. Spurr, *The Restoration Church of England, 1646–1689* (New Haven, CT: Yale University Press, 1991), p. 204.

12. J. A. Sharpe, "'Such Disagreements Betwyx Neighbours": Litigation and Human Relations in Early Modern England', in J. Bossy (ed.), *Disputes and Settlements: Law and Human Relations in the West* (Cambridge: Cambridge University Press, 1983), pp. 167–87.

13. N. Penney (ed.), *Record of the Sufferings of Quakers in Cornwall 1655–1686* (London: Friends Historical Society, 1928), pp. 17–19; compare P. Mack, *Visionary Women* (Berkeley, CA: California University Press, 1992), p. 196; M. Coate, *Cornwall in the Great Civil War* (Truro: D. Bradford Barton, 1963), p. 348. Anne went on to become a prominent Quaker in the town, and married the Quaker preacher Thomas Salthouse; her brothers became fierce persecutors of local Friends: Penney, *Record*.

14. M. Storey (ed.), *Two East Anglian Diaries, 1641–1729: Isaac Archer and William Coe*, Suffolk Record Society, 36 (1994), pp. 65–88, 127.

15. C. G. Crump (ed.), *The History of the Life of Thomas Ellwood* (London: Methuen, 1900), pp. 26–50; quotation on p. 35.

16. Ibid., pp. 2–4, 8–9, 41, 72.

17. Ibid., pp. 56–70.

18. *John Bunyan*, pp. 85–7.

19. E. Hobby, *Virtue of Necessity: English Women's Writing 1649–88* (London: Virago Press, 1988), pp. 54–75; F. A. Nussbaum, *The Autobiographical Subject* (Baltimore, MD: The Johns Hopkins University Press, 1989), pp. 154–77.

20. Owen Watkins does not discuss the narrative, and omits it from his list of spiritual autobiographies: O. C. Watkins, *The Puritan Experience* (London: Routledge and Kegan Paul, 1972), pp. 241–59.

21. See especially Mack, *Visionary Women*; see also I. Grundy and S. Wiseman (eds), *Women, Writing, History, 1640–1740* (London: B. T. Batsford, 1992); M. Nevitt, *Women and the Pamphlet Culture of Revolutionary England, 1640–1660* (Aldershot: Ashgate, 2006); J. Holstun (ed.), *Pamphlet Wars. Prose in the English Revolution* (London: Frank Cass, 1992).

22. Hobby, *Virtue of Necessity*, pp. 66–75; Nussbaum, *The Autobiographical Subject*, pp. 154–77; compare S. Smith, *A Poetics of Women's Autobiography* (Bloomington, IN: Indiana University Press, 1987), pp. 3–62.

23. J. Turner, *Choice Experiences* (London, 1653), sig. A–B8v; quotations at sig. A4v–5, B8–v. Their pastor was John Spilsbury, his colleague John Gardiner. Compare Hobby, *Virtue of Necessity*, pp. 68–9; Watkins, *Puritan Experience*, pp. 88–91. Gardiner, and Turner's husband, John, were officers in the New Model army: M. Tolmie, *The Triumph of the Saints* (Cambridge: Cambridge University Press, 1977), p. 158.

24. See, for example, J. R. Knott, 'Joseph Besse and the Quaker Culture of Suffering', in T. N. Corns and D. Loewenstein (eds), *The Emergence of Quaker Writing* (London: Frank Cass, 1995), pp. 126–41, and more generally W. C. Braithwaite, *The Beginnings of Quakerism*, 2nd edn (Cambridge: Cambridge University Press, 1955) and W. C. Braithwaite, *The Second Period of Quakerism*, 2nd edn (Cambridge: Cambridge University Press, 1961).

25. N. H. Keeble, *The Literary Culture of Nonconformity in Later Seventeenth-Century England* (Leicester: Leicester University Press, 1987), pp. 187–214.

26. M. McKeon, *The Origins of the English Novel 1600–1740* (Baltimore, MD: The Johns Hopkins University Press, 2002), pp. 95–6.

27. *The Narrative of the Persecutions*, p. 9.

9 Williamson, 'Parish Politics, Urban Spaces and Women's Voices in Seventeenth-Century Norwich'

1. See, for example, M. Ingram, *Church Courts, Sex and Marriage in England, 1570–1640* (Cambridge: Cambridge University Press, 1987); S. Amussen, *An Ordered Society: Gender and Class in Early Modern England* (Oxford: Blackwell, 1988); G. Walker, 'Expanding the Boundaries of Female Honour in Early Modern England', *Transactions of the Royal Historical Society*, 6:6 (1996), pp. 235–45; J. Kamensky, *Governing the Tongue: The Politics of Speech in Early Modern New England* (Oxford: Oxford University Press, 1997). Keith Thomas provides descriptions of honourable ideals at all levels of the hierarchy: K. Thomas, *The Ends of Life: Roads to Fulfilment in Early Modern England* (Oxford: Oxford University Press, 2009), pp. 147–86.

2. L. Gowing, *Domestic Dangers: Women, Words, and Sex in Early Modern London* (Oxford: Oxford University Press, 1996).

3. Steve Hindle highlights the risks associated with making accusations against others, in S. Hindle, 'The Shaming of Margaret Knowsley: Gossip, Gender and the Experience of Authority in Early Modern England', *Continuity and Change*, 9:3 (1994), pp. 391–419.

4. For more on women in legal contexts, see N. Z. Davis, *Fiction in the Archives: Pardon Tales and their Tellers in Sixteenth-Century France* (Cambridge: Cambridge University Press, 1987); L. Roper, *Oedipus and the Devil: Witchcraft, Sexuality and Religion in Early Modern Europe* (London: Routledge, 1994); G. Walker, 'Just Stories: Telling Tales of Infant Death in Early Modern England', in M. Mikesell and A. Seeff (eds), *Culture and Change: Attending to Early Modern Women* (Newark, DE: University of Delaware Press, 2003), pp. 98–115.

5. For more, see B. Capp, *When Gossips Meet: Women, Family and Neighbourhood in Early Modern England* (Oxford: Oxford University Press, 2003).

6. See L. Foxhall and G. Neher, *Gender and the City before Modernity* (Chichester: Wiley-Blackwell, 2013); L. Cowen Orlin, *Locating Privacy in Tudor London* (Oxford: Oxford University Press, 2008); A. Flather, *Gender and Space in Early Modern England* (Woodbridge: The Boydell Press, 2007); R. B. Shoemaker, 'Gendered Spaces: Patterns of Mobility and Perceptions of London's Geography, 1660–1750', in J. F. Merritt (ed.), *Imagining Early Modern London: Perceptions and Portrayals of the City from Stow to Strype, 1598–1720* (Cambridge: Cambridge University Press, 2001); L. Gowing, '"The Freedom of the Streets": Women and Social Space, 1560–1640', in P. Griffiths and M. Jenner (eds), *Londinopolis: Essays in the Cultural and Social History of Early Modern London* (Manchester: Manchester University Press, 2000), pp. 130–53; and D. Romano, 'Gender and the Urban Geography of Renaissance Venice', *Journal of Social History*, 23:2 (1989), pp. 339–53.

7. Ralph Kingston has argued that the 'spatial turn' is not a passing phenomena but a historiographical method that will continue to influence social historians for the foreseeable future: R. Kingston, 'Mind Over Matter? History and the Spatial Turn', *Cultural and Social History*, 7:1 (2010), pp. 111–21.

8. Flather, *Gender and Space*, p. 1.

9. M. Camille, 'Signs of the City: Place, Power, and Public Fantasy in Medieval Paris', in B. A. Hanawalt and M. Kobialka (eds), *Medieval Practices of Space* (Minnesota, MN: University of Minnesota Press, 2000), pp. 1–36, on p. 9.

10. Classic examples include J. Dod and R. Cleaver, *A Godlie Forme of Householde Government: For the Ordering of Private Families* (London, 1612) and W. Gouge, *Of Domesticall Duties* (London: John Haviland, for William Bladen, 1622).

11. The expression 'politics of the parish' was popularized by Keith Wrightson: K. Wrightson, 'The Politics of the Parish in Early Modern England', in P. Griffiths, A. Fox and S. Hindle (eds), *The Experience of Authority in Early Modern England* (Basingstoke: Palgrave Macmillan, 1996), pp. 10–46. For more on ideals of masculinity and manhood, see A. Shepard, *Meanings of Manhood in Early Modern England* (Oxford: Oxford University Press, 2003), esp. pp. 1–7, 152–213; E. Foyster, *Manhood in Early Modern England: Honour, Sex and Marriage* (London: Pearson Education, 1999); A. Fletcher, 'Manhood, the Male Body, Courtship and the Household in Early Modern England', *History*, 84 (1999), pp. 419–36, or M. Breitenburg, *Anxious Masculinity in Early Modern England* (Cambridge: Cambridge University Press, 1996).

12. Capp, *When Gossips Meet*, p. 188.

13. For example, B. Waddell, 'Neighbours and Strangers: The Locality in Later Stuart Economic Culture', in F. Williamson (ed.), *Locating Agency: Space, Power and Popular Politics* (Newcastle: Cambridge Scholars Publishing, 2010), pp. 103–32 and S. Hindle, *On the Parish?: The Micro-Politics of Poor Relief in Rural England, c. 1550–1750* (Oxford: Clarendon Press, 2004).

14. N. Tadmor, 'Friends and Neighbours in Early Modern England: Biblical Translations and Social Norms', in L. Gowing, M. Hunter and M. Rubin (eds) *Love, Friendship and Faith in Europe, 1300–1800* (Basingstoke: Palgrave Macmillan, 2005), pp. 150–76.

15. Gowing, "Freedom of the Streets", p. 136.

16. Church court records have been mined by many scholars, including several of the contributors to this collection, but surprisingly few have focused on the rich Norwich records, with the notable exception of Susan Amussen, whose research on Norwich's church court depositions formed the basis of *An Ordered Society*, and Donald Spaeth, who has worked extensively on the sixteenth-century Norwich Diocese records.

17. K. Wrightson, *English Society, 1580–1680* (London: Routledge, 1982), p. 51.

18. Norfolk Record Office (hereafter NRO), C/S3/21, Articles against Joane Mackam, loose papers, 1617–18.

19. For early modern perceptions of public and private, see M. McKeon, *The Secret History of Domesticity: Public, Private, and the Division of Knowledge* (Baltimore, MD: The Johns Hopkins University Press, 2005). See also S. Handley, 'Sociable Sleeping in Early Modern England 1660–1760', *History*, 98:329 (2013), pp. 79–104, esp. pp. 91–102.

20. NRO, DN/DEP, 32/25, fol. 834r, *Amyes* v. *Ansten*, 23 June 1607.

21. NRO, DN/DEP, 51/55, fol. 349r, 26 January 1680. *Faireman* v. *Metcalf*.

22. NRO, DN/DEP, 51/55, fols 349r–v, 26 January 1680. Evidence of John Lawes of Norwich, weaver, and Samuel Salmon of Norwich, barber.

23. It is not entirely clear whether the sisters were related to Katherine Goodwin by blood, or if the prefix 'Cozin' was a term of familiarity and friendship, as was common at that time.

24. NRO, DN/DEP, 47/51 fol. 8r, 23 September 1664. The information of Mary Frogg.

25. Ibid.

26. Ibid.

27. NRO, DN/DEP, 47/51, fol. 135r, 4 November 1664. *Frogg* v. *Austin*.

28. Ibid.

29. NRO, DN/DEP, 47/51, fol. 12v, 18 December 1664. *Austin* v. *Frogg*.

30. Ibid, fol. 209r.

31. Ibid.
32. NRO, DN/DEP, 47/51, fol. 210r, 18 August 1665. The information of Samuel March.
33. Ibid.
34. NRO, DN/DEP, 47/51 fol. 7v, 23 September 1664. The Information of John Morton.
35. P. Millican (ed.), *The Register of the Freemen of Norwich, 1548–1713* (Norwich: Jarrold & Sons Ltd, 1934), p. 153.
36. The laws surrounding marriage to a dead spouse's relative lacked clarity. Prohibited originally by canon law, the practice continued in the Anglican Church after the Reformation. However, the law was not enshrined into common law until the Marriage Act of 1835. Hence, there was some ambiguity over whether or not a marriage of 'affinity' as opposed to the taboo of 'consanguinity' might be allowable. The most notorious case in the early modern period was of course the marriage between Henry VIII and Katharine, his dead brother's wife. The law was not repealed until 1907.
37. P. Seaman (ed.), *Norfolk and Norwich Hearth Tax Assessment: Lady Day, 1666*, vol. 20 (Norwich: Norfolk and Norwich Genealogical Society, 1988), p. 72. To contextualise, aldermen serving in Frogg's ward (Fyebridge) during the 1666 hearth tax assessment were Henry Hyrne and Christopher Jay, who were rated at seven and sixteen hearths respectively: Seaman, *Norfolk and Norwich Hearth Tax*, pp. 71, 76. There is a large discrepancy between the respective ratings of these two men, yet both held the positions of sheriff and mayor, and Jay was a burgess-in-parliament from 1660 until his death in 1677: T. Hawes (ed.), *An Index to Norwich City Officers, 1453–1835, Norfolk Genealogy*, vol. 21 (Norwich: Norfolk and Norwich Genealogical Society, 1989), pp. 82, 88 and B. Cozens-Hardy and E. A. Kent, *The Mayors of Norwich, 1403–1835* (Norwich: Jarrold & Sons, 1938), pp. 89, 95.
38. In 1659 a Nicholas Frogg was listed as a collector and a William Austin was listed as a constable, but I am not entirely convinced that these are the Frogg and Austin of our case. The names and dates fit, but neither man served his office in St Saviour's parish: Hawes, *Index to Norwich City Officers*, pp. 7, 64.
39. NRO, DN/DEP, 47/51 fol. 14v, 1664. *James Denew* v. *Mary Frogg*, and NRO, DN/CON/21, Miscellaneous Court File, loose sheets, 1663–6.
40. For an introduction to the symbolism of church interiors and the importance of pew allocation, see C. Marsh, 'Order and Place in England, 1580–1640: The View from the Pew', *Journal of British Studies*, 44 (2005), pp. 3–26; C. Marsh, 'Sacred Space in England, 1560–1640: The View from the Pew', *Journal of Ecclesiastical History*, 53:2 (2002), pp. 286–311; R. Tittler, 'Seats of Honour, Seats of Power: The Symbolism of Public Seating in the English Urban Community, *c.* 1560–1620', *Albion*, 24:2 (2002), pp. 205–23; J. Merritt, 'The Social Context of the Parish Church in Early Modern Westminster', *Urban History Yearbook*, 18 (1991), pp. 10–31; Amussen, *An Ordered Society*, pp. 134–51; P. Graves, 'Social Space in the English Medieval Parish Church', *Economy and Society*, 18:3 (1989), pp. 297–322 or R. Gough, *The History of Myddle* (Firle: Caliban Press, 1979).
41. S. Hindle, 'A Sense of Place? Becoming and Belonging in the Rural Parish, 1550–1650', in A. Shepard and P. Withington (eds), *Communities in Early-Modern England* (Manchester: Manchester University Press, 2000), pp. 96–114, on p. 110.
42. NRO, DN/DEP, 43/47B fol. 156r, 5 February 1638. *Martyn* v. *Hunt*.
43. NRO, DN/DEP, 53/58A, fol. 15r, 29 July 1696. *Kett* v. *Nicholls*.
44. Ibid.
45. This case is also interesting for the fact that although both women were married, the language that both used conveyed a sense that their perception of credit and worth was

based on their own merits, not the social ranking of their respective husband, as is often assumed to be the case. For more on this, see A. Shepard and J. Spicksley, 'Worth, Age, and Social Status in Early Modern England', *Economic History Review*, 64:2 (2011), pp. 493–530.

46. Seaman, *Norfolk and Norwich Hearth Tax*, p. 71. Susan Denew's compurgators – Anna Dingle, Lidia Hellwys and Mary Curle – were married to men rated at one, four and six hearths respectively.

47. Pepys was assessed for five hearths in the 1666 hearth tax assessment and he was later to become a common councillor: Seaman, *Norfolk and Norwich Hearth Tax*, p. 72 and Hawes, *Index to Norwich City Officers*, p. 120.

48. Langley does not appear in the 1666 hearth tax assessment (or exemptions) for St Saviour, or any other parish of the city.

49. NRO, DN/DEP, 47/51, fol. 222r, 23 October 1665. *Frogg* v. *Austin*.

50. NRO, DN/DEP, 47/51, fol. 214r, 23 October 1665. *Frogg* v. *Austin*. Thurrold was rated at six hearths in the 1666 assessment and in 1672 pays £80 for a dispensation from all local offices. Todd was also assessed on six hearths and he later became a councillor, alderman and sheriff of the city: Seaman, *Norfolk and Norwich Hearth Tax*, p. 72 and Hawes, *Index to Norwich City Officers*, p. 152–3.

51. NRO, DN/DEP, 47/51, fols 213r and 222r, October 1665. *Frogg* v. *Austin*.

52. NRO, DN/CON/20/1, Loose sheets, October 1665.

53. NRO, Norwich Consistory Court (hereafter NCC) Administration Act Book 1673–88 fol. 152.

54. NRO, NCC Administration Act Book 1673–88 fol. 52.

55. NRO, MC 500/59, 762X2, fol. 11, 1622–1773. The 1670 'Act for the Better Settling of Intestates Estates' stated that the court, after settling any debts and funeral expenses, should distribute what remained to the wife and children, and on the occasion that the wife was also dead, only then should money be passed solely to the children. See *Statutes of the Realm, 1628–80*, ed. J. Raithby, vol. 5 (1819), pp. 719–20.

56. W. Moens (ed.), *The Walloons and their Church at Norwich, 1565–1832* (Lynington: Huguenot Society, 1887–8), pp. 186–7, W. Rye, *The Norwich Rate Book: Easter 1633 to Easter 1634* (London, 1910), p. 77.

57. Gowing, "Freedom of the Streets", p. 134.

58. R. Laitinen and T. Cohen, 'Cultural History of Early Modern Streets: An Introduction', *Journal of Early Modern History*, 12 (2008), pp. 195–204, on pp. 195–6.

59. For more on civic performance in Norwich, see M. A. Blackstone, 'Walking the City Limits: The Performance of Authority and Identity in Mary Tudor's Norwich', in G. Clark, J. Owens, and G. T. Smith (eds), *City Limits: Perspectives on the Historical European City* (Montreal: McGill-Queens University Press, 2010), pp. 106–38.

60. In Norwich, people could watch entertainments in the market square; walk in pleasure gardens and tree-lined avenues; hear news at the market cross; take part in street celebrations with bonfires, music and singing; or watch one of the grand civic processions, perhaps the annual mayoral inauguration parade.

61. Anne Tarver notes that 'under English law, every individual was entitled to a good name; to undermine this in public ... was an offence against both the secular law and that of the church'. Thus a public location and an audience were two of four legal qualifiers for a case to be considered defamation. For details, see A. Tarver, *Church Court Records: An Introduction for Family and Local Historians* (Chichester: Philimore Press, 1995), pp. 113, 116.

62. Laura Gowing's research on defamation in early modern London suggested that domestic thresholds held particular significance for women, functioning as a place where female identities and reputations could be evaluated, contested and mediated: Gowing, "Freedom of the Streets", p. 136. This may have been the case in London, but in Norwich thresholds do not appear to have held the same gendered symbolism. Popular with both sexes as places to work and socialize, the threshold was more often than not where a witness to defamation, rather than the parties involved, was situated. For more, see F. Williamson, 'Space and the City: Contesting Public and Private in the Seventeenth Century', *Cultural and Social History Journal*, 9:2 (2012), pp. 169–85.
63. NRO, DN/DEP, 47/51, fol. 12b, 18 December 1664. *Austin* v. *Frogg*.
64. NRO, DN/DEP, 47/51, fol. 12r, 26 September 1664. *Officum* v. *Austin*. 'Officium' was a case presented by the court, rather than an individual: an office, as opposed to an instance cause.
65. NRO, DN/DEP, 47/51, fol. 136r, 4 November 1664. *Frogg* v. *Austin*.
66. NRO, DN/DEP, 47/51, fol. 12r, 26 September 1664. *Officium* v. *Austin*.
67. For more on the practice of office holding, see M. Goldie, 'The Unacknowledged Republic: Officeholding in Early Modern England', in T. Harris (ed.), *The Politics of the Excluded, c. 1500–1850* (Basingstoke: Palgrave Macmillan, 2001), pp. 153–94, 162.
68. NRO, DN/DEP, 34/36B, fol. 50r, 1608. *Thull* v. *Skott*.
69. NRO, DN/DEP, 42/47A, fol. 501v, 25 January 1635. *Ingram* v. *Greenwood*.
70. NRO, DN/DEP, 45/48B, fol. 104r, 1640. *Inman* v. *Meen*.
71. NRO, DN/DEP, 51/55, fol. 209r, 12 February 1682. *Gothan* v. *Russell*.
72. NRO, DN/DEP, 52/56 and 57, fol. 1r, 31 March 1690. *Browne* v. *Tarnell*.
73. For more on this, see D. Lord Smail, *Imaginary Cartographies: Possession and Identity in Medieval Marseille* (Ithaca, NY: Cornell University Press, 1999).
74. Based on an investigation of Norwich's City Sessions, Mayor's Court and Norfolk Quarter Sessions records.
75. NRO, DN/DEP, 43/47b, fol. 220v, 13 July 1638. *Edwards* v. *Broome*.
76. NRO, DN/DEP, 53/58a, fol. 3r, 27 October 1696. *Horne* v. *Warren*.
77. James argues that the concept of honour lost its last vestiges of the medieval chivalric tradition during the seventeenth century, emphasizing civility over prowess as the benchmark for honourable status. This, combined with a rising 'middle-class' seeking to consolidate their own position in the face of external pressure and prejudices, resulted in a potentially explosive mix: M. James, 'English Politics and the Concept of Honour, 1485–1642', in M. James (ed.), *Society, Politics and Culture* (Cambridge: Cambridge University Press, 1986), pp. 308–415, 309.

10 Whyte, '"With a Sword Drawne in Her Hande": Defending the Boundaries of Household Space in Seventeenth-Century Wales'

1. A. Shepard, *The Meanings of Manhood in Early Modern England* (Oxford: Oxford University Press, 2003), pp. 64–8; A. Flather, *Gender and Space in Early Modern England* (Woodbridge: The Boydell Press, 2007).
2. G. Markham, *The English Housewife: Containing the Inward and Outward Virtues which ought to be in a Complete Woman*, ed. M. Best (Canada: McGill-Queen's University Press, 1986); G. Walker, 'Expanding the Boundaries of Female Honour in Early Modern England', *Transactions of the Royal Historical Society*, 6:6 (1996), pp. 235–45.

3. Flather, *Gender and Space*, pp. 42, 44.

4. G. Walker, *Crime, Gender and Social Order in Early Modern England* (Cambridge: Cambridge University Press, 2003), pp. 75–6; also G. Walker, 'Keeping it in the Family', in H. Berry and E. Foyster (eds), *The Family in Early Modern England* (Cambridge: Cambridge University Press, 2007), p. 87.

5. C. Muldrew, 'Social Identity, Wealth and the Life-Course', in H. French and J. Barry (eds), *Identity and Agency in Early Modern England* (Basingstoke: Palgrave Macmillan, 2004), pp. 147–77; C. Muldrew, *The Economy of Obligation: The Culture of Credit and Social Relations in Early Modern England* (Basingstoke: Palgrave Macmillan, 1998), esp. ch. 9.

6. S. Hindle, 'Persuasion and Protest in the Caddington Common Enclosure Dispute, 1635–39', *Past and Present*, 158 (1998), pp. 37–78, esp. pp. 50–2.

7. Muldrew, 'Social Identity', p. 149.

8. See also A. Shepard, 'Honesty, Worth and Gender in Early Modern England, 1560–1640', in French and Barry (eds), *Identity and Agency*, pp. 87–105; L. Gowing, *Domestic Dangers: Women, Words, and Sex in Early Modern London* (Oxford: Oxford University Press, 1996); Walker 'Expanding the Boundaries'.

9. For a succinct introduction, see I. Hodder, 'The Social in Archaeological Theory: An Historical and Contemporary Perspective', in L. Meskell and R. W. Preucel (eds), *A Companion to Social Archaeology* (Oxford: Blackwell, 2004), pp. 31–4.

10. M. Johnson, *English Houses 1300–1800 Vernacular Architecture, Social Life* (Harlow: Longman, 2010), pp. 153–4; for a discussion of witch bottles, see R. Merrifield, *The Archaeology of Ritual and Magic* (London: Batsford, 1987), pp. 163–75.

11. For an introduction to theoretical approaches to landscape see, for example, J. Thomas, 'Archaeologies of Place and Landscape', in I. Hodder (ed.), *Archaeological Theory Today* (Cambridge: Polity Press, 2001), pp. 165–86. See also Julie Sanders's excellent *The Cultural Geography of Early Modern Drama 1620–1650* (Cambridge: Cambridge University Press, 2011).

12. P. Bourdieu, *Outline of a Theory of Practice* (Cambridge: Cambridge University Press, 1977); Hodder, 'The Social in Archaeological Theory', pp. 34–6.

13. N. Whyte, '"Custodians of Memory: Women and Custom in Rural England *c*. 1550–1700', *Cultural and Social History*, 8:2 (2011), pp. 153–73; N. Whyte, 'Landscape, Memory and Custom: Parish Identities *c*. 1550–1700', *Social History*, 32:2 (2007), pp. 166–86.

14. A question also raised in J. Whittle, 'The House as a Place of Work in Early Modern Rural England', *Home Cultures*, 8:2 (2011), pp. 133–50.

15. L. Gowing, '"The Freedom of the Streets": Women and Social Space, 1560–1640', in P. Griffiths and M. Jenner (eds), *Londinopolis: Essays in the Cultural and Social History of Early Modern London* (Manchester: Manchester University Press, 2000), pp. 130–53; S. Mendelson and P. Crawford (eds), *Women in Early Modern England* (Oxford: Clarendon Press, 1998), pp. 205–8.

16. L. Cowen Orlin, 'Boundary Disputes in Early Modern London', in L. Cowen Orlin (ed.) *Material London ca. 1600* (Pennsylvania, PA: University of Pennsylvania Press, 2000), pp. 433–77; Gowing, *Domestic Dangers*, pp. 56, 70–1.

17. Flather, *Gender and Space*, pp. 42–3, 52–3; L. Cowen Orlin, *Locating Privacy in Tudor London* (Oxford: Oxford University Press, 2007), esp. pp. 152–92.

18. But see also M. Johnson, *Housing Culture: Traditional Architecture in an English Landscape* (London: University College London Press, 1993); and his *English Houses*; see also

B. A. Hanawalt, '*Of Good and Ill Repute*': *Gender and Social Control in Medieval England* (Oxford: Oxford University Press, 1998).

19. P. Smith, 'Rural Housing in Wales', in J. Thirsk (ed.), *The Agrarian History of England and Wales IV, 1500–1640* (Cambridge: Cambridge University Press), pp. 767–813, on pp. 767, 774; Johnson, *English Houses*.

20. Flather, *Gender and Space*, p. 107; D. Underdown, 'Regional Cultures? Local Variations in Popular Culture during the Early Modern Period', in T. Harris (ed.), *Popular Culture in England c. 1500–1850* (Basingstoke: Palgrave, 1995), pp. 28–47.

21. R. Houlbrooke, 'Women's Social Life and Common Action in England from the Fifteenth Century to the Eve of the Civil War', *Continuity and Change*, 1:2 (1986), pp. 171–89; J. Walter, 'Grain Riots and Popular Attitudes to the Law: Maldon and the Crisis of 1629', in J. Brewer and J. Styles (eds), *An Ungovernable People* (London: Hutchinson, 1980), pp. 47–84; S. Howard, *Law and Disorder in Early Modern Wales: Crime and Authority in Denbighshire c. 1660–1730* (University of Wales, 2008).

22. For other discussions of this category of litigation, see Walker, 'Keeping it in the Family'; J. Tait (ed.) *Lancashire Quarter Sessions Records* (Manchester: The Chetham Society, 1917); F. G. Emmison, *Elizabethan Life and Disorder* (Chelmsford: Essex Record Society, 1970), pp. 117–31.

23. Walker, 'Expanding the Boundaries'; see also Gowing, *Domestic Dangers*.

24. A point also made by Walker, 'Keeping it in the Family'.

25. Ibid., and see also Walker, *Crime, Gender and Social Order*, p. 77.

26. Contemporary accounts record the coastal flooding of Monmouthshire in 1607.

27. The National Archives (hereafter TNA), Stac8/176/20.

28. K. Warner Swett, 'Widowhood, Custom and Property in Early Modern North Wales', *Welsh History Review*, 18:2 (1996), pp. 189–227.

29. Walker, 'Keeping it in the Family'.

30. The rights of men of lower social standing, including those of yeoman status, to carry swords were called in to question. See, for example, the deposition of 30-year-old David Thomas, yeoman, TNA, Stac8/116/12.

31. TNA, Stac8/189/21.

32. Flather, *Gender and Space*, pp. 44–5; Gowing, *Domestic Dangers*, p. 98.

33. TNA, Stac8/177/7.

34. Flather, *Gender and Space*, p. 106.

35. For further discussion of women's role in forcible rescues, see Walker, *Crime, Gender and Social Order*, pp. 76–7, 89–90, 95–6, 249–62; Emmison, *Disorder*, p. 174.

36. TNA, Stac8/116/11; F. Heal, *Hospitality in Early Modern England* (Oxford: Clarendon Press, 1990).

37. TNA, Stac8/116/12.

38. For architecture and building traditions, see J. Alfrey, 'Deserted Rural Settlement: The Architectural Evidence', in K. Roberts (ed.), *Lost Farmsteads: Deserted Rural Settlements in Wales*, CBA Research Report (2006), p. 148; Smith, 'Rural Housing in Wales', pp. 767–813.

39. TNA, Stac8/8fF0/2.

40. TNA, Stac8/249/26.

41. TNA, Stac8/177/7.

42. Flather, *Gender and Space*, pp. 53–4.

43. TNA, Stac8/249/26.

44. TNA, Stac8/168/6.

45. TNA, Stac8/249/26.
46. A. L. Erickson, *Women and Property in Early Modern England* (Abingdon: Routledge, 1993); T. Stretton, *Women Waging Law in Elizabethan England* (Cambridge: Cambridge University Press, 1998).
47. L. B. Smith, 'Towards a History of Women in Late Medieval Wales', in M. Roberts and S. Clarke (eds), *Women and Gender in Early Modern Wales* (Cardiff: University of Wales Press, 2000), pp. 14–49, esp. 23–30.
48. Walker, 'Expanding the Boundaries', p. 241.
49. Walker, *Crime, Gender and Social Order*, p. 77.
50. TNA, Stac8/134/4.
51. TNA, Stac8/123/11.
52. TNA, Stac8/196/6.
53. Flather, *Gender and Space*, pp. 160–73; S. Amussen, *An Ordered Society: Gender and Class in Early Modern England* (Oxford: Blackwell 1988), pp. 137–44; D. Underdown, *Revel, Riot and Rebellion: Popular Politics and Culture* (Oxford: Oxford University Press, 1985), pp. 29–33; C. Marsh, 'Order and Place in England, 1580–1640: The View from the Pew', *Journal of British Studies*, 44 (2005), pp. 3–26.
54. TNA, Stac8/88/6.
55. TNA, Stac8/286/22.
56. Whyte, 'Custodians of Memory'.
57. TNA, Stac8/177/7.
58. TNA, Stac8/76/8.
59. A. Wood, *Riot, Rebellion and Popular Politics in Early Modern England* (Basingstoke: Palgrave, 2002), esp. pp. 100–12.
60. Walker, 'Keeping it in the Family'.
61. TNA, Stac8/141/15.
62. TNA, Stac8/168/10.
63. TNA, Stac8/133/11.
64. TNA, Stac8/88/6.
65. On the notion of the moral landscape, I have found the collection of essays in L. Dowler, J. Carubia and B. Szczygiel (eds), *Gender and Landscape* (Abingdon: Routledge, 2005) particularly useful. On the construction of court narratives, see N. Z. Davis, *Fiction in the Archives: Pardon Tales and their Tellers in Sixteenth-Century France* (Stanford, CA: Stanford University Press, 1987).
66. Shepard, *Meanings of Manhood*; see also S. Amussen, 'Punishment, Discipline and Power: The Social Meanings of Violence in Early Modern England', *Journal of British Studies*, 34 (1995), pp. 1–34. See also E. Ewan, 'Disorderly Damsels? Women and Interpersonal Violence in Pre-Reformation Scotland', *Scottish Historical Review*, 89, 2:228 (2010), pp. 153–71.
67. Shepard, *Meanings of Manhood*, p. 150.
68. N. Whyte, 'Enclosure Breaking and Household Space' (forthcoming).
69. Walker, 'Expanding the Boundaries'; Walker, *Crime, Gender and the Social Order*, pp. 75–7; Ewan, 'Women and Interpersonal Violence', pp. 159–60.
70. TNA, Stac8/123/11.
71. TNA, Stac8 /77/17.
72. K. Wrightson, 'The Politics of the Parish in Early Modern England', in P. Griffiths, A. Fox and S. Hindle (eds), *The Experience of Authority in Early Modern England* (Basingstoke: Palgrave Macmillan, 1996), pp. 10–46, on p. 16.

73. TNA, Stac8/168/6.
74. G. Walker, 'Strange Kind of Stealing: Abduction in Early Modern Wales', in M. Roberts and S. Clarke (eds), *Women and Gender in Early Modern Wales* (Cardiff: University of Wales Press, 2000), pp. 50–74.
75. TNA, Stac8/177/21.
76. TNA, Stac8/177/21; see also Stac8/146/11.
77. TNA, Stac8/168/2.
78. TNA, E134/9Jas1/East17.
79. Davis, *Fiction in the Archives*.

INDEX

Aberedw, Radnorshire, 169
Acomb Grange, Yorkshire, 39
Aldham, Essex, 110
Anagol, Padma, 3
Andover, Hampshire, 60–1
Andrewes, Lancelot, 119
Anglican, Anglicanism, 104, 114
Ansten, Albert, 128
arbitration, 45, 63, 96
Archer, Isaac, 118–19
Arden, John de, 57–8
Arminghall, Norfolk, 129, 132
Arminian, 104, 108
    Arminianism, 105
Arnold, John, xvi, 4, 7–8, 31, 33
Askham Brian, Yorkshire, 66
Austin, Anne nee Roberts, 129–32, 135, 137
Austin, William, 129–35
Awne, Avice de, 50
Awne, William, 50

Bailey, Joanne, 6, 10, 18–19
Bainton, East Riding, 65–6, 71
Bakhtin, Mikhail, 8
baptism, 101–3
Baptist, 122, 124
Barbour, Alice, 27
Bardsley, Sandy, 11, 58, 93–5
Baskervill, Sara, 153–4
Bassett, Lady Eleanor, 57–8
Bassett, Sir Ralph, 57–8
Bawde, Humphrey, 18, 22–9, 157
Bawde, Johanne, 18, 22–9, 157
Beare, Elizabeth, 110
Beaumont, John (junior), 113–14
Beaumont, John (senior), 113–17, 119–20
Beauwater, Elizabeth, 110

Beattie, Cordelia, xv, 8, 15, 45
Bedale, Yorkshire, 66
Beleby, Alice de, 38–9, 41
Bell, William, 131–2, 134, 140
Bellamy, J. G., 89
Bennett, Judith, 1–3, 55, 90
Biggleswade, Bedfordshire, 115–7, 121
Biller, Peter, 51
Black Death, 3, 39, 41
Bleythyn, Morgan, 152–3
Bodvell, John, 147
borough courts, 32, 111
Bosworth, 66–7
Boteler, Ralph, 67
boundaries
    boundary breaking, 15, 143–4, 149–52,
        154
    parish, 59, 126–7, 138–9
    symbolism of, 15, 138–9, 141–6, 153–5
Boverton, Glamorgan, 77
Bradelay, Maud de, 37
Braden, Flintshire, 153
Brafferton, North Yorkshire, 59
Braudnam, Elizabeth, 27
Brayn, John, 92
Bread Street, London, 82, 84
Brettle, Ellen, 102
Bringham, Robert, 60
Brotherhood, Katherine, 137–8
Brown, Sir Richard, 146
Brun, William, 58
Bulkley, Richard, 150
Bunyan, John, 113–4, 117, 120–1, 123
burial, 32, 103–5
    see also funeral
Butler, Sara, 5

Caerleon, Gwent, 77
Calthorpe, Elizabeth, 65
Calthorpe, William, 65
Camber, Mariam, 111
Cambridge University, 118
Camille, Michael, 125–6
Cannon, Christopher, 19
canon law, 31–3, 36, 38, 40–1, 46, 48, 50–4,
    57, 61
Canons Ashby, Northamptonshire, 57
Cant, Bridget, 110
Capp, Bernard, 5, 12, 13, 113, 126
Cardiff, South Glamorgan, 78–9
Carne, Jane, 79–80
Carow, Margaret, 52
Carter, Elizabeth, 110
Carter, Prudence, 107
Carue y Thiffithe, Trevelyne, 149
Catholic, Catholicism, 99, 104
    popery, 102–4
Chancery, Court of, 8, 10–11, 17–23,
    25–29, 63, 69, 71–3, 75–7, 82
Charles I, 99, 104
Charles II, 113
Chaucer, Geoffrey, 51
Chaytor, Miranda, 25
Chelmsford, Essex, 103, 112
Cheriton, Gower, 84
Cholmondley, Dame Marie, 153
church calendar, 106–7
church court, 32, 37, 46, 48, 50–2, 57, 61, 104
    of Canterbury, 32, 41, 44–5, 47–8, 52–4,
        57
    of London, 19, 23, 27, 32
    of Norwich, 14, 127, 129
    of York, 32–4, 39, 41, 44–5, 48, 50,
        52–3, 59–60
churching, 101–2
Claxton, Thomas, 128
clerical vestments, 99, 104, 106
Cley-Next-The-Sea, Norfolk, 131–2, 139
Clifford, Lord Henry, 68
Cliftlands, Bill, 108
Clopton, Agnes de, 52
Coale, Jennett, 151
Cobbler, William, 92, 94
Coke, Amy, 77
Committee for Scandalous Ministers, 108

'common fame', 60
common land, 141–2, 149–50, 152
Common law, 7–11, 15, 17, 31, 55, 58,
    63–4, 72–5, 85
Common Pleas, Court of, 7
Common Prayer, Book of, 99, 102, 104, 118
Cook, Joanna, 90
Cook, Susan, 106
Cooper, John, 92
Cotherstone, County Durham, 66, 72
Cotwin, Mary, 131–2, 134
Council in the Marches of Wales, 75–6,
    79–80
coverture, 4, 6–7, 10, 45
Cradock, John, 84
Cradock, Sir Matthew, 76, 78–9
Cram, Elizabeth, 102
credit, 6–7, 90, 92, 94, 96, 125, 133, 135,
    138, 142
    see also honour
Cressy, David, 106
Cromwell, Thomas, 76–7, 85
Crowley, D. A., 89, 91
Croxton, Joan, 107
Curteys, Oliver, 149, 151
Cwrt-Rhyd-Hir, Glamorgan, 80, 83–4

Dafydd, Hopkyn ap, 78
Davell, Charles, 129
David, John ap Howell ap Lewis, 148
David, Katherine verch, 79
David, Mary, 146–7
Davies, Maurice, 149, 152
Declaration of Indulgence, 113, 117
Dedham, Essex, 106
defamation, 7, 12, 14, 27–8, 32, 45, 47, 50,
    58–9, 126–8, 133, 135, 139–40
Defoe, Daniel, 139
Denbigh, Denbighshire, 150
Denew, James, 131, 134–6
Denew, Susan, 133–6, 138
Devereux, William, Lord Ferrers, 79
DeWindt, Anne Reiber, 89
DeWindt, E. B., 89
Dinley, Caernarvonshire, 148, 150, 153
disseisin, 144, 151, 154
Dolan, Francis, 5
Dolbenmaen, Caernarvonshire, 154

Domesday Book, 91
doorways, 14, 127, 136–7, 143, 145–6
Douglas, Mary, 112
Dowse, John, 59
Drake, Richard, 105
Drayton, Worcestershire, 57
Dunn, Caroline, 83
Dunn, Penny, 89
Dynsdale, Elizabeth, 138

Eaton, Elizabeth, 107
Edgefield, Norfolk, 132, 139
Edmund, David, 144–5
Edward IV, 67
Edworth, Bedfordshire, 113–14, 116–7
Ellwood, Thomas, 119–20
Elton, Geoffrey, 73
enfeoffment, 63, 69
equity court, 7, 8, 18, 143–4
Erickson, Amy, 6, 148
Evans, Richard, 151
Evesham, Worcestershire, 57

Faireman, Andrew, 128–9
Fairfax, William, 38
Falconer, Daniel, 110
Felbrigg, Elizabeth, 65
felony, 76–7, 79–80, 82–3, 89, 91, 94, 138
Fentress, James, 46
Fiennes, Celia, 139
Finch, A. J., 93
Flather, Amanda, 5, 13, 14, 125, 143
Fletcher, Sara, 151
Fowler, Johanne, 17, 22
Foxcott, Lady Isabella de, 61
Foxholes, Richard, 52
frankpledge, 11, 89–92
Frogg, Mary, 130–40
Frogg, Nicholas, 132–6, 139–40
Frohock, Mary, 136
Frost, William, 109–10
funeral, 68, 101, 104, 114–15
    see also burial

gadding, 107–8
Gamlingay, Cambridgeshire, 113–16
Gaskill, Malcolm, 5, 8

Glamorgan, South Wales, 73, 75–80, 83–4, 143, 152
Gloucester, Richard Duke of, 66–7
Glover, Henry, 92
Glynneath, Glamorgan, 78
Goldberg, Jeremy, xv, 2, 5, 9, 27, 46, 49–50, 53
Golden Dog Inn, Norwich, 133, 137
Goldhangar, Essex, 106–7
Goldsmith, Alice, 93
Goodwin, Katherine, 129–30
Gothan, Francis, 138
Gower, John, 43
Gower, West Glamorgan, 73, 75–6, 78–9, 84
Gowing, Laura, 4–5, 11, 14, 19, 60, 111, 127
Gramsci, Antonio, 1
Grantham, Agnes, 39
Gratian, 50, 53
Great Holland, Essex, 107
Great Maplestead, Essex, 110
Great Middleton, Essex, 109–10
Great Saling, Essex, 109–10
Great Stambridge, Essex, 107
Great Totham, Essex, 111
Great Wakering, Essex, 107
Great Waltham, Essex, 106, 112
Green, I. M., 108
Griffith, Owen, 82
Grindal, Edmund, 105
Gros, Denise, 17, 22
Gruffith, Humffrey, 153
Gruffudd, Owen, 78–84
Gruffudd, William ap, 78–84
Gunter, Philip, 77
Gwydry Esq, Caernarvonshire, 147
Gwyn, Felice, 77

Haddon, Derbyshire, 82
Hadley, Essex, 111
Hailes, Abbot of, 68, 70, 72
Hailes, Gloucestershire, 63, 68, 71–2
Hall, Bartholomew, 109
Hall, Margaret, 109
Halsted, Essex, 101, 106, 112
Hammer, Randle, 153
Hanawalt, Barbara, 2, 17, 93
Harcourt, Christopher, 65–6
Harcourt, Simon, 72

Harcourt, Sir Richard, 65–6
Harrie, Thomas, 151
Harries, John, 151
Harris, Elizabeth, 137
Harris, Margaret, 147
Hart, Thomas, 23
Haskett, Timothy, 20–1
Hawkins, Anne, 151
Hawkyne, John, 151
Helmholz, R., 53
hengwite, 91
Henllan, Denbighshire, 146
Henry VII, 67–8, 70, 74
Henry VIII, 73–5, 78, 85
Herbert, Katherine, 145, 151
Herbert, Sir George, 76, 79
Herbert, Sir Walter, 80
Herdman, Alice, 47
Herdman, Dulcia, 47
heresy; heretic, 4, 8, 31
Herthill, Maud de, 35
Heybridge, Essex, 101
Hicks, William, 110
Hindle, Steve, 14
Hinteworth, Sibilla de, 55
Hitchin, Hertfordshire, 115
Hoebel, Adamson E., 95
Hogan, Patricia M., 88
Holeput, Joan, 59
Holmes, Clive, 108
honour, 12, 15, 25, 56, 59, 90, 93, 124–5,
    133, 140–2, 144, 152
    see also credit
Horne, Anna, 140
Horrox, Rosemary, 10–11
household, 6, 9, 12–15, 25, 57–9, 61, 87, 90,
    110, 136, 141–55
Howell, Joanne ap (of Ogmore), 79
Howell, Johanne ap (of Istradevoduck), 149
Howell, Martha, 6
Howell, Morgan ap, 153–4
Huddleston, John (I), 66–7
Huddleston, John (II), 67, 69–71
Huddleston, John (III), 68–71
hue and cry, 11–12, 58–9, 77, 80, 87–8, 90–6
Hugh, Katherine verch, 146
Hughe, Andrew ap, 150
Hughes Dayton, Cornelia, 46

Humffrey, Evan ap, 150
Humfrey, Humfrey ap, 148
Hunt, John, 134
Hurterigg, Phillip de, 47
Hyams, Paul, 45

iconoclasm, 5, 14, 99–101, 103–6, 112
    see also protest
Ingham, Norfolk, 64–5
Ingram, Martin, 11–12
Inns of Court, 63

James I, 144
Jeffrey, Gwen verch, 150
Jegon, John, 108, 110
John, Dafydd ap Gruffudd ap, 78–80
John, Gruffudd ap, 78
John, Margaret verch, 150
Jones, Alexander, 77
Jones, Karen, 27
Jones, William, 77
Josse, William, 94

Kane, Bronach, 9, 12, 27, 32
Katersouth, Maud, 37–8
Kebell, Margaret, 82
Kebell, Thomas, 82, 84
Kempe, William, 138
Kendall, Elizabeth, 107
Kermode, Jenny, 4, 9
Kett, Phillipa, 134
King's Bench, Court of 7, 10, 73, 82
King's Lynn, Norfolk, 88
Kingsley Kent, Susan, 3
Kirkham, North Yorkshire, 60
Knight, Charity, 103, 112

Lake, John, 109–10
Lakenham, Norfolk, 132, 139
Lamanva, Elizabeth, 17
Lancedell, Glamorganshire, 151
Langley, Christian, 135
Larkwell, Essex, 107
Laud, William, 99, 102
Laudian, 102, 104, 106–7
Leek, John, 54
Leek, Matilda, 54
leet, court, 11, 87–90, 95
Lewes, Robert, 82

Lexden, Essex, 109
Lincoln, John de, 94
Littester, John, 52
Little Baddow, Essex, 106
Llangiwg, Glamorgan, 79, 82, 84
Llangower, Gwynedd, 150
Llanllawddog, Carmarthenshire, 146
Llywelyn, John ap, 78
Lloyd, John, 146
Lloyd, Lewis, 77
Lloyd, William, 150
Lollard, 106
London, 3, 17, 19, 22–3, 26–9, 32, 60, 67,
    69, 75, 82–4, 104–5, 115, 143
lordship, 64, 76, 79
Lye beside Asthall, Oxon, 66
Lytle, Johanne, 22

Mackam, Joanne, 128
Maitland, Frederick, 6, 88
March, Katherine, 131
Marrays, John, 32, 36–7
marriage, 5–7, 10, 32, 37, 43, 45, 47, 50–9,
    64–8, 81, 83, 99, 101, 125, 130, 132,
    148, 152
Martyn, Alice, 134
martyr, 123
masculinity, 2, 59, 87, 95–6, 141
Mathern, Monmouthshire, 77
Matthew, Elizabeth, 77
McIntosh, Marjorie, 1, 18, 89
memoria, 43, 44, 49
    ars memoria, 48
memoriale presbiterorum, 67
memory, 1, 9, 12, 15, 33, 38–9, 43–4, 46–9,
    52, 55–62, 96, 127, 139, 142
Menuge, Noël James, 5
Merioneth, Merionethshire, 150
Metcalf, Michael, 129
Millom, Cumberland, 67–8
Mirour de l'Omme,, 43
Mitchell, Elizabeth, 110
Mitchell, William, 129, 132
More, Sir Thomas, 78
Morland, Beatrix de, 38
Morris, Jenkin John, 144
Morris, W. A., 89
Morton, John, 130, 132

Muldrew, Craig, 142
Müller, Miriam, 7, 45, 88, 94–5
Murray, Jacqueline, 62
Mycholson, John, 54

Neal, Derek, 5, 59
Neath, Glamorgan, 77, 80–4
Nesfeld, Margery, 40–1
Nesfeld, Thomas, 40–1
Nettles, Stephen, 109
Newsted, Christopher, 108
Nicholls, Susan, 134
nonage, 56–7
non-conformism, 13, 113, 115, 117–8,
    120–1, 124
North, John, 92
North Walsham, Norfolk, 88
Norwich, 14, 88–9, 126–9, 132, 134, 136,
    139

Olson, Sherri, 89–90
Olyff, Maud, 23, 28, 157
Osborne, Joan, 110
Owen, John, 150
Owen Edwards, Ifan ab, 75

Peasants Revolt (1381), 49, 88
Pepys, William, 135
Perkins, William, 119
pew disputes, 101, 133–4, 149
Philip, Amy, 77–8
Philips, Thomas, 76
Phillips, Margaret, 151
Piers, Edward, 148
Piers, Marie, 148
Pole, William de la (Duke of Suffolk), 64–5
Pollock, Frederick, 6
Poole, Grace, 112
Poole, Jonathan, 112
Poos, L. R., 89
protest, 74, 77–8, 105, 112, 142–143, 147–54
    see also iconoclasm
Porter, Richard le, 92
Postles, D., 90
Pottell, William, 36–8
Poyer, David, 151
Protestantism, 99, 104, 112, 141
Pulleyne, John, 111

Quaker, 118–20, 122–3
quarter sessions courts, 5, 143–4
Quysteler, Agnes, 36

Radwinter, Essex, 103
Randulf, Robert, 61
Ratley, Warwickshire, 57–8
Rawcliffe, Yorkshire, 34, 38
Rayleigh, Essex, 107
Reformation, 4, 13, 99–100, 139
Requests, Court of, 15, 19, 76
Reyf, Rolland, 94
Reyf, Troye, 94
Rhetorica novissima, 56
Rhys, Rolland, 92
Richard III, 66–7
Richard, Anne verch, 149
Richard, John, 152
Richard, John ap, 154
Richard, William, 152
Richards, William ap, 77
Richardson, Samuel, 124
Rigby, Stephen, 1
Robert, Kathryn, 73, 80–5
Roberts, Simon, 90
Rodziewicz, Janka, xv, 11, 87
Rogers, Elizabeth, 147
Rogers, Thomas, 147
Root and Branch Petition, 104
Roper, Lyndal, 4
Rouclif, Alice de, 32, 35–6, 38–9, 41
Rouclif, Eufemia de, 36
Rouclif, John de, 38
Rouclif, Lady Margery de, 38–9
Rouclif, Sir Brian de, 32, 34
Rutledge, Elizabeth, 89

Saint Austell, Cornwall, 118
Saint Clair, Edith, 65
Saint Fagan, Glamorgan, 152
Saint John, Emma, 61
Saint John, John, 61
Saint Woollos, Monmouthshire, 144
Salthouse, 129, 131, 139
Sandon, Essex, 106
Saul, Anthony, 89
Schofield, Phillipp, 45, 89
Scott, James C., 1

sequestration, 108, 111
settlement
    dispersed, 143
    nucleated, 143
Shepard, Alexandra, xv, xvi, 2–3, 6, 152
Shephard, Edward, 110–11
Sible Hedingham, Essex, 108
Signa, Boncompagno da, 56
Silkwoman, Joanna, 90
Skott, John, 138
Smith, Elizabeth, 110
Smith, Thomas, 132
Somerset, Henry, Earl of Worcester, 76
Southwell, Sir Robert, 68, 70
space
    and gender, 3, 12–15, 25, 100–1, 106,
        112, 141, 151–2
    household, 136, 141, 143–4, 151–2, 154
    private, 128, 136, 146, 149, 154
    rural, 15
    sacred, 100–1, 106, 112
    social, 134, 136–7
    theory of, 13, 125–6, 141, 143
    urban, 14, 126–7, 139–40
Speight, Margery, 40
Spurgeon, Elizabeth, 110
Stapleton, Brian, 66
Stapleton, Jane, 11, 63–6, 68–72
Stapleton, Sir Miles, 64, 66
Star Chamber, 10, 73–8, 80–2, 84–5,
    144–149
Steane, Northamptonshire, 57
Stede, Alice, 94
Stisted, Essex, 108
Stow, John, 105
Stratton Strawless, Norfolk, 139
Stretton, Tim, xv, 8, 15, 19
Sudeley, Gloucestershire, 67–8
Supraboscus, Gower Wallicana, 79
Swaffham, Norfolk, 88
Swansea, West Glamorgan, 79, 84
Sweyn, Alice, 93

Tadmor, Naomi, 126
Tailor, William, 93
Tancred, Archdeacon of Bologna, 48, 50
Tapster, Catherine, 94
Tapster, Kati, 92

Thaxted, Essex, 101
Thetford, Norfolk, 88
Thicket, convent of, East Riding, 61
Thomas, Hopkyn ap Rees ap, 82
Thomas, Roger, 144–5
Thomas, Thomas ap, 151
Thomson, Ellen, 59
Thurrold, Robert, 135
Tir Pen y Lan, Monmouthshire, 144–6, 148
tithe disputes, 15, 32–3, 43, 45, 59–61, 108, 152
tithing, 11, 89–93
Todd, John, 135
Tracy, William, 70
Turberville, Christopher, 79
Turnay, Robert, 60
Turner, Jane, 122, 124
Tyndale, John, 110

Union, Acts of (1536–42), 85
Upcott, Anne, 118
Urswick, Christopher, 70
Usk, Monmouthshire, 149, 152
Utting, John, 140

Vernon, Roger, 82
Vickery, Amanda, 13

Wade, Henry de la, 57
Waden, George, 151
Walengfeld, Thomas de, 54
Walker, Garthine xv, 2–4, 8, 9, 19, 25, 81, 144, 148
Walkyngton, John de, 37
Wallensköld, A., 26
Walter, Jane, 151
Walter, John, 100
Warren, Esther, 140
Wascelyne, Anabilla, 35
Weldon, Northamptonshire, 57–8
Welshry, The (Gower Wallicana), 79
Weston, Hugh de, 57

Weston, Ralph, 57
Weston-by-Welland, Northamptonshire, 57–8
Westrupp, Ambrose, 111
Weybread, Suffolk, 64
Whately, William, 119
White, Joan, 40
Whitup, Joanna, 102
Whyte, Nicola, 13–15
Wickham, Chris, 46
widow, 10–11, 17, 22, 31–2, 38–9, 45, 51, 58–9, 61, 65, 72, 75, 78–9, 82, 87, 100–1, 104–6, 108, 145, 149, 152, 154
Wilding, Thomas, 140
William, Robert ap, 81
Williams, Denise, 78–80, 83–5
Williams, Eleanor, 154
Williams, Glanmor, 76
Williamson, Fiona, 12, 13, 14
Wilson, John, 113, 115
Winchcombe, Gloucestershire, 68, 70–1
Witham, Annas, 151
Witherley, Edmund, 131
Wolsey, Sir Thomas, 74–5
Wood, Andy, 15
Wrightson, Keith, 1, 12, 128

Yale, Denbighshire, 147–8
Yarmouth, Norfolk, 11, 87–96
York, Yorkshire, 32–34, 37, 39–41, 44–5, 48, 50, 52–53, 59–60, 66
Younge, Joan, 151
Youngs, Deborah, 10
Ynys Derw, Gower Wallicana, 79
Ynysmeudwy, Glamorgan, 82
Ynystawe, Gower, 78
Ysceifiog, Flintshire, 147
Yssa, Caernarvonshire, 150

Zemon Davies, Natalie, 7, 19
Zouche, William de la, 39

Lightning Source UK Ltd.
Milton Keynes UK
UKHW020628221121
394385UK00004B/22